DEAF AND DISABLED,
OR DEAFNESS DISABLED?
Towards a human rights perspective

Mairian Corker

Open University Press
Buckingham · Philadelphia

Open University Press
Celtic Court
22 Ballmoor
Buckingham
MK18 1XW

and
1900 Frost Road, Suite 101
Bristol, PA 19007, USA

First Published 1998

A catalogue record of this book is available from the British Library

ISBN   0 335 19699 3 (pb)   0 335 19700 0 (hb)

Library of Congress Cataloging-in-Publication Data
Corker, Mairian.
    Deaf and disabled, or deafness disabled? : towards a human rights perspective /
Mairian Corker.
        p.   cm. — (Disability, human rights, and society)
    Includes bibliographical references and index.
    ISBN 0-335-19700-0 (hardcover). — ISBN 0-335-19699-3 (pbk.)
    1. Deaf—Social conditions.   2. Deaf—Civil rights.   3. Discrimination against
the handicapped.   4. Sociology of disability.   5. Marginality, Social.   I. Title
II. Series.
HV2380.C69 1997
305.9'08162—dc21   97-20448
                                                                                                  CIP

Copy-edited and typeset by The Running Head Limited, London and Cambridge
Printed in Great Britain by Biddles Ltd, Guildford and King's Lynn

DEAF AND DISABLED,
OR DEAFNESS DISABLED?

Disability, Human Rights and Society

Series Editor: Professor Len Barton, University of Sheffield

The *Disability, Human Rights and Society* series reflects a commitment to a particular view of 'disability' and a desire to make this view accessible to a wider audience. The series approach defines 'disability' as a form of oppression and identifies the ways in which disabled people are marginalized, restricted and experience discrimination. The fundamental issue is not one of an individual's inabilities or limitations, but rather a hostile and unadaptive society.

Authors in this series are united in the belief that the question of disability must be set within an equal opportunities framework. The series gives priority to the examination and critique of those factors that are unacceptable, offensive and in need of change. It also recognizes that any attempt to redirect resources in order to provide opportunities for discriminated people cannot pretend to be apolitical. Finally, it raises the urgent task of establishing links with other marginalized groups in an attempt to engage in a common struggle. The issue of disability needs to be given equal significance to those of race, gender and age in equal opportunities policies. This series provides support for such a task.

Anyone interested in contributing to the series is invited to approach the Series Editor at the Division of Education, University of Sheffield.

Current and forthcoming titles

M. Corker: *Deaf and Disabled, or Deafness Disabled?*
M. Moore, S. Beazley and J. Maelzer: *Researching Disability Issues*
A. Roulstone: *Enabling Technology: Disabled People, Work and New Technology*
C. Thomas: *Female Forms: Disabled Women in Social Context*
A. Vlachou: *Struggles for Inclusive Education: An Ethnographic Study*

For Kavita
May you be the mother of a hundred differences

Contents

Series editor's preface

The Disability, Human Rights and Society series reflects a commitment to a social model of disability and a desire to make this view accessible to a wide audience. 'Disability' is viewed as a form of oppression and the fundamental issue is not one of an individual's inabilities or limitations but, rather, a hostile and unadaptive society.

Priority is given to identifying and challenging those barriers to change, including the urgent task of establishing links with other marginalized groups and thus seeking to make connections between class, gender, race, age and disability factors.

The series aims to establish further disability as a serious topic of study, one in which the latest findings and ideas can be seriously investigated.

This is an extremely important book. It is a most stimulating and questioning analysis presented in an accessible, coherent and integrated way. The complex issues concerning the relationship and tensions between disabled and deaf people are investigated in an open and refreshing manner. Corker provides a series of thought-provoking insights concerning difference and diversity in which she endeavours to resist the legitimation of a reified construction of deafness and an essentialist view of disability.

Motivated by a desire to encourage a dialogue between deaf and disabled people, Corker discusses the question of collective empowerment and the pursuit of change. Points of common interest, needs and rights are explored in a highly reflective process of deconstruction, demystification and reconstruction.

This is a very challenging book, one which I have no doubt will stimulate debate. It is essential reading for all those engaged in disability/deaf issues, studies and research.

Professor Len Barton
Sheffield

Acknowledgements

This book is the product of many individual discussions, numerous pieces of correspondence and a few arguments! In particular I would like to thank Colin Barnes, Jenny Corbett, Sally French, Rachel Hurst, Colin Low, Mike Oliver, Tom Shakespeare, Brenda Smith, Graham Turner, Ayesha Vernon and Gerry Zarb; all of whom, in different ways, have helped to mould it.

I am especially grateful to the series editor, Len Barton, for his careful and constructive criticism of the original manuscript, and for opening a very substantial door; also to Jacinta Evans and Joan Malherbe at Open University Press, for keeping it open.

I must also give a very special thanks to Julia and Alex Caprara who just go on supporting and encouraging in such wonderful ways, and to Geoff Pine and Jamie Phillips for memories of Provence, where it all began, and Brighton, where it certainly developed.

And, finally, as always, I have to thank my partner Janet, and the cats Humpty Dumpty, Tweedledum and Tweedledee for giving me a constant stream of riddles and reintroducing me to Wonderland and the Looking Glass.

Introduction: curiouser and curiouser...

'You see it's like a portmanteau – there are two meanings packed
up into one word.'
(Lewis Carroll, *Through the Looking Glass*, 1872)

One of the chief practical problems facing us in our attempts to achieve
real understanding and insight is the problem of how to be open without
being self-indulgent – how to remain actively willing to consider new
ideas without falling into the trap of believing whatever appeals to us ...
The temptation to believe that something is true because it could be and
we would like it to be is a destroyer of honest thinking that never goes
out of business. Furthermore, it offers a resting place, whereas true
enquiry has no resting place.

(Magee and Milligan 1995:182)

It is fitting in many ways that this book should begin with the above quotation, which is taken from *On Blindness*, a fascinating dialogue between two
philosophers, one sighted (Brian Magee) and the other blind (Martin Milligan). Magee initiated this dialogue following the death of another blind
philosopher and close friend, Rupert Cross. The exchanges were intended to
begin from the premise that anything which lies outside our direct experience – 'anything that exists that we cannot apprehend or conceptualise or feel
– has no being *for us*, real though it is' (p. x). The aim of the dialogue then
became to examine the nature of our relationship to the unknowable, and
whether, indeed, it was possible to understand this relationship. I do not pro-
fess to comprehend at first reading, and probably even after several readings,
all the levels of analysis in Magee and Milligan's attempt to examine the
nature of blindness. I am a philosopher of the organic kind; I neither have the
benefit of their particular kind of knowledge and experience, nor do I share
these two academics' command of their particular ways of using language.
Even if I were to educate myself in their concerns, I would still be at a disadvantage because – in relation to *their* worlds – I am an outsider and my perspective is, in Antonio Gramsci's terms, a ***positional*** one. (Please note that
words in bold italics are defined in the Glossary.) I cannot *know* what it is to be

blind, for example; I can only attempt to understand how a blind person experiences blindness. If I try to understand it from my perspective, the quality of my understanding is immediately bound up with my own experience, specifically the fact that I am deaf, and so blindness has particular connotations for me. It is the acknowledgement of the limits to my ability to understand both my own experience and the experience of others which often makes me react frustratedly to people who say, from a positional perspective, 'this is the way it is' – as if this 'way' is carved in stone, and immutably true. They seem to forget that even monoliths weather with time, and that history is largely a catalogue of tensions between the **individualism** and **collectivism** that initiate social and political change. This is why, for me, enquiry – particularly enquiry which relates to the human, social and political sciences – 'has no resting place', because standing still denies the tenets of history and the inevitability of change.

History is full of dissenters, of varying levels of effectiveness and conviction. There are also 'silent' voices who go with the flow because they lack the ability to think critically about themselves and the effect their actions have on others, or because they fear persecution if they follow their own paths. I have never been of the latter disposition – the voice of my social conscience is too demanding – but I have worked alongside many deaf people who are, and my own experience of oppression has suggested many reasons for why their 'silence' might feel safe. Nor is my dissent always of the kind so beloved of political activists: this, again, is bound up with knowing my boundaries. In facing up to and attempting to solve the challenges which the environment throws at me and other deaf and disabled people, I cannot pretend to engage in apolitical activity, or to be able to separate the personal and the political. But I do not think strategies for challenging oppression or other kinds of political activity can be effective unless we 'take the masses with us' *willingly*, and demonstrate an understanding of the kinds of barriers we erect which stop many people joining us in our struggles. These barriers concern us as deaf and disabled people directly and are additional to those which society uses to obstruct our path to social transformation.

Most of my work is centred in the intellectual arena – creating and developing theory, and suggesting *how* change might be achieved through challenging stereotyped and restrictive thought and practice by highlighting and emphasizing diversity. This tendency to want to open things up rather than narrow them down is perhaps what creates a conflict in the political arena. It also means that, paradoxically, in some quarters I am labelled as a liberal and in others as a radical. However, since the loudest 'voices' of deafness are those framed by the thinking and experience of positional outsiders or by that of political activists who are not always able to strike a reasonable balance between being where the action is and making sense of it, liberalism is often a pseudonym for the voice of the 'silent' majority, and radicalism is synonymous with the experience of threat. Nevertheless, these labels bemuse me. When I meditate on my reasons for writing, I realize that they are intricately bound up with issues of meaning and representation, specifically with the

roles of dissent and silence in creating new meanings and challenging outdated ones; perhaps I write from a vantage point which allows me to see the
wood *and* the trees. Dissent may seem too strong a word to use in this context,
but if I did not have something different to say, it seems to me that writing
would be pointless; if there were no dissenting voices, however 'silent', there
would be nothing for me to say which was anything other than a reflection of
my own experience or a regurgitation of the past.

This is not to diminish that experience, or to deny the past. When we point
to something outside our immediate frame of reference, three fingers point
backwards to remind us of where we are. My perspective has not been found
on a shelf and picked off simply because it seemed attractive and in need of
dusting, nor is it *the* deaf perspective. It has been arrived at by a long, sometimes painful and certainly ongoing process: observing, participating in,
learning from, critically analysing both my environment and my/others'
(including other deaf and disabled people) relations to it. The reference to the
role of my own experience is to emphasize that I do not claim to represent
anything other than that experience, though I am in a position to provide a
commentary on the experience of others. As deaf and disabled people, we
have become accustomed to what McNay (1992: 191) calls the 'indignity and
misguidedness of speaking for others'. But, as Chadwick (1996: 37) suggests,
our experience of such practice 'can be used to guard against the dangers of
incorporating the worst elements of "majority rule" and to work towards a
participatory democratic form of organisation which reflects difference'.
However, I would also be wary of the conflation of democracy and participation, because there are many types of democracy, some of which merely
involve participation that is imposed by force, or the threat of force, and
others where participation is a result of uncritical allegiance to a particular
set of beliefs and values in the absence of knowledge of alternatives. Close
examination of our homelands in the deaf and disabled communities can
sometimes reveal flawed reflections of the outside world that eat away at the
heart of our communities, and it can therefore be both more enlightening
and more traumatic to turn our gaze in this direction. This is especially so
when our communities have, historically, been marginalized from mainstream society, and draw their strengths from collective bonding through
self-determination, political action or social cohesion. As insiders of marginalized groups, we therefore have to be particularly careful, and also courage-
ous, when we begin to formulate questions around our disenchantment with
characteristics of our communities, *and the way in which these characteristics are
described*, which we may feel are confusing or damaging the lives of people
who are our natural allies.

Although this is not the first book I have written, and probably will not be
the last, in many ways it is the one which I have struggled most to write
because it reaches very deep inside me and comes closer to the core of both
my personal and my professional experience than any of my other work to
date. I am often asked to give subjective accounts of my life, and for the most
part I decline, because I suspect that the majority of requests are born out of

voyeurism or the need for a subjective and often isolated deaf perspective to bulk out the incomplete, insubstantial and unfounded theories of others, rather than out of a genuine desire to understand my experiences in context or to inform thinking in particular areas. I am also acutely aware of how often labels are used in relation to my experience to reflect the position of the user in a way that bears little resemblance to the meaning I associate with those labels. This is true of all the characteristics which are fundamental to who I am – all of these identities sit comfortably in my own psyche and in my own framework of meaning, and all of them have relevance for the way in which I perceive, respond to and learn from the multiple and simultaneous oppressions I experience. But for those who make up my social environment, they are more likely to cause discomfort, create a barrier to communication and to symbolize something alien. When this discomfort is then projected onto me, I somehow become responsible both for the cause *and* for the effect of these oppressions, a psychic meeting place where contradictions can coexist – but they cannot easily be translated into a single physical reality.

I don't believe that any of us, oppressor or oppressed, can take the hat of personal or collective experience on and off at will, though some of us seem remarkably adept at justifying oppression as 'normal', spontaneous thoughts and actions which just happen to take place, and over which 'most people' have no control. But explanations which locate oppression either within the personalities of the oppressed or within those of the oppressors are distractions: prejudice and discrimination are widespread and institutionalized phenomena based on deep-rooted oppressive power relations. Reducing everything to individual 'idiosyncrasies' is deeply offensive because if institutionalized oppression is consciously denied, this denial removes the last remaining possibility of its **deconstruction**. I would further emphasize that because language and communication are the fabric of every single interaction that ever existed – every relationship, every community and every society and culture are founded on these things – and because they are the substance of the way in which deaf people are oppressed, it is a nonsense to suggest to me that I can ever move beyond or deny my sense of my self or that this self could ever be an appendage, something that is 'out there'. So, I have no choice but to live with it and to strive to understand it.

This is why I describe myself as a philosopher of the 'organic' kind. My deafness – to use one of the visual analogies I am so fond of – is a light that illuminates everything, including how I think, how I perceive and how I express myself; I value the different perspective it brings enormously. However this light is in itself a multicoloured rainbow of merging and mutating tones and hues which would be quite meaningless if I were to try to separate them from each other. I recognize that there are times when this particular way of *being* deaf brings me into conflict with the different social worlds of which I am a part – or not a part, depending upon whose gaze I fall under. This tension between self and environment means that in the social context there is at present no sense in which these worlds share a collective experience or boundaries which overlap and engage in the mutual or fluid transfer of information, perhaps because each is defined by collective experiences of qualitatively *different* oppressions. In other words, they have all been socially and culturally constructed as separate and largely autonomous collectivities, each embracing its own conditions for belonging, its own pursuit of authenticity through the construction of *archetypes* of what is desirable, and all have their own strategies for dealing with oppression and for isolating anyone who is seen as different or who engages in dissent. Unsurprisingly, it is rare to find such separate social worlds subject to the gaze and framework of exploration and analysis which are based on a conception of the public realm as common ground where people pass each other from many directions and thus have much to share.

The *social model of disability* separates disability from impairment and attributes the creation of disability to the dominant sociocultural environment. The model, for example, describes deafness, or not-hearing, as an impairment, but a lack of access to 'visually produced' information is a disability which might be countered by removing communication and information barriers in society. Impairment is an individual phenomenon framed largely by medical categories and terminology. However, though the physical and psychological consequences of impairment are clearly part of the reality of disabled peoples' lives, particularly when our relationships to different concepts of 'normalcy' are considered, the analysis of impairment has been marginalized from sociological and cultural discourse on disability (Morris 1992a; Crow 1996). Similarly, there are some ideological disagreements as to whether disability should be conceptualized and explored from within a *phenomenological* framework which takes account of meaning and representation and views disabled people as a social grouping (Shakespeare 1994), a minority group or *community* framework which espouses notions of alternative culture (Padden and Humphries 1988; Ladd and John 1991; Lane 1995; Lane *et al.* 1996), or a *materialist* framework which is focused on the social and economic structures which create disability oppression and describes disabled people as a *social movement* (Oliver 1990, 1996).

Ideological tension is further complicated by social and political tension arising from the diversity which exists in our communities and which has resulted in the marginalization of particular groups such as people with learning difficulties (Brechin and Walmsley 1989), people who are marginalized by virtue of multiple *Others* – such as disabled black and ethnic minority people (Stuart 1992; Vernon 1996), disabled women (Begum 1992; Morris 1996), disabled gays and lesbians (Hearne 1991; Corbett 1994; Shakespeare *et al.* 1996) and deaf people (Padden and Humphries 1988; Ladd and John 1991; Lane 1995; Lane *et al.* 1996).

This book is primarily concerned with deaf people. In terms of self-definition, deaf people are caught at different points in a linguistic and cultural web made up of spoken languages, sign languages, deafness and hearingness. Different locations in the web therefore become associated with different meanings of language and identity, and these meanings are not always static or consistent. Of particular significance, however, is that group of deaf people who define themselves or are defined by others as having a minority group status based on their linguistic and cultural difference, and who distance themselves from notions of deafness as hearing impairment and disability. This group is commonly referred to as the *Deaf* community; in view of this distancing, its existence poses some very difficult and challenging questions for disability dialogues and theory.

There is, further, some evidence of marginalization of *deaf* people from the Deaf community on the basis of impairment, social identification, language use and by the degree of what is called *attitudinal deafness*. The marginalization of deaf people has certainly been exacerbated by the lack of coherent and common frameworks for understanding, and by the limited constructive dialogue both between deaf and disabled people and between academics, researchers and service professionals working in the deaf and disability fields. However, it must be emphasized that *all* deaf people have, in different ways, posed challenges to our thinking about disability, particularly in relation to how disability should be defined. They have also questioned whether or not existing definitions, such as those described by disability legislation or the social model of disability, can include the diversity of deaf experience in a meaningful and acceptable way without discrediting the considerable advances which have been made by both deaf and disabled people in terms of self-definition, self-determination and political action.

A failure to address these issues fully has created a number of paradoxes which, when considered together, have two main implications for deaf and disabled people:

- What are the consequences for collective empowerment as a result of limitations placed on both deaf and disabled people's ability to engage in co-ordinated struggles for participation in key areas of social and political life?
- How might deaf and disabled people challenge (effectively and politically) and reorganize policies and services which appear confused in their philosophy, inconsistent and uncoordinated in their structure and delivery, and which sometimes encourage unhelpful competition for resources both within and between our communities?

Within a climate of division, little attention is paid to common interests, oppressions, needs and rights, or the implications of the specific barriers faced by each group in developing constructive dialogue. But a deeper understanding of the underlying issues could conceivably contribute a great deal both to academic debate and to the future development of services and effective legislation.

This book aims to explore what Oliver (1996: 157) describes as 'the fine line between marginalisation and incorporation (Oliver 1990) which remains one which the disabled people's movement must address'. In this context, the book examines the origins of tensions between deaf and disabled people, the contribution which a number of new frameworks might make to the further development of the social model and to our understanding of disability in society, and, finally, how the *inclusion* of deaf people in disability theory, disability *discourse* and the multitude of discourses which make up the social world might be usefully achieved to our mutual benefit. Many of the issues which are discussed are complex and stimulating, and in order to explore them fully, we need to reach across disciplines and schools of thought, some of which will be unfamiliar to some readers. This complexity must be acknowledged, but is not the intention to use it to mystify the reader. To facilitate access, the book has been structured in a particular way. Terms which appear in bold italic type, both specialist jargon and terms which some readers may use in a taken-for-granted way, are explained further in the Glossary at the end of the book. Each chapter has an introduction, which outlines the main thrust of the chapter and links it to the themes of the book as they are developed, along with boxed information and a chapter summary; these highlight the main issues which have arisen from the discussion so far. And finally, information is presented (where appropriate) in diagrammatic or other forms of visual representation. There are, of course, limitations of such representation, particularly when it is restricted to two dimensions when it seems fixed in space and, in particular, when it represents a particular way of seeing, but all of these illustrations should be regarded as frameworks which are open to modification in the reader's mind.

Though the book is primarily about deaf people, and their different visions, we are viewed in the context of the various linguistic, social and cultural environments which include, alienate or oppress us. As such, it is not a book which seeks to *reify* a given construction of deafness – this makes its analysis different from many which have preceded it. This is perhaps because we need to move away from the idea of culture, society and ideology as a straitjacket if we are to be able to take collective responsibility for starting to assure self-determination and social justice *for all*. When oppressed identities are restricted, and framed by the tenets of cultural backlash and received wisdom, their deconstruction often reveals that oppressor and oppressed are two sides of the same coin.

 1

First principles

'Or madly squeeze a right-hand foot
Into a left-hand shoe.'
(Lewis Carroll, *Through the Looking-Glass*, 1872)

'Contrariwise,' continued Tweedledee, 'if it was so, it might be;
and if it were so, it would be: but as it isn't, it ain't. That's logic.'
(Lewis Carroll, *Through the Looking-Glass*, 1872)

Introduction

In this and the following two chapters, I want to set out my own analysis of
the structures and processes through which deaf and disabled people have
become divided, and to suggest an alternative framework for thinking which
adds to and develops the current frameworks and identifies our common
ground. This chapter is particularly concerned with structural fragmentation
and how this has become the foundation of particular sets of ideas and practices to which members of different communities consent – *paradigms*. It
also deals with the *essentialist* pursuit of different 'truths' about deafness and
disability – *ideologies*. It is important that I stress from the start that I am
questioning paradigms and ideologies, in so far as they represent world-
views belonging to particular times, particular cultures and particular groups
of people, and which can therefore be used to create the particular 'realities'
which, given certain circumstances, constitute *hegemony*:

> To say that some situation has arisen by virtue of hegemony is to say that
> the beliefs of one group have achieved the status of 'the truth' not
> through imposition, the use of wealth, physical coercion, and the active
> oppression of those holding non-conformist views, but through any
> other means which lead to the wiser population giving its consent to a
> certain set of ideas or a certain world-view. This set of ideas thereby
> becomes the common-sense view, is articulated from a point of popular
> strength on behalf of the community, and may be passed on as received
> wisdom (i.e. 'the facts') within the community.
>
> (Turner 1994: 117–18)

I am not disputing the claims of individuals and groups that they have the right to self-determination or the desire to develop a world-view within which they can feel intrinsic value or experience social justice and equity – these, I feel, must be fundamental human rights. It is not my intention either to engage in an iconoclastic challenge of the existing frameworks which we use to explain and understand deafness and disability, and which seem to be at the roots of many of our apparent differences. I am, however, deliberately echoing Nietzsche's comment that 'All truths are bloody truths for me!' (Kaufmann 1950) along with Foucault's (1978) belief that 'truth is no doubt a form of power', in suggesting that they do not always represent frameworks to which we can all be totally committed because of the 'truths' they exclude. Frameworks and theories are, in my view, meant to assist and develop our thinking, not restrict it. Much of how useful they are often depends on which comes first, the framework or the ideas, evidence or people which shape it, particularly in terms of frameworks which describe people. One simple example of a restricting framework might be a research project which starts with the premise that deaf and hearing people are different and that, for deaf people, being deaf is better. In order to test this hypothesis, a series of statements are developed which carry *either* positive overtones when they relate to deaf people (for example, 'Socializing with deaf people is easy') *or* negative overtones when they relate to hearing people (for example 'Hearing people make me angry'). Deaf respondents are then asked to agree *or* disagree with each statement, often with the predictable outcome that being deaf is preferable to being hearing *or vice versa*. In such circumstances our thinking is restricted because the fixity of the states of deafness and hearingness is assumed in the way in which statements are made and, in particular, by statements which are not made. This probably says quite a lot about my own theoretical orientation, but it also reflects to a very large extent the particular set of experiences which make up my world and my own personal and professional history.

It is evident from work published in the last ten years relating to deaf people that only a small section of the deaf population, currently ranging from between 40,000 and 60,000 individuals in Britain, regard themselves as a linguistic and cultural minority group and distance themselves from impairment and disability in its medical/individual construction. It is clear that the alternative discourse on self-definition posited by this group is extremely visible and articulate and finds much favour with both the dominant culture and the disability movement; this more than makes up for the group's limited numbers. However, not all members of this group define themselves *only* in terms of minority group status; many, indeed probably the majority, are unfamiliar with the proposed distinction between minority group status and disability status in its social construction, nor are they aware that alternative disability discourses such as the social model exist or are being manufactured. This is perhaps reflected in the fact that the membership of the British Deaf Association (BDA) – where political activism emerging from linguistic and cultural minority status is most salient – stands at about one-tenth of the estimated total number of British Sign Language (BSL) users.

The remainder of the deaf population, whose numbers range from 1.4 to 8.4 million people, depending on the source and purpose of the statistics and which levels of hearing loss are included in them:

- are aligned with the dominant culture's individual/medical construction of disability, not always by choice;
- define themselves in terms of the disability movement's social construction of disability; or
- are uncommitted in their self-definition, again sometimes because they do not feel sufficiently included in dialogue, theory or practice to make such a commitment.

For the moment, it is convenient to refer to the linguistic minority using the term 'Deaf', to the latter groups as 'hearing impaired' people, and the terms 'deaf' and 'deafness' to refer to both groups together. However, as will become clear, it is not always a simple matter to use terminology consistently, which itself presents a powerful argument against totalizing definitions. I therefore use these terms reservedly.

The cultural backdrop

All models of disability and deafness implicitly or explicitly forge some kind of relationship between the deaf or disabled individual and the dominant culture, and the differences reside mainly in the question of how we understand this relationship. This question has revolved around the issue of the direction of influence – does society influence the individual or does the individual influence society? – and who, ultimately is responsible for the way in which disability and deafness are experienced. The current debate between Deaf and disabled people, for example, concentrates on issues of disability and deafness in different contexts and in different cultures; at the level of theoretical frameworks, there are many similarities across Western societies. I want to begin my analysis with looking at some of the characteristics of the culture in which we live in twentieth-century Britain, which like most Western societies is built on individualism. In individualist societies, individuals are assumed to be discrete, autonomous and independent; *liberal humanism*, the philosophy which delineates conception of the self and society, predominates. From this perspective, individuals are considered to be rational and universal entities who are focused on their rights to choose, define and search for self-fulfilment freely. Individualist cultures emphasize the *I* versus *you* distinction (Kim 1995: 27). In such cultures, relationships are built on contracts such as economic contracts fuelled by the law of supply and demand, and individual 'rights' are of primary importance. Substantive rights – that is, those rights which apply to everyone – are considered to be beyond the bounds of individual duty (Scanlon 1978; Miller 1984; Taylor 1985).

However, these cultures are not necessarily universal in their boundaries, internal structures, interrelationships among individuals and the character- istics of the group. On the basis of these factors, Kim (1995) has identified three main kinds of individualist society which he calls *aggregate*, *distributive* and *static*, and suggests that the main difference between them lies in the flu- idity of the group boundaries. Of critical importance is that individuals in the *aggregate* mode are bound by normative and ethical principles on which they base their claim to 'rights' that all people should have but which do not enjoy legal endorsement (Feinberg 1973), whereas individuals in the *static* mode are bound by law (for further discussion of this in relation to deaf people, see Corker 1996b). Paraphrasing an example developed by Brown (1986), the dis- tinction might be described as follows. When we see another person in phys- ical, psychological or emotional pain or social and economic disadvantage, though we may be compelled by a normative or ethical principle to relieve their pain or help them in some other way, we are not bound by any law to do so. If we fail to respond to that person, we have not committed a crime, but we have violated a moral principle. In most circumstances, however, if we delib- erately contribute to an increase in that person's pain or disadvantage, we have both violated an ethical principle and committed a crime punishable by law.

When important moral and ethical principles are not widely upheld, they are sometimes formalized into laws, of which equality, abortion, incest taboo and child abuse laws are all current examples. Thus aggregate individualism can become static individualism, or these two forms of individualism can coexist. In the USA, for example, which is often described in terms of static individualism, the Bill of Rights and the Constitution of the United States guarantee and protect the inalienable rights of all individuals, and are seen as the cornerstone of America's individualism – 'individuals have rights when, for some reason, a collective goal is not a sufficient justification for denying them what they wish, as individuals, to have or to do, or not a sufficient justi- fication for imposing some loss or injury upon them' (Dworkin 1977: 188). In Britain it is sometimes assumed that because we have the Disability Discrim- ination Act 1995, the Children Act 1989 and various legislation related to equal opportunities, special education and community care, we are the same as the USA. There are, however, major differences in the way in which the concept of 'rights' is translated into law. British law confuses moral and eth- ical principles with 'rights', because what is ultimately formalized in the con- cept of legal rights is *the rights of the dominant culture*. In legal terms, this is reinforced by the suggestion that society accommodates particular ethical or moral principles 'wherever possible' – and this includes the principles of equality and social justice. This is not the same as *guaranteeing* protection of the inalienable rights of *all* individuals in society to equality and social jus- tice. Indeed, in reality, it is about as effective as not formalizing moral and eth- ical principles at all since, in such conditions for example, deaf and disabled people do not have 'rights' – apart, that is, from the 'right' to benevolence, charity or scientific intervention. The contractual relationship between us and the dominant society is driven by the law of benevolence and need, or what Mithaug (1996) calls the need–problem–solution cycle which fuels the monopoly held by the 'massive human services that drive our economic system [and which] identify social problems embedded in individuals and their social relationships, reify them, and make them and their solutions commodities to be bought and sold in the marketplace' (Albrecht 1992: 20, 27). Mithaug (1996: 121, my italics) describes this cycle as one which, in the past,

> freed individuals from their fixed positions in the social structure to improve their prospects for self-determination. To the extent that these individuals could solve *the problems of production valued by the community*, they could also improve their positions of control over production and, as a consequence, improve their prospects for getting what they wanted in life.

The human services are characteristic of *distributive* individualism where individuals have often joined together to protect and propagate their interests in the service of others. But, in developing their own subculture and socializing mechanisms, they have maintained their viability and have competed so successfully with other groups that they often epitomize goals which conflict with those of other individuals and of a changing society. By law, monopolies are not allowed unless they are subject to strict governmental and judicial control. But if government and the judiciary is in agreement with or dictates the values and goals of the service monopoly, the latter becomes relatively autonomous, preserving existing power structures, acting as an agent of social control, providing 'solutions' to social problems, and furthering particular political ideologies (Dalrymple and Burke 1995). In such circumstances, Kleinman (1980), Zola (1983) and, more recently, Fancher (1995) argue that the monopoly serves the existing interests of its members at the expense of consumers' changing interests. When set against the rights of the monopoly, all other 'rights' pale into insignificance. In this cultural context – which, it must be emphasized, all deaf and disabled people share, irrespective of ideology, identity and social identification, and which many willingly collude with or internalize – social fragmentation is rife. To mirror such a culture in our own communities, however, is not helpful to our status as oppressed peoples, nor does it assist us in our challenge of oppression and the pursuit of social justice for all.

The emphasis on conflict and divisions which permeates our communities has, in my view, disguised other substantial commonalities which might be used in this pursuit, and this has been detrimental to our understanding of peoples and cultures in contact. Such an emphasis may soon no longer be relevant at a time of rapid social and cultural change. As we approach the new millennium, however, we must be aware that groups form for different reasons and that different kinds of interrelationships are effective in diverse cultural contexts. We might, for example, compare two forms of collectivism:

- the collective, though independent pursuit of a common political goal which is at the root of social movements (Shakespeare 1993; Oliver 1996);
- the collective interdependence of minority or ethnic groups which are formed on the basis of a particular society, culture or world-view.

There will be a number of critical differences in the implications of these two forms for the relationship between the personal and the political. The first is a form of political collectivism based on social *un*relatedness, whereas the second hinges on social interrelatedness. Both, however, are suspended in a culture which is politically and socially individualist. Whereas we can learn a considerable amount from cultural contexts which are different to our own, we cannot simply or easily take the belief and value system and social relationships – the cultural identity – of another culture or time in history and transpose it onto that in which we live now, because this would be to ignore cultural *historicity* (Fishman 1982). A comment made by Elisabeth Bumiller in her book about women in India, *May You Be the Mother of a Hundred Sons*, is relevant to the present analysis:

> I decided that the question of whether it was intellectually consistent to be in favor of a woman's right to abortion yet opposed to sex-selective abortion had, for me, a different answer in the United States than in India. I can't resolve the contradictions and can only conclude that there are no universally applicable answers in this world.
>
> (Bumiller 1991:121)

The logic of essentialism

Individualistic narratives seek to promote a particular viewpoint, frequently at the expense or to the detriment of others. In some cultures, wars are still fought over ideology and religion which are framed in this way. In Western cultures, the term 'acts of terrorism' reinforces this because it suggests that there is something which has been set up as an established principle or belief which is being 'terrorized'. But terrorism is not confined to physical aggression; in so-called 'civilized' Western society, the most pernicious form of terrorism is attitudinal and intellectual oppression which persuades people that they must think in a particular way to reap the benefits of their culture. For example, it is often remarked in the media that British politics is currently much more about the success with which one political party can damage the reputation of the other by subversive means than it is about democracy and getting things done. And yet, the differences between the main political parties in terms of policies are becoming less and less noticeable – the terms 'right of centre' and 'left of centre', though they still undoubtedly exist on the backbenches, are no longer so readily visible at the level of governance, which has become more and more concentrated on the centre. The suggestion here seems to be that conflict, or perhaps the need for conflict, is deeply rooted in our culture; so much so that if one set of differences are resolved, they are sure to be replaced by another. Certainly, narratives of conflict, of which the issues discussed in this book are fairly characteristic examples, do appear to reflect Western culture's predilection for **empirical positivism** which rests on a world-view that has persisted for centuries, and is prevalent in both traditional psychology and sociology. This world-view is based on the metaphor of linear progress, absolute truth and rational planning (Harvey 1989; Reason 1994) and has five important components (Box 1.1).

Box 1.1 The essential beliefs of empirical positivism

- Logocentrism – the belief that scientific rationality provides the absolute truth about the world and that reason is the highest form of knowledge and understanding;
- phonocentrism – the belief that the spoken word is the ultimate communication;
- ethnocentrism – the belief that one's own culture or race is superior to all other races or cultures;
- phallocentrism – the belief that the archetypal qualities of the masculine such as language, concepts and analysis, are primary;
- physicalism (or materialism) – the belief in the primacy and priority of physical properties and the laws that govern them.

These beliefs generate their own logic of binary oppositions (Featherstone 1990) or 'either/or' (Burr 1995), as epitomized by questions such as 'Do we have free will *or* are we determined?', 'Are we individuals *or* the product of society?', 'Do we analyse our experiences in terms of the subjective *or* the objective?', 'Do we act through reason *or* through emotions?' These questions lead directly into the more specific questions with which this book is concerned: 'Are we disabled *or* does society disable us?', 'Is deafness (or disability) best explained within the social model *or* a minority group framework?' 'Do we seek inclusion *or* coexistence?' and 'Is identity singular and finite *or* multiple and complex, fixed *or* transitional?' Moreover, deaf and disabled people are not completely immune from thinking in this way.

For example, Colin Barnes's justification for the social model of disability is heavily grounded in the search for the historical origins of 'able-bodied' ideals and values. Although he refers to 'the myth of bodily and intellectual perfection' (1996b: 57), his analytical focus, along with that of many other disabled analysts, is very much on the body. This in itself seems to reflect the materialism and logocentrism of Western culture, since physical properties, in many ways, lend themselves more readily to rational explanation and tend to be more predictable. Yet for deaf people, this emphasis is problematic, as we will see in the following chapter. Moreover, other disabled people such as Sally French (1993: 17) argue that various 'profound social problems' that she encounters, in this instance as a visually impaired person, influence her life far more than material barriers, and are 'more difficult to regard as entirely socially produced or amenable to social action'. The dual gaze of the binary is also evident in a somewhat circular argument concerning progression and causality of empowerment. Oliver (1996) believes that the key to understanding self-empowerment is the notion of collective empowerment, and this progression underpins the conceptualization of the social model of disability. Fenton (1989) reverses this progression, and so echoes the minority group position.

Binary oppositions such as these suggest that disability and deafness have some inherent, essential nature, which can be discovered and which is therefore given the status of 'the truth'. Put another way, they are characteristic of *essentialism*, which hinges on the belief that the world can be understood in terms of underlying structures, and that such structures can be explained by all-embracing world-views or *metanarratives*, such as those described in Box 1.1. In this sense the economic structure exemplified in the work of Marx is no different from the psychic structures of Freud and Piaget. It is not difficult to understand why people cling to this way of seeing the world. Shakespeare (1996: 108) suggests that it is 'comforting and secure' to be able to define and understand people and their worlds within clear boundaries. Certainly there is no harm in simplistic *reductionism* as long as it is understood that theories and frameworks which are based on it cannot provide a total explanation of individual or collective reality. There is generally a gap between what a theory can do to explain our own reality and what we need to know – a so-called experiential learning gap – because theories designed according to particular perspectives do not always mirror our own, and they are not always addressed to things that we are concerned with or interested in. We are often involved with unique or context-specific situations and so find many theories limited in their relevance or application (Lee 1990).

The primacy given to that side of the equation which reinforces the metanarrative becomes the 'norm', and this 'norm' designates anything outside it or contrary to it as non-existent or meaningless:

> Once the normal is constructed, its explanation organises our understanding of all other variations by moving us to conceive of all other outcomes as violations or variations of the logic of the normal. The power of the normal is its ability both to establish 'difference' and, then, to disguise 'difference' by transforming it either into 'variation' or 'deviance'. In doing so, all instances falling within a category become understandable in terms of the contours of some instances. Differences within a conceptualised category are rarely to be seen as requiring different explanations, but only as variations of an already established theme. This process of developing explanations is particularly irresistible when we start the process with already defined and differentially evaluated outcomes, that is, when there is a preexisting commitment to what at the moment is defined as normal.
>
> (Simon 1996: 14)

The dominant culture's perceived dichotomy between normalcy and **Other** underpins many metanarratives in Western society. The term 'Other' has a number of different, specific meanings within philosophy. It is here used in its broadest sense to describe aspects of people which cannot be embraced by the thought-forms of Western philosophy without giving them primacy in some way. As such they compromise the dominant world-view of normalcy. Structural fragmentation is present in both the dominant culture and in deaf and disabled communities, largely *as a response to* the pressure to deny difference.

Social diversification, which is one factor in the production of social fragmentation, generally takes two main forms: **pluralism** and **individuation**. Individuation is a consequence of the multiplication and separation of roles available to or in some cases imposed upon the individual by oppressive forces, whereas pluralism refers to the increased visibility of social diversity. I will return to these concepts in the following chapter. The literature on disability and deafness is currently preoccupied with structural divisions relating to social diversification, both in terms of pluralism and in terms of individuation, which are described in the context of how deaf and disabled communities deal with multiple identities. For example, Ladd (1992: 85), in his own analysis of the structural divisions in the deaf population, suggests that they are socially produced:

> One of the major manifestations of oppression is the creation of divisions within a culture. In the Deaf community, there are three major strands. One is the marginalisation of partially deaf and deafened people, hearing children of Deaf parents, and hearing parents of Deaf children, in what would be a very sizable community. The second strand, which overlaps with the above in pertinent ways, is the division between those with a 'better' education (or other characteristics that lead them to look down on BSL (British Sign Language) users, and grassroots Deaf people. The third strand is the divisions between mainstream Deaf life and the lives of Deaf minorities; the latter including Black Deaf, gay and lesbian Deaf, disabled and Deaf-Blind people.

He attributes social divisions to oppression, but he is careful not to identify the oppressor. Shakespeare (1996: 109), on the other hand, suggests that the lack of awareness of similar divisions in the disabled population is not without its problems:

> there is a danger of ignoring the fact that disabled people are also men and women, straight and gay, and come from various ethnic groups. Just as white feminists were accused by black women of ignoring the specificities of black women's experience, and even of being racist, so disabled people risk ignoring difference.

There is also reference to the tendency to define the relationships between deafness, disability and the dominant culture in terms of a binary opposition. For example, Davis (1995: 1) suggests that 'one is either disabled or not', and

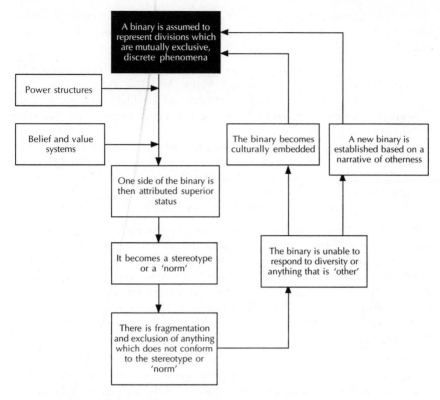

Figure 1.1 The dilemma of essentialism

Oliver (1996: 150) talks about the 'distinction between movement and community'; whereas Lane *et al.* (1996: 413) insist that 'Deaf people do not see themselves as being disabled', and that 'there is no continuum between Deaf and hearing'. The links between binary oppositions and the process of social fragmentation are illustrated in Figure 1.1.

Figure 1.1 shows that social diversification *itself* is problematized by essentialist world-views since, as I implied above, it is not amenable to social control or *cultural regulation* by the dominant culture without giving it primacy. It is seen as individualism out of control; and control, as we have seen, is necessary to individualist cultures. Simon (1996: 1) continues:

> The problematics posed by [pluralism and individuation] for the individual also exist for the individual theorist as well as for communities of theorists. Individuation at the individual level and differentiation at the collective level make it increasingly difficult to continue to maintain the illusion that science can achieve some privileged position of neutral observation reported in unbiased language.

Control must then be manufactured, but in a way which is ***legitimated*** within the dominant culture. So far as deaf and disabled people are concerned there are two forms of control open to the dominant culture, which may interact:

- overt control and social oppression through the imposition of a different, 'objective' and more manageable structure which is divorced from deaf and disabled people's multiple realities, and which cons them into believing that medicine and science know best because these are given the culture's stamp of 'truth';
- subtle control through the manufacture and perpetuation of 'split subcultures', which may or may not be based on deaf and disabled people's multiple realities, and the attribution of value to one side of the dichotomy. Control is achieved because struggles are turned inwards towards self-discipline; if taken to the extreme, this can result in self-destruction.

The term 'split subcultures' is drawn from Susan Griffin's (1984: 175) concept of 'split cultures', which she describes as cultures in which we are 'divided against ourselves. We no longer regard ourselves as part of this earth. We regard our fellow human beings as enemies. And, very young, we learn to disown parts of our own being.' As indicated earlier, one of the processes by which cultures become 'split' is linked to the attribution of value, where one side of a duality is given a more privileged position or greater 'truth' or 'value' than the other:

> Though this device is convenient, it produces stereotypical and distorted pictures of a complex social reality. When a whole society or culture is pigeonholed in dichotomous categories . . . subtle differences and qualitative nuances that may be more characteristic of these social entities are glossed over. Such descriptive labels evoke unduly fixed and caricature-like mental impressions of cultures or societies rather than representative pictures of their complexities. Also, when cultures are presented in black-or-white terms, not only does this cloud our understanding of them, but it inevitably leads to our making good/bad comparisons.
>
> (Sinha and Tripathi 1995: 123)

'Good' and 'bad' are arbitrary and relative value categories, but when the 'good' or more powerful consciousness becomes locked in a power struggle with the 'bad' or weaker consciousness, it can become an attempt by one to eliminate the other in the pursuit of survival. For example, whereas Shakespeare (1994) suggests that the Marxist origins of the social model reduce everything to social and economic factors, Barnes argues that a focus on the cultural production of prejudice 'reduces explanations for cultural phenomena such as perceptions of physical, sensory and intellectual difference to the level of thought processes' (1996b: 49). Each has problems with the other's reductionisms. Elements of this are also in evidence in the tensions between Deaf and hearing impaired people, and the disability movement and the individual model of disability. Ladd (1994: 6, my additions in brackets), arguing from a Deaf perspective, uses a similar reductionism in his comment that 'If you look at people who are deafened later in life, you see how miserable their lives are. They may be no more or less deaf than we, audiologically, yet while we are connected through our language and our culture, [which is a tremendous source of positivity and pride] they are cut off from the society with which they identify' [and this is the source of their misery]. These 'miserable' lives, moreover, are only worthy of the pages of 'a very large . . . clinical literature' (Lane *et al.* 1996: x). Similarly, Crow (1996: 208) asks, 'Why has impairment been so excluded from our analysis? Do we believe that admitting there could be a difficult side to impairment will undermine the strong, positive (SuperCrip?) images of our campaigns?' She seems to imply intentionality in the failure of disability discourse to include impairment because it means weakening the tenets of the social model.

A backlash is somewhat inevitable, however, which might be summed up in Ingstad and Reynolds-Whyte's (1995: 10) question, 'We ask if and how impairment affects one's value as a human being and one's position as a social person. Are persons with impairments impaired persons?' Hence Golan (1995: 11) derides the suggestion that by not adopting the positive, proud Deaf identity, 'I am living a marginal life with no identity . . . that I have no self-esteem . . . that I am pretending to be a hearing person . . . that I am ashamed of being deaf', and French (1993: 19) says that being told 'my definitions are wrong, that I have not quite grasped what disability is, tends to close the discussion prematurely; my experiences are compartmentalised, with someone else being the judge of which are and which are not worthy of consideration'. This is certainly an example of the 'struggle' that Lane (1995) refers to – a struggle for the right to self-definition; at its roots it is a struggle for the dominant discourse on deafness and disability. But if Golan's and Crow's views are read carefully, the rejection of 'negative' labels and the acknowledgement of the difficulty of including impairment in analysis implies also a rejection of the dominant discourse of deafness and disability as framed by the dominant culture. However, these, perhaps, are not issues about positivity and pride versus negativity, but about where 'pride' is placed in relation to other ways of experiencing deafness and disability.

The distinction between the two forms of control, as outlined above, marks the difference between what French philosopher Michel Foucault called ***sovereign power*** and ***disciplinary power*** (see for example Kritzman 1988: 96–109), which I will return to in the following chapter. It seems to be the case that there is more emphasis on the structural and material elements of sovereign power than on disciplinary power, which has obvious parallels with the comments I made about terrorism at the start of this section. Both Colin Barnes (1996b) and Harlan Lane (1992) emphasize the substantial historical evidence for governments and their officials' exercise of sovereign power – through practices such as institutionalization, eugenics, genocide and infanticide – aimed at the pursuit of the 'perfect' and 'pure' model of humanity. Such practice still exists, though modern-day equivalents of sovereign power uphold the dominant world-view of what is moral or ethical. In other words, technically, the practices which constitute intervention have not changed very much – they still involve invasion of the body or the mind in some way – but perceptions of what is 'right' have changed, as has the sophistication of the technology and thought behind the practices.

In the discussion of deafness and disability, disciplinary power is marginalized perhaps because it includes a recognition of *internalized oppression* as a form of self-discipline. Internalized oppression, like impairment, is Other. In general no one wants to accept the downside of disability as experienced by individuals – it must either be 'cured' because it is 'not normal' or it must be hidden because it is a threat to the survival of a strong identity. But the emphasis on sovereign power is itself legitimated by the dominant culture, since disciplinary power is only effective while it remains underground. Foucault (1976: 86) says that 'power is tolerable only on condition that it mask a substantial part of itself. Its success is proportional to its ability to hide its own mechanisms.' He provides us with a parallel example in relation to sexual practices, noting that with the power to say which practices were permissible, and which not, inevitably came the idea of 'normal' sexual practice. The practice of scrutinizing the population's sexual behaviour and of encouraging people to confess to the 'inquisitors' their sexual 'sins' developed into a powerful form of social control as people began to internalize this process. They were encouraged to scrutinize their own behaviour, to ask questions about their own 'normality' and to adjust their own behaviour accordingly.

Barnes (1996b) and Oliver (1996) agree that some of the 'splitting' into impairment categories is a form of social control which identifies people as 'problems' because they are seen to deviate from the dominant culture's view of what is desirable, 'normal', socially acceptable or safe; the dominant culture sees these 'problems' as requiring different 'solutions' which are provided by medicine and science. As a result, hearing impaired and disabled people are compelled to live as an individualist, disparate subculture of 'unrelated strangers' – unrelated not only because these categories are arbitrary but also because from a social perspective, we are without the benefit of relationships based on longstanding trust and cooperation. As such we are reminiscent of the *Gesellschaft* tradition of industrial urban settings which evolved from the sixteenth century onwards (Tönnies 1957, first published 1887). The Deaf community, on the other hand, could be described as a 'culture of relatedness' (Kagitçibasi 1995) which is more like the *Gemeinschaft* tradition. However, sociologist Joshua Fishman (1989: 303–4) warns:

> The return to origins, to purity . . . is part of a more general yearning for Gemeinschaft, part of a hope or pretence that in the simplicity of Gemeinschaft may be found the solutions to the complex problems of Gesellschaft. The long-ago is a desirable point of departure for several reasons. It is relatable to religious and temporal glories . . . It is uncontaminated by the currently stigmatised anti-models. Finally, for the man [*sic*] in the street, any claims made for it are less confirmable and therefore . . . it is infinitely more manipulable than those closer to hand.

As a community which seems to be based on *essentialist* collectivist values, the Deaf community is marginalized by the individualism of the dominant culture, and itself marginalizes 'unrelated' hearing impaired and disabled people. Gregory (1995: 22) feels that 'the distinction [between Deaf and hearing impaired] has been important in order to establish notions of Deaf identity, Deaf community and Deaf culture, as, without such recognition, the rights of Deaf people are not clear'. In making the link between social differences and different rights, she alludes to questions of power and control, which is further reinforced when she goes on to say that 'in establishing a clear identity for one group, those on the outside become excluded and marginalised' (p. 22). French (1993: 19) agrees that 'this gives rise to feelings of estrangement and alienation', but some commentators argue that perhaps this *should* be the case because the Other is 'alien'.

The social agenda and the 'right' to self-definition

Any attempt to develop ideas which takes the larger variety of human capacities or histories and transforms them into a smaller number of possible outcomes (or reduces most of existing diversity into non-consequential variations) produces alienation and fragmentation when it is linked to questions about the boundaries to group identity and the nature of social identification, social networking, and group beliefs and values. Significantly, Vernon (1996a: 51) notes, with reference to race and disability, that 'the fact that someone is oppressed does not mean they are free of prejudices against other oppressed groups in society . . . For as long as we are divided and fighting our own exclusive causes, we will continue to be oppressed.' This, again, raises the important question of relationships between deafness, disability and narratives of otherness related to gender, race and sexuality, for example. Questions about what is 'like' and what is 'not like' – or issues of **identity** (Turner 1994; Corker 1996b) – are clearly influential, if not critical, in the social stratification of deaf and disabled communities, as is shown in Figure 1.2. Being 'like' something or someone is also a matter of degree, and, as Shakespeare (1996) indicates in his distinction between 'identity and identity choices', issues of identity are not always about what is given. We can choose to be more 'like' someone than 'like' someone else, or we can be compelled to conform to a particular identity, because we are often under pressure to fit, or perhaps because we have been rejected from an alternative framework which we would have chosen given the choice. Thus, for many deaf and disabled people, choosing between Deaf *or* hearing *or* disabled does not represent a real choice of *social* identification at all.

Social identification is subsumed by a discourse on 'clear' or 'pure' identities – that is, identities which are defined in terms of essentialist, usually singular parameters which assume 'master [*sic*] status' (Goffman 1968). By implication, identities which are not 'clear' or 'pure', such as those of people who are of mixed racial parentage (Katz 1996), bisexual (Firestein 1996) or multiply disabled, for example, are problematized. When new identities are forged, this process is often combined with an attempt to draw from the experience of other groups in order to justify the creation of a different concept of 'purity'. There are a number of references in the literature to which particular group similarities can be drawn, as, for example, when Lane *et al.* (1996: 417) suggest that Deaf people are 'like other language minorities' and when Oliver (1996: 148) draws parallels between the collective empowerment of the disabled people's movement and that of other 'new social movements'. However, Ladd and John (1991: 15, my addition in brackets) present a slightly different scenario when they say that 'Many disabled people see Deaf people as belonging with them outside the mainstream culture. We, on the other hand, see disabled [and hearing impaired] people as "hearing" people in that they use a different language to us, from which we are excluded, and see them as being members of society's culture'. This scenario is more reminiscent of Shakespeare's reference to an 'us' and 'them' approach (1996: 108).

This is reinforced when we look at the history of parallels in the Deaf community. Arthur Dimmock (1980, 1986), one of the original chairmen of the National Union of the Deaf (NUD), moved from the view that Deaf people constituted an 'independent and ethnic group' to say that 'I quite like the phrase "Linguistic Minority" . . . I used Ethnic Minority in the past, but it raised a lot of objections because of the alien tag' (quoted in Ladd and John 1991:10). The particular parallels which are emphasized in trying to establish a coherent group, identifiable in some recognizable category, can be implicitly associated with strengthening our identity and our boundaries such that we are distanced from the Other *and* legitimated by the dominant culture. The fact that many ethnic minorities are also linguistic minorities does not seem to come into the equation. Developing the idea that the minority group construction of deafness effectively dichotomizes diversity by contracting the individual/medical construction of deaf experience still further into two discrete and often opposing world-views – Deaf *or* hearing – illustrates this. The Deaf Other – hearing impairment – within such a framework, becomes a subcategory of *hearing* and so is distanced. But the 'positive' image of Deaf people finds favour with the dominant culture because it is 'unlike' that presented by disabled people, 'who are thought to be physically repulsive or mentally inadequate' (Christiansen and Barnarrt 1995: 215). In the context of 'purity', this approach becomes reminiscent of the phallocentrism inherent in notions of sexual dimorphism – the division of sexuality into male and female – for example. It seems to impose its own metanarrative. Whereas Deaf people are seen to have a 'right' not only to their language, but also to their 'roots' and 'culture', which are given to them by the Deaf community, hearing impaired people seem to have no such 'right' to belong and are caught between the opposing sides of the dichotomy.

Interestingly, Shakespeare (1996) goes on to suggest that the history of disability is *not* like that of race and gender – a parallel which is more usually drawn. In my own work (Corker 1996b) I express a concern that the

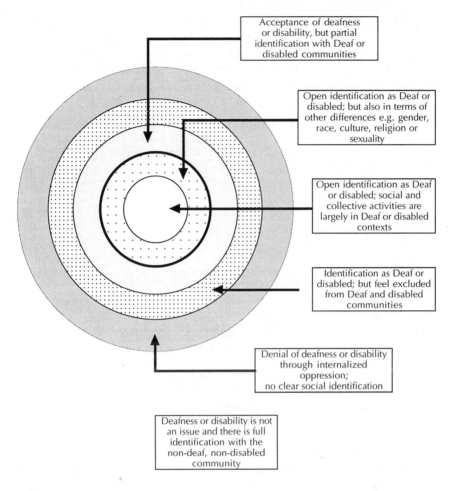

Acceptance of deafness
or disability, but partial
identification with Deaf or
disabled communities

Open identification as Deaf or
disabled; but also in terms of
other differences e.g. gender,
race, culture, religion or
sexuality

Open identification as Deaf
or disabled; social and
collective activities are
largely in Deaf or disabled
contexts

Identification as Deaf or
disabled; but feel excluded
from Deaf and disabled
communities

Denial of deafness or disability
through internalized
oppression;
no clear social identification

Deafness or disability is not
an issue and there is full
identification with the
non-deaf, non-disabled
community

Boundary of Deaf community/disability movement

Figure 1.2 The social agenda – identity and social identification in the Deaf
and disabled population

generalized parallels that Deaf people are drawing between their history and
that of black people are somewhat tenuous. Part of this concern is because
such parallels underrate the fact that the vast majority of deaf children are
born to hearing parents who have not experienced deafness before and who
have usually internalized the dominant phonocentric values of Western culture. These children do not often have the benefit of Deaf role models from
within the family nor the community *of their origin*. Though they may subsequently find such role models later in life in the Deaf community – in effect
the Deaf community is adopted as the family or community *of choice* – this is

frequently a harrowing journey. Its outcome may rest on how they resolve the conflict between the values of the family of origin, which for the most part reflect those of the dominant culture, and those of the family of choice, which in this case advocates an existence which is separate from the majority culture, from the family of origin, *and from disability*:

> we do not wish mainstream society to restructure so we can be *part* of it. Rather, we wish for the right to exist as a linguistic minority group within that society . . . Labelling us as 'disabled' demonstrates a failure to understand that we are not disabled in any way within our own community . . . Many disabled people see Deaf people as belonging, with them outside the mainstream culture. We, on the other hand, see disabled people as 'hearing' people in that they use a different language to us, from which we are excluded, and see them as being members of society's culture, as 'consumers' when active participation is restricted by society's attitude to 'its own'.
>
> (Ladd and John 1991: 14–15)

However, the obvious struggle which exists between these different sets of values means that I strongly support Shakespeare's (1996) view that deafness and disability, *excepting the situation where both child(ren) and parents are Deaf or disabled*, are more 'like' sexuality than they are 'like' race, where the family of origin is also the racial family, or gender where, in most communities, different gender roles are clearly visible. Moreover, the parallel can be taken further. In recent years, philosophers and sociologists such as Thompson (1987, 1994), Herdt (1993) and Roscoe (1995) have been urging gay men to challenge the assumptive structure of sexual dimorphism and begin to define themselves as a 'third gender' which can learn from the intersexual role of the *berdache*, who, in some cultures, is a powerful shamanic figure. It seems, however, that we are now seeing a similar situation in the increasing visibility of borderline deaf (and hearing) people who do not see themselves as Deaf or hearing, and feel restricted by essentialist notions (see Chapter 5 for further explanation). Another parallel which might be made is between the Deaf community and Jewish Hasidim, particularly in relation to some more militant views on segregated education, employment and training and the 'right' to exist as a minority group with its own cultural, linguistic and social practices. Sexuality discourses and minority group discourses, like disability discourses, are at present regarded as neither socially acceptable nor safe. In such circumstances, parallels may be more often about placing our social identities alongside other identities which have been legitimated within the dominant culture, than they are about real likenesses.

Looking at the development of group boundaries in terms of dichotomies, then, particularly when it is connected with issues of the legitimacy of an oppressed group within the dominant culture, tends to result in internal fragmentation. This raises further questions about the nature of our communities, such as 'What or who is dominant or powerful?', 'What is the right way to exist?', 'Who fits or doesn't?' and 'How do we make decisions about and act on these issues?' For example, Lane (1995: 173) refers to a 'struggle' between the linguistic minority and 'disability' constructions and says that there is 'no simple criterion for identifying most childhood candidates as clients of the one position or the other'. The reference to deaf children as 'clients of one construction *or* the other' is an indirect reference to the way in which the power and 'rights' held by children, as we will see in Chapter 4, are largely a function of adult agendas, both Deaf and hearing, because children are the key to survival in every community. It illustrates how far deaf and disabled children are behind in the race for 'rights', which, for these children, seem to remain hooked on the outdated notion of what is in the best interests of the child, as determined by adults, and which are a reflection of Western society's tendency to divide its members' life cycles into two broad age states: child-hood and adulthood. However, adult 'cocoons can stifle and oppress as well as comfort' (Franklin 1995: 7). I will argue in a later chapter that, for this reason, it is necessary to consider childhood as a factor when exploring the rocky ground of simultaneous and multiple oppressions. These questions of power move the analysis into the political realm.

The political agenda

When 'rights' are established in territorial fashion around social agendas that many groups could claim to share, such as the 'right' to self-expression, self-determination, intrinsic worth, or the 'right' to social justice, it can result in open conflict simply because different and sometimes contradictory mean-ings are placed on these 'rights'. One important example of contradicting 'rights' is the discrepancy which can arise from the struggle between the right to self-determination *for all* and the expression of that right by *a few*:

> We are as likely to experience contradictions between what we believe is fair in the moral sense and what we experience as constituting fair treat-ment in the practical and social sense. The discrepancy between the right and the experience of self-determination is an example of what is more rather than less likely to trouble us now and in the future.
>
> (Mithaug 1996: 240)

Dichotomizing diversity can contribute to this struggle when one group becomes associated with a doctrine of 'all' which ultimately rules a culture of dissatisfaction and discomfort. The conflict over 'rights' within this culture goes hand in hand with a pressure to conform to the dominant group's ver-sion of normalcy, which itself is portrayed as the most fundamental of 'rights'. Different perceptions of normalcy imply different relationships with the dominant culture; since that culture, for deaf and disabled people, is an oppressive one focused on social control, the nature of these relationships will to a large extent determine whether and how oppression is perceived and challenged, and whether and how we regain self-control and self-determination.

Williams (1989: 258–60), with particular reference to people with learning difficulties, has identified three main political strategies which people use to liberate themselves from oppression:

- fitting into and, sometimes uncritically, adopting the norms, values and culture of the world as it is;
- withdrawal from society into a separate culture and the assertion of the positive attributes of that culture;
- entering the world and collectively organizing around changing it on one's own terms.

Deaf and disabled people can be further fragmented by contradictions in or the priorities given to these strategies, as is illustrated in Figure 1.3, because

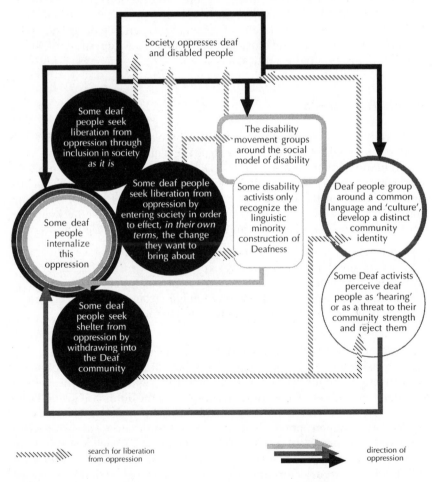

Figure 1.3 The political agenda: cycles of oppression and fragmentation – origins, responses and strategies employed for liberation

each implies a different balance between social and political agendas, which can itself become confused with the search for community belonging and expectations of the kind of community that is searched for. Shakespeare (1996: 107) notes that

> there are . . . contradictions internal to the political strategies, for example with the clash between the social model and the minority group notions of disability . . . There are in fact two, contradictory goals of disability politics: firstly, demolish the processes which disable; second defend disabled people.

Oliver (1996: 166) suggests that the struggle between the individual and the collective is particularly acute in the sphere of disability politics because 'seeing the end of the separation between personal and public spheres is central to disabled people's world view'. I would add to this, however, that in the search for community, often the pull of social belonging is more persuasive and more important than the promise of political action for oppressed groups who are excluded from mainstream social life. The Deaf community and the disability movement might be described as the powerhouses of collective political activism. Deaf and disabled *individuals* nevertheless have a variety of perceptions of the function of political activism and what this means for their social relationships. In other words, the social fragmentation of the deaf population could be said to be produced in a similar way to that which can be observed among women, where varied relationships to being female and to feminism produce different groupings such as housewives, professional women, liberal, radical or lesbian feminists. These perceptions will, moreover, be different for people in the process of finding community and identity to those who have already found it and are committed to it. For the former, the social and political agendas may be interrelated, whereas for the latter a political agenda can more easily be pushed to the fore. Equally, a singleminded pursuit of a social agenda can lead to the marginalization of the political agenda and vice versa. Yet I would suggest that both agendas are critical to the survival of oppressed groups, because how they interact has consequences for the strength of collective organization and political action. But it also has potential consequences for the experience of internalized oppression when individual expectations are not realized, as I will explain later in this section.

For example, the disability movement has traditionally focused on the political agenda framed by the social model of disability. In establishing and being committed to an essentialist dichotomy between the individual and society, the movement argues that the main responsibility for their liberation from oppression is located in the dominant culture, which must change its conceptualization of normalcy. At the same time the movement recognizes that it has responsibility for the **collective empowerment** of disabled people through 'consciousness raising' and the mobilization of campaigning resources. But the strength of *collective* empowerment itself hinges on the kind of relationships that are developed within the movement. Disabled people in transition, and even those who have committed themselves to the movement, can be given a great deal of information and access to resources but may still be prevented from using them if relationships within the movement do not accommodate unconditional social support and networking. I want to emphasize the term 'unconditional' here because many deaf and disabled people have grown up in a climate where love and social support is *conditional* on how 'well they cope with their disability' or how far they are successful in maintaining a facade of being non-disabled. The movement does of course have a social element, largely in its involvement in its own form of cultural production through disability arts for example, but this too has a political aim in the fight against disabling culture (Campbell and Oliver 1996). Finkelstein (1996: 111) expresses the dilemma between the social and political agendas from the perspective of a disabled activist when he says that

> there is a great deal of uncertainty amongst disabled people about whether we do want 'our own culture'. After all, we all have had the experiences of resisting being treated as different, as inferior to the rest of society. So why now, when there is much greater awareness of our desire to be fully integrated into society, do we suddenly want to go off at a tangent and start trying to promote our differences, our separate identity? . . . a cultural identity will play a vital role in helping us to develop the confidence necessary for us to create the organisations which we need to promote the social change we all want.

The movement has, however, resisted a role in more direct forms of individual social support:

> If a person's physical pain is the reason they are unhappy there is nothing the disability movement can do about it. All that BCODP [British Council of Organizations of Disabled People] can do is facilitate the politicisation of people around these issues. Of course this politicisation is fairly difficult to make practical progress with – much easier to achieve anti-discrimination legislation than a total review of how society regards death and dying, I imagine. This might explain why these subjects haven't been made a priority, but their day will come.
>
> (Vasey 1992: 43)

The Deaf community, on the other hand, is firmly rooted in a social agenda which cherishes interdependence and community support networks which extend beyond national boundaries, because the community is itself an international community made up of nation states. As with the disability movement, however, there is a tension inherent in the support role of the community, because unconditional support is not readily extended to deaf people in transition nor to those who experience oppression within the dominant culture. Deaf people must abide by the rules of the culture to benefit from its support. With the growth of Deaf Studies departments in universities and colleges and other forms of Deaf sector employment, particularly that which is focused on the teaching of sign language, it is sometimes suggested that if deaf people 'choose' to exist in the dominant culture, then they only have themselves to blame for their oppression, when an alternative, and 'better' lifestyle is available in the Deaf community. Awareness of the wider political agenda is largely confined to the educated Deaf elite, and this can in itself lead to social fragmentation in the Deaf community and between Deaf and disabled people. For example, Padden and Humphries (1988: 44) say that

> the modern language of 'access' and 'civil rights,' as unfamiliar as it is to Deaf people, has been used by Deaf leaders because the public under-stands these concerns more readily than the ones specific to the Deaf community. Knowing well the special benefits, economic and otherwise, of calling themselves disabled, Deaf people have a history, albeit an uneasy one, of alignment with other disabled groups.

The last few years have seen a great deal of anger in the community about the demise of Deaf clubs, which, along with residential schools, are at the heart of Deaf cultural life. In particular, it has been noted that Deaf young people are finding different ways of coming together, and that Deaf profes-sionals tend to congregate more around professional activities such as work-shops and conferences. This separates the main growth areas from the grassroots and is epitomized in the development of new signs – DEAF-GRASSROOTS and DEAF-PROFESSIONAL – which are spatially opposite to each other in the way they are signed. (Signs are usually capitalized in this way to distinguish them from words as there is often no simple word-for-sign translation; the capitalized signs are called *glosses* of English). This cannot help education about alternative political agendas. However, because most Deaf professionals are under tremendous pressure from multiple role demands and role conflicts, which are themselves symptoms of individua-tion, this change in the social stratification of the community is perhaps not surprising.

In distancing themselves from hearing society and hearing impaired people, Deaf people claim to represent a different kind of 'norm' and a dif-ferent 'truth'. This effectively means, as we saw earlier, that because they are already 'normal', they 'do not wish society to change so that we can be included in it' (Ladd and John 1991: 14). This is ultimately unsatisfactory on a political level for two main reasons.

Firstly, in apparently accepting society as it is in order to justify an internal focus on a defence of the group's 'norm', the risk is that attention is drawn away from oppression as a widespread societal phenomena, and away from the power relations that are fundamental to it. That is, the allusion to with-drawal from mainstream society suggests withdrawal from something; all accounts suggest that this something is cultural and linguistic oppression. But Western society, together with the dominant human services culture and its governance and legal systems which at present control to a large extent how we live, still view *all* deaf people, including those who are Deaf, in terms of the *individual/medical* model. Hence, though sign language is increasingly acknowledged as a viable means of communication, it does not follow that there is widespread *cultural* acceptance within such frameworks for thinking and service development. We could, in such circumstances, perhaps equally well say that the need to define oneself in terms of a distinct culture and language is one consequence of disability oppression. The suggestion that Deaf people are *not* disabled, at least not within the framework of the social model of disability, therefore confuses the political issues.

Secondly, when a minority group strategy is combined with the marginalization of the Other – in this case, the marginalization of hearing impaired people and disabled people within the individual/medical straitjacket – and that Other is the same Other that the dominant culture seeks to marginalize in exactly the same way, this risks colluding with the dominant culture in their oppression of hearing impaired and other disabled people. It allows that culture 'to believe that essential biological or cultural differences *do* exist between them and oppressed groups' (Williams 1989: 259). Imposing an artificial division between Deaf and hearing impaired people therefore means competition for the same resources, which ultimately means less for everyone because it becomes entrenched in decisions about which group of deaf people has the *greatest need*. On both counts, then, society is exonerated from the outcomes of social control.

Community marginalization or rejection, it must be remembered, has consequences for internalized oppression, more so when the community itself represents the community of choice, and this strengthens the disciplinary power of the oppressor because it encourages social fragmentation within oppressed communities. The use of counter-essentialism and counter-hegemony to maintain minority group notions of deafness or disability simply means that in our attempts to create a more acceptable 'truth' we may end up covertly using the same tactics which we so despise in the dominant culture. As a consequence, the content of our self-fulfilment as an oppressed group can vary widely, from self-actualization or the achievement of what *we* perceive to be as our potential, to hedonism where we are only concerned with our own desires and pleasure. In such circumstances, an essentialist agenda which manufactures or is built on a division between the social and political in some ways corresponds to Rogers and Wrightsman's division of rights into the 'nurturance' versus 'self-determination orientations' (1978: 61) – a division between social support and socially motivated political action – which finds its present day equivalent in the distinction between welfare and liberty rights. As such, I am not sure that an essentialist agenda clarifies the issue of different 'rights' at all, because it seems to be saying that rather than aiming for unconditional 'rights' for all, we must engage in the right-wing doctrine of competition for the exclusive 'rights' of the few who are deemed 'fit' to have them.

Summary

This chapter has suggested that the roots of the apparent divisions between Deaf and disabled people lie in the logic of essentialism, which is embedded in Western society. However, as Box 1.2 suggests, many of the divisions can be

Box 1.2 Deconstructing the relationship between Deaf and disabled people

The Deaf community	*The disability movement*
Differences	
Embraces a minority group notion of deafness, which makes a clear distinction between Deaf and hearing	The movement is founded on the social model of disability which separates the individual and society
Accepts the individual definition of disability, and does not make a distinction between disability and impairment	Rejects the individual definition of disability and makes a distinction between disability and impairment
Strong belief in segregated education and the right to coexist as a separate group or subculture of society	Strong belief in inclusive education and inclusion in society, though some acceptance that this is difficult for some groups of disabled people
Seeks liberation from oppression by setting up an alternative community and vigorously asserting the positive attributes of being Deaf while largely denying the negative attributes	Seeks liberation from oppression by putting the responsibility for change on the oppressor and spelling out what changes should be made through direct action and other strategies

Commonalities

A history of cultural oppression in Western society, with specific reference to eugenics, institutionalization and genocide, for example

Theory is based on essentialist notions of deafness/disability, for example 'one can only be Deaf or hearing', 'disability is located in the individual or in society'

The main specific legislation is the 1981 Education Act and its amendments, The Children Act and the Disability Discrimination Act, all of which use the individual model of disability

Distancing from the concept of impairment

Difficulty in dealing with pluralism and individuation

Self-definition in terms of social identity, social movement and community

Strong belief in self-determination

Recognition for the linguistic minority construction of Deafness attributed to the lack of constructive dialogue between the different communities or are manufactured by essentialist notions of deafness and disability.

This has two main outcomes. Firstly, very substantial areas of commonality between deaf and disabled people are disguised or ignored. Secondly, the complex experiences of people are reduced to simple categories, often binary oppositions, which are both a result of and determine how these experiences are controlled or regulated by the dominant culture. Two main forms of regulation are identified: the sovereign power of medicine and science which focuses on overt control, and the more subtle disciplinary power which directs community concerns inwards towards self-regulation and self-discipline. Essentialism is such a powerful driving force in contemporary Western culture that it also appears to influence how Deaf people and the disability movement develop ideological and cultural frameworks for representation and identity. It can be demonstrated, for example, that both the social model of disability and the linguistic minority construction of deafness hinge upon binary oppositions – between the individual and society and between Deaf and hearing respectively. The construction of these binaries is actually very similar in that Deaf = individual and hearing = society. But because cultural production and political strategies which aim to achieve liberation from oppression are then focused on further reinforcing and giving value to *opposite sides* of the different dichotomies, these strategies, to a certain extent, cancel each other out. Cultural production and the particular strategy used can further be a function of whether and how they are legitimated by the dominant culture. Differences in legitimation can result in a discrepancy between the 'right' to self-determination and its expression, which creates social and political tension within communities. However, tension also exists because individuals are expected to 'fit' one side of the dichotomy, and this leads to social fragmentation because issues of identity are more complex than those which can be defined in terms of a binary. Social fragmentation is the enemy of effective political action, especially when there are differences in the way in which the power imbalance between oppressor and oppressed is the focus of such action.

 **2**

Refocusing

'It's a poor sort of memory that only works backwards,' the
Queen remarked.
(Lewis Carroll, *Alice's Adventures in Wonderland*, 1865)

'The question is,' said Humpty Dumpty, 'which is to be master –
that's all.'
(Lewis Carroll, *Through the Looking Glass*, 1872)

Introduction

The title of this book could equally well have been *Deaf and Disabled or Deafness Disabled or . . .?* That is to say, in using the title I have used, I do not wish to give the impression that I intend to become preoccupied with the same 'either/or' agenda which seems to have overtaken the preceding pages. The title poses a complex, multidimensional question, which is intended to challenge the hypothesis that deafness and disability, or the individual and society, for example, are discrete entities which can be reduced to something which is easily and accurately described, measured and analysed. To understand this challenge fully means that we have to start from a different place, and perhaps pose a different question. The first step in this process has been achieved in bringing deaf and disabled people under the same spotlight, and this did not happen by accident. It has been suggested that Western culture constructs disability and deafness as deviance, damage, dependence – the so-called 'sick role' – and perpetuates labels and stereotypes which stigmatize, disempower, deskill and marginalize deaf and disabled people. These frameworks for interpretation, or discourses, are not simply descriptive, however; they create meaning. Moreover, they are not the only frameworks which exist. Some cultures and societies, for example those described by Connors and Donnellan (1993) and Ingstad and Reynolds-Whyte (1995), consider disabled people to be no different from anyone else; in others, we are revered, even given God(dess)-like status. This evidence can certainly act as a resource in exploring different ways in which we might change the dominant world-view in such a way that it constructs deafness and disability differently, ways which recognize the human rights of deaf and disabled people – rights which at present we do not share with the rest of the population. Further, as long ago as 1954, Allport noted that prejudice is reduced when:

* common goals are pursued;
* persons of similar status work together;
* interactions with out-group members are frequent and varied so that stereotypes are more likely to be broken down.

The dual spotlight of essentialism does not allow these conditions to prevail, since it fragments both our communities and the way in which we define ourselves – it disguises with narratives of conflict our relationships to each other, to each other's Others, and to the dominant culture. However, social fragmentation based on alienation, inequality and prejudice, and social diversification based on pluralism and individuation are not the same thing though they do influence each other. Social diversification can be construed as a contemporary response to a rapidly changing social world. This world has seen a massive explosion in its population, which has provided more of each possible variety of individual. The parallel growth in the removal of territorial boundaries, mass media, new global information systems and flows, and new visual forms of communication have made it easier for individuals to form recognizably distinct groups or *contingencies* (Simon 1996); these then connect, sometimes temporarily, to challenge existing social categories. They have a substantial impact on the ways our lives are organized and on the ways in which we understand and relate to each other. du Gay *et al.* (1997) refer to these as *substantive factors*, or those which have empirical substance and influence the *turn to culture*. The isolation of individuals from each other and their marginalization from mainstream life (through their allocation to arbitrary categories based on the primacy given to *one* characteristic of a complex whole) has now become a form of *social resistance* as different wholes begin to merge and to locate each other within different frameworks in the pursuit of social change. This is reminiscent of Foucault's view that power and resistance always go together, and it means that the system of social stratification is becoming increasingly important for the future of Western society:

> With increases in size and complexity, the number of social categories multiply. In simple systems, one's kin affiliation (lineage and clan), age and sex are the most relevant categories, but in more advanced systems, these distinctions are supplemented by ethnic, economic, religious, political and class categories. Each of these categories locates individuals in the social web, dictates the resources available to them, controls their perceptions and actions, and circumscribes how others respond to them.
>
> (Maryanski and Turner 1992: 109)

Increased social diversification also means the cultural production of alternative knowledge, ideas, intellectual trends and identities, each of which demands speaking rights or 'warrants voice' (Gergen 1989). These are the *epistemological* influences on the development of cultural discourses (du Gay *et al.* 1997). As more individuals *position* themselves in relation to these alternatives they find the binary to be equivalent to a cultural straitjacket. In such circumstances, Simons and Billig (1994: 3), drawing on Gramsci (1971), note that 'in place of a single ruling class within a given society, there are multiple and competing factions', and 'ruling-class hegemony is never complete; there is always the opportunity for oppositional readings'.

In a sense, then, it is being suggested that the logic of 'either/or' is, itself, an intellectual artefact, and that each side of the various dichotomies do not after all represent discrete entities; existing divisions are relative and therefore meaningless. If this were so, it reinforces the view that both the social model of disability, with its 'top-down' emphasis on the individual–society dichotomy and its inherent conflicts of agency *versus* structure, and the linguistic minority construction of deafness, with its 'bottom-up' view that individuals determine society, and its insistence that Deaf and hearing are discrete, are essentialist. Each excludes substantial elements of the other and each hides a variety of marginalized and repressed discourses which might provide clues to our tensions and how they can be removed.

Refocusing

The inherent tensions of thinking in terms of absolute 'truths' and essentialist grand theories are evident throughout the literature on deafness and disability, and many commentators seem to have difficulty with their own quests for definitive answers. For example, Lennard Davis (1995: 4, 2) on the one hand suggests that disability is an absolute category – 'one is either disabled or not' – and, on the other that:

> disability is not an object – a woman with a cane – but a social process that ultimately involves everyone who has a body and lives in the world of the senses. Just as the conceptualisation of race, class and gender shapes the lives of those who are not black or female, so the concept of disability regulates the bodies of those who are 'normal' . . . Normalcy and disability are part of the same system.

Likewise, Padden and Humphries (1988) make a strong case for Deaf people's cultural uniqueness, and their definition of Other as 'hearing' (though not in the sense of being able to hear sound, since Deaf and hearing are *cultural* categories). Their argument is placed within an implicit narrative of **nature–nurture**, and questions are asked about whether one must be born into Deaf culture or whether one can grow into it. Within this framework, hearing children of Deaf parents then become 'an ongoing contradiction in the culture' because they can hear but have absorbed Deaf cultural values. The authors go on to say that the boundaries between *deaf* (which they have defined as 'the audiological condition of not hearing') and *Deaf* are not clear 'because Deaf people are both Deaf and deaf, and their discussions even arguments, over issues of identity show these two categories are often interrelated in complex ways' (pp. 2–3). The admission that Deaf people are also deaf is a reference to sensory impairment or difference in relation to the audiological condition of hearing. Yet '"Disabled" is a label that historically has not belonged to Deaf people. It suggests political self-representations and goals unfamiliar to the group' (p. 44). Other commentators have framed this tension rather differently, however. For example Preston (1994: 236), a hearing child of Deaf parents, refers to 'the fallacy of cultural dichotomisation: you must be Deaf, or you must be Hearing', and Kyle (1991: 45) says that 'Deaf people have to accept hearingness in one way because it is only through an understanding of it that they can progress in life . . . The Deaf identity has to be seen along a dimension of deafness and hearingness.'

Let us suppose that we could resolve some of these dilemmas by posing two further questions: 'Why can't Deaf people, if they are both Deaf and hearing impaired, also be disabled?' and 'If disability and being Deaf are cultural constructions, though perhaps in different ways, and hearing impaired people are disabled, might it not be useful to develop discourses which frame the experience of hearing impaired people in terms of cultural referents?' Further, if, in attempting to answer these questions, we were to suggest a different framework which moves away from the logic of 'either/or', what implications would this have for existing ways of thinking which are so deeply embedded in our culture? How can we achieve an alternative without simply taking an oppositional position or creating what Paul Ricœur (1986) calls 'the **hermeneutics** of suspicion', and therefore slipping into further essentialism or total **relativism** – a situation where there is no 'truth' at all? And most importantly, why do we need an alternative framework in the first place? Radicalism is radically suspect if it claims to know 'the truth'. So perhaps we need to work towards something which is not simply reactive and aimed at exposing unwarranted foundationalist claims about 'the real'.

If we take the last question first we could begin by emphasizing that it is not just an academic question which is only of interest to those who reside in the towers of academe. There are a number of reasons, in my view, why we need to approach the deaf–disabled divide in a different way. Firstly, the descriptions in the preceding chapter are a clear indicator that despite its profound, though not always altruistic achievements, essentialism 'has become philosophically untenable and liberalism politically exhausted' (Simons and Billig 1994: 2). The Disability Discrimination Act 1995, which we will explore further in Chapter 6, is testimony to this. The continued adherence to arbitrary medical rather than sociocultural categories – which separates disability from race and gender, for example – and the legal status granted to justifiable discrimination against disabled people, makes a mockery of the Act's prohibition clauses and is a flagrant abuse of human rights. Barnes (1996b) and other disabled writers have equated the oppression of disabled people in Western society with **Social Darwinism** and the rooting out of the 'weakest' in the pursuit of survival. But this seems to collude with the view of disabled people as 'weak'; this plays into the hands of those who wish to link disability and 'the sick role'. It is also a somewhat limited reading of the work of Darwin, who among other things uncovered the huge capacity of natural populations to respond to extreme or unpredictable conditions through diversification. This was a major contribution to our understanding of evolution through change and a precursor of what we now know as ecology and systems theory. The suppression or control of pluralism and individuation within deaf and disabled communities is a manifestation of perceived threat to the 'one true voice' of disability. But as long as a singular 'voice' is loudest, there will be dissent because institutionalized oppression is also experienced and responded to in a multiplicity of ways.

Secondly, the division between Deaf and hearing impaired, which is seen by some commentators as representing a division between 'normal' and Other, is already in evidence in the service and employment sectors and is being used as the basis for divisions in local service philosophy, planning, prioritizing and delivery. Moreover, as resources are reduced, there is a great deal of pressure on local authorities to downsize, unify or streamline services. This carries with it the risk that deaf people will be stereotyped and moulded to 'fit' whichever model is dominant in any given authority, often under the guise that some groups are more disabled, and therefore more needy, than others. National policy, though it remains orientated towards arbitrary classifications of individual impairments, is so totally ineffective in its ability to enforce legislation and guarantee full legal rights that it encourages different and sometimes equally arbitrary interpretations at local level. Divisions are also beginning to be more visible in the media. For example, the national press has conducted an ongoing, polarized, largely simplistic and ill-informed debate on the subject of whether deaf children should be helped to be 'hearing' through the use of *cochlear implants* or be allowed to become Deaf through sign language in education. But interestingly divisions are also evident in the separation of deaf and disabled people in BBC Television's specialist programming, and in the provision of Deaf-only programming on Channel 4 television; at the time of writing, though, changes seem to be in the pipeline.

More surprisingly, however, the disability movement itself reflects the hearing impaired–Deaf division, though not quite in the way we might expect. In the last four years, work by disabled activists has expressed a clear bias towards the Deaf stereotype (see, for example, Morris 1992b; Campbell and Oliver 1996; Finkelstein and Stuart 1996; Morris 1996; Oliver 1996; Shakespeare *et al.* 1996), with the example of Martha's Vineyard in the USA (Groce 1985) providing the most commonly quoted historical context. This in fact was also very unusual, since it referred to a small and geographically separate island community. On Martha's Vineyard as a whole, the percentage of deaf people was 0.6 per cent, though in one town it was as high as 25 per cent, and yet sign language was used throughout the island (Ladd and John 1991). When the island was later subject to an influx of settlers from the mainland, the deaf gene, and the use of sign language, died out. In terms of its positive imagery – watching Deaf people sign fluently is a more æsthetic experience than listening to Deaf voices, as many Deaf people themselves point out – this certainly 'fits' with the kind of identity which the disability movement wants to project. However, because the movement is grouped around political goals, and the goals of the Deaf community have a very different emphasis, this bias is, in other ways, strange. It certainly means that some of the movement's strongest political and moral aims are compromised, notably that of inclusive education (British Council of Organizations of Disabled People Update 1996, Autumn).

In spite of this apparent bias, there is no doubt in my mind that deaf people, whatever their social, linguistic or cultural affiliations, have been marginalized or excluded from the development of social model theory and dialogues, because of the diminished role of language and discourse in social model theory, and the mind–body split inherent in some social model thinking.

As such, the social model does not go as far as it might in providing a radical and rounded alternative to the individual model of disability. The materialist emphasis of *praxis* in social model theory sidelines philosophical discourses which are concerned with cultural processes (Shakespeare 1994), though this perhaps reflects the inferior role that cultural processes have occupied in the explanatory hierarchy of the social sciences in general, and sociology in particular:

> In contrast to economic and political processes, for example, which were routinely assumed to alter material conditions in the 'real' world – how people thought and acted – in ways which could be clearly identified and described, and hence to provide 'hard knowledge of the social world, cultural processes were deemed rather ephemeral and superficial. Because cultural processes dealt with seemingly less tangible things – signs, images, language, beliefs – they were often assumed, particularly by Marxists theorists, to be 'superstructural', being both dependent upon and reflective of the primary status of the material base and thus unlikely to provide social scientists with valid, 'real' knowledge.
>
> (du Gay *et al.* 1997: 1–2)

However, without the full integration of cultural processes into the model, reference to the cultural construction of disability and deafness seem somewhat hollow:

> In order to conduct a social practice we need to give it a certain meaning, have a conception of it, be able to think meaningfully about it. The production of social meanings is therefore a necessary precondition for the functioning of all social practices and an account of the cultural conditions of social practices must form part of the sociological explanation of how they work.
>
> (du Gay *et al.* 1997: 2)

Cultural description and analysis is very much linked to cultural *discourse*, which resides in the philosophical branches of *metaphysics* and the philosophy of language, in particular, hermeneutics, the *intersubjective theory of meaning* and *poststructuralism* as epitomized in the work of philosophers such as Wittgenstein, Foucault, Derrida and Ricœur. The need to consider these ways of thinking becomes critical when we begin to examine the inclusion of groups of disabled people both within the mainstream culture and within the disability movement, whose very existence is bound up in issues of identity, language and communication. In recognition of this, I will devote the whole of the following chapter to discussion of these issues. For the moment, what is clear is that because human agency is lost in the materialism of the social model and because discourse is seen to be a side-effect of social structure, neither can be the focus for social change. Deaf people, whatever their linguistic and cultural affiliations, are necessarily preoccupied with issues of language; they might conceivably have difficulty with this perspective.

Because praxis is concerned with the philosophy of materialism, discourse on impairment and the individual experience of impairment is marginalized by some social model thinkers perhaps because it echoes the legacy of Descartes's *mind–body doctrine*. It creates an image of a division between thought processes or ideas and the act of oppression – a sort of mind–body split – which has been highlighted by Mike Oliver, in a slightly different sense. He refers to 'the tension between intellectuals whose role is to create theory, and political activists whose role is to produce social change' (1996: 166–7). However, just as Oliver feels the solution is the organic intellectual, some contemporary philosophers have put forward the view that intellectual activity (*theoria*) is itself a form of praxis, first and foremost an act (Cheney 1987). Moreover, anyone who has read Jung Chang's *Wild Swans* (1991), a historical biography of twentieth-century China, will recognize the human consequences of trying to reinforce a mind–body split through the promotion of a materialist doctrine. It raises questions such as 'Even if pain or oppression should turn out to have a single physical or social correlate across all individuals, how can the painfulness of pain or the extremity of oppression *be* a physical or social property?' In this context, to suggest that attitudinal oppression is the most pernicious form of oppression is similar to saying that it is entrenched without looking at the processes whereby it becomes entrenched, or explaining why it is that some elements of attitudinal oppression are extremely resistant to change and others are changed quite rapidly relative to the human lifespan. In swinging from one extreme to the other – from an individualist state of mind to collectivist materialism – we lose, it has been argued, the distinctiveness of mental properties such as their qualitative character, their special accessibility to our awareness, and their privacy. An overemphasis on 'the body' happens not only because of the personal struggles of many of the most prominent disabled academics and activists, but also perhaps because to focus on 'the mind', or even on consciousness, reduces the distance between the individual and society and makes it more difficult to explain disability oppression solely in the language of materialism and structuralism. However, this is perhaps not surprising since it reflects the early differences between Marx on the one hand and Hegel and Feuerbach on the other on such concepts as *alienated* and *false consciousness*, the resolutions of which remain outstanding.

This is not to suggest, however, that the Deaf agenda succeeds in incorporating discourse perspectives more fully. The Deaf agenda is a monocultural framework, and as such does not do justice to its own emphasis on the role of language and cultural processes in identity formation, nor does it answer a number of very difficult questions about the development of deaf children in the family context. Moreover, going back to one of my original questions, there is something of a paradox in Deaf people's strong promotion of cultural values and their denial of hearing impaired and disabled people's involvement in the five major cultural processes of representation, identity, production, consumption and regulation (du Gay *et al.* 1997), outside of the pathological framework. What is the difference, for example, between Elton's (1996) considered study of cross-cultural communication between Deaf and hearing people and Kenyon's (1994) account of 'reaction–interaction' between hearing impaired people and hearing people, or Coleman and DePaulo's (1991) analysis of communication between disabled people and non-disabled people? These are the final reasons why it may be important to refocus our thinking. But, returning to our original questions, what alternative frameworks might we use in the process of refocusing?

The postmodernist agenda

Foucault suggested that instead of compressing diversity we might take the reverse position and celebrate our heterogeneity alongside the multitude of alternative possibilities that it creates for change by freeing us from our usual ways of understanding ourselves. These ideas seem more at home in the context of the cultural and intellectual movement of *postmodernism*: this includes a variety of approaches aiming to understand people as social beings, such as *social constructionism*, critical psychology, *discourse analysis*, *deconstruction* and *poststructuralism*. All of these disciplines embrace a number of key assumptions, which are presented in Box 2.1.

Postmodernism challenges the very foundation of essentialism that there can be an absolute 'truth' or 'reality' which can be discovered through reason and rationality, arguing that such an approach was more appropriate to the Enlightenment period, which began in the mid-eighteenth century. Thus it acknowledges the legitimacy of historicity, and is of relevance to the idea that deafness and disability are constructed in time-honoured, culturally specific and context-dependent ways. The postmodernist movement ranges between a view that completely rejects the dominant belief of Western cultures, that the world can be understood in terms of underlying structures along with the supposition that such structures can be explained by all-embracing grand theories or metanarratives, to one which accepts the need for some form of social structure and standards. It is this range, together with the difficulty in producing a clear definition of postmodernism, that leads perhaps Barton (1996: 9) to refer to the need to 'guard against . . . the regressive relativism of particular forms of postmodernism'. However, this is somewhat different

---

Box 2.1 The key assumptions of the postmodernist movement

- It takes a critical stance towards taken-for-granted ways of under-standing the world and the people in it, or *knowledge*, and challenges the assumption that knowledge is based on objective, unbiased obser-vation of this world. Significantly, this means that the categories with which we apprehend the world do not necessarily refer to real divi-sions.
- The way in which we construct knowledge is contextually, historically and culturally specific and relative.
- Knowledge is something that people *do*, rather than something that they *have*. Shared versions of knowledge, or what we regard as 'truth', are negotiated and constructed between people through the dynamics of social interaction and *discourse*. The processes by which forms of knowledge are achieved by people are therefore more important that the structure, and the way people think, and the categories and con-cepts that provide meaning for them, are provided by the language they use.
- Each construction brings with it a different kind of human agency, and sustains some patterns of social action while excluding others. Discourse has not just an expressive role but an active, performative role also.

---

from Riddell's (1996: 89) comment, in the same volume, that 'postmodernists question whether it is possible to sustain accounts of oppression since it is impossible to establish one account of events as being superior to another'. Some postmodernists undoubtedly do question that there can ever be a 'true reality', but this is mostly in the sense that what is one person's or group's reality is another person's or group's fiction at a given moment in time. The common example cited is that when a group views a painting, the assump-tion can reasonably be made that there will be many similarities and many differences in how each individual forms a critique of that painting. But who is to say which of those critiques is the 'real' one and which is closest to the artist's truth, especially if the artist is disinclined to state what it is they are saying through the image. I feel that the literature strongly supports the view that there are different deaf and disabled 'realities', and though we may see 'deaf' on the one hand and 'hearing' on the other, since this view is legit-imated in the dominant culture, we cannot claim they are unrelated any more than we can suggest that 'society' and 'individuals' are. I like Burr's (1995: 104) analogy, when she says that 'It is not like looking at an egg and a hot frying pan and asking what effects each has on the other – the frying pan hardens the egg, and the egg makes the frying pan eggy.'

However, in its focus on pluralism and individuation, which are seen as the dominant characteristics of the postmodern world, postmodernism rests uneasily within disability discourse. These characteristics, as we have seen, are inherently difficult for oppressed communities already threatened by fragmentary discourses, structures and practices. When couched in more extreme postmodernist terms, the social model's construction of an archæ-ology of institutionalized oppression in Western society and Deaf people's alternative cultural and linguistic production would perhaps be no more 'truthful' or valid than the dominant culture's construction of a hierarchy of impairments in the disabled population. However, Burr (1995: 102) con-tinues, echoing some social model theorists:

> In theories of prejudice, explanations which locate the problem either within the personality of the victim or within that of the prejudiced draw attention away from prejudice and discrimination as widespread societal phenomena, and away from the power relations that are funda-mental to them.

What Burr implies is that the archæology of oppression is to be found in the *relationship* between deafness, disability and 'normalcy', which echoes the earlier comment by Lennard Davis. In other words, the specific meaning of impairment, disability and deafness only emerges through their relationship to the many ways in which 'normalcy' is perceived, and *one* possible meaning of this relationship – albeit the dominant one in Western society – is social or economic oppression. However, studying the relationship in different con-texts allows us to identify other meanings and different forms and sources of oppression. This does not prevent us differentiating 'the oppressor' from 'the oppressed', suggesting rather that the *process* of oppression and the dynamics of power lie in the relationship between the two, and oppression can be most effectively challenged if the specifics of that relationship are understood.

Another perspective that arises from beginning to examine process in this way is one which has already taken root within disability studies and, to a lesser extent, in Deaf studies. This concerns the relationship between 'the researcher' and 'the researched' – specifically that the process of research often means that the answers we get, as researchers, frequently depend on the questions we ask and how we ask them, rather than on *reflexivity*, where the researched are given the opportunity of equal status in the research and their commentary on their contribution and that of the researcher gives added value to the research process. If we begin with preconceived assump-tions about deafness and disability, as was suggested in Chapter 1, we often limit ourselves to answers that are framed by these assumptions. I have explored this in the context of identity research in an earlier work (Corker 1996b) and will look at a more specific example in Chapter 6. Lane (1992) also gives a very clear account of research which is based on assumptions about deaf people in his discussion of whether or not there is 'a psychology of the deaf'. The social model effectively proposes a postmodernist alternative to the 'ultimate truth' of the individual view of disability (see Oliver 1996), since there is some further evidence that the field has begun to respond to the postmodern dilemma in disability research. For example, it is now being advocated that there cannot be 'pure' measures of things as, inevitably, to arrive at 'purity' involves filtering out the normal social context of a person's life: a practice which itself encourages distortion. Disabled researchers such as Abberley (1991) and Barnes (1996b) challenge 'the myth of the independent researcher' and advocate the development of an *emancipatory research* paradigm, which is based on a *participatory* world-view (Reason 1994). The Deaf notion of 'purity', in its incorporation into theories of culture and identity, is more difficult to unravel, but it relies heavily on empirical justification and would perceive emancipatory paradigms as weakening its fundamental tenets.

Clearly, the essentialist and postmodernist agendas are diametrically opposed to each other in a number of ways, and as such there *is* a risk that postmodernism slips into a different kind of essentialism if it only seeks to dismantle established ideas about 'truth' and 'reality'. It is also true that *any* challenge to something that has been regarded as 'given' for a very long time and by a very large number of people involves relativism, and as Brown (1994: 26) points out, this 'brings with it the fear that usually accompanies the view of the world as uncertain'. As an example, I remember in the 1980s the shock of having the certainty of my cosy little world and the apathy of my political beliefs turned upside down by the growing number of references to a horribly different, post-nuclear holocaust world. However, with respect specifically to social constructionism, Shakespeare (1996: 108) says that

> Crude dichotomies between social constructionism and essentialism are perhaps not particularly helpful, as Diana Fuss (1989) argues. Social constructionism can itself be quite determinist and fixed. At other times, in the rejection of biological thinking as essentialist, it can become idealist and totally decentred.

The uncertainty created by relativism depends very much on how we use it, as there are also different forms of relativism. Bhaskar (1979), for example, distinguishes between epistemic or epistemological relativism and judgemental relativism. The first relates to the historicity of knowledge and, while rejecting the idea of a 'purity' that can be described, it does allow for both the need and the possibility of making determinations about the validity of knowledge systems. Judgemental relativism, on the other hand, suggests that because all forms of knowledge are epistemically relative they are therefore all equally valid or invalid, and we cannot compare them or discriminate among them. Brown (1994: 28) continues:

> relativism does not entail a society without standards. Rather, the conjoining of deconstruction and epistemology helps us to recognise when, where and how the standards are to be established cooperatively, constantly renewed and periodically reshaped. Hence, unlike absolutism, relativism is reflective about its own limits.

The logic of 'both/and' and cultural processes

There are a number of issues raised by the above discussion, and many of them, I feel, take us back to the original problem of ideologies based on dualistic notions which exclude by giving one side of the binary a more privileged position than its opposite. Indeed, French philosopher Jacques Derrida (1974, 1978, 1981) and others have argued that *any* way of thinking based on binary oppositions works against inclusion. Attempts to describe the meaning of human existence in these terms, as we have seen, become embroiled in questions of 'who fits where?', when most people probably lead a more fluid existence which hinges to a large extent on what Hall (1994: 32) describes as 'tacit' culture:

> We are all imprinted by personal (or tacit) culture, which is why it is so personal. It is this highly personalised experience, the 'me' quality that makes it so difficult for people to come to grips with the reality of tacit culture. When different ethnic groups interact en masse, tacit cultural differences can be devastating . . . Behind the power of culture lies the power of the self in the membership in a group. But the self can only be formed around symbols that are shared with others. The symbols and how they are used determine how people organise their worlds – how they think, how they communicate, and the feeling and tone of the communication . . . Any discourse on language and culture faces the problem of separating the language from the culture and vice versa.

The current challenges to social model thinking are perhaps evidence of this, but the experience of deaf people shows us why it is important to respond appropriately to these challenges. These situations arise because we do not pay sufficient attention to how things happen and the space between two parts of a given dichotomy, because it is often from that space that the challenges emerge. Derrida says that an alternative way is to adopt the logic of 'both/and', because in order to understand any phenomenon fully, we should take as our unit of study both what that phenomenon is taken to be and what it seems to exclude:

> Derrida argues that in whatever we take to be immediate and present there is always already difference and deferral. If presence always contains absence, there cannot be a neatly drawn line of opposition between these two notions. It is not that presence and absence are opposite, not that there is either presence or absence, but rather that there is an inevitable defining of the one through the other: there is both presence and absence.
>
> (Sampson 1989: 12)

This is what is meant by *deconstruction*. Derrida suggests, moreover, that something cannot exist without its Other, and certainly the numerous examples given above of the difficulty of separating the two sides of a dichotomy seem to support this view. We could say, for example, that the concept of

'Deaf'excludes that of hearing and vice versa. This is why the notions of 'Deaf identity' and the 'Deaf family' embraced by the minority group construction, like those of 'black identity' and the 'black family' embraced by anti-racists (Katz 1996), are close to the non-translatability of discourses posited by some postmodernists (Corker 1996c). In such circumstances, both the minority group construction and phonocentrism share the same discourse of totality and exclusion, which is considerably enhanced by the failure to define 'hearing culture', as Woodford (1993: 13) explains:

> I want to put the word 'hearing' in front of culture. How much of what you have been putting into the outline [of hearing culture] depends on hearing, and, because culture is expressed through and shaped by language, how much of that fleshing out that you have been making depends on the fact that the language of that 'hearing' culture is a word form? – spoken or written. We must, if we are to have any perception of hearing culture and its relationships with deaf culture, answer those two questions: first – How much of hearing culture depends on hearing?, second – How much of hearing culture depends on language being in word form? Messages in communication are only useful if understood by the recipient and understanding is culture bound and influenced.

Sampson (1989), drawing on Bateson (1972), suggests that one way of exploring relationships is to view the individual and society unit and, therefore, the Deaf–hearing continuum as an interacting system where all dimensions contribute to the interaction. For example, if we go back to the mind–body dichotomy described earlier, it becomes important to emphasize that the distinction between the person and the physical body must be transformed into a way of recognizing that the self and Other are, within 'both/and' logic, mutually defined. This way of looking at people-in-systems is already at the heart of an attempt to explain the difference between women's and men's sense of self (Gilligan 1984) which argues that Western notions of the individual are phallocentric. Women's sense of self is that of the 'self-in-relationship', and the dividing line between self and other is less clear than it is for men (Corker 1996b). Sampson (1990: 124) describes this 'self-in-relationship' as 'the embedded individual':

> Embedded individuality requires a constitutive view of the person, re-embedding, free-standing modern individuals in their social worlds and thereby emphasising ensembles of relationships and communities of belongingness rather than isolated nomads . . . the reformulation is a perfect example of seeking to use our discipline in order to constitute a different kind of social reality . . . But . . . an embedded individuality is not designed with current conceptions of societal management in mind; rather, it responds to a different kind of historical urgency.

Though I will somewhat inevitably be accused of gender bias, I wonder if it is a coincidence that the founders of the social model of disability are men and the main contemporary challenges to the supremacy of the social model from within the disability movement are from women. Interestingly, however, in current dialogues about the linguistic minority construction of deafness, which are largely concerned with the processes of language, identity formation and social affiliation, the gender divisions are less clear.

The systemic approach and simultaneous oppressions

So, rather than thinking of the individual or society, self or Other, Deaf or hearing, and sign language or English as forming opposite sides of a dichotomy, rather than viewing disability, race, gender, age, sexuality and class as discrete characteristics, we should instead think of them as the inseparable components of a *system*, none of which can make sense without its 'opposite' or the other components of the system (Corker 1990). This accommodates the postmodernist view that the relationships between these components are 'complex and fractured, rather than hierarchical' (Brah 1992). By the same token, all of these aspects of personhood and cultural identity, in the different relationships they have with the dominant culture, produce an archæology of oppression, much like the ***archæology of knowledge*** proposed by Foucault (1972). It is worth emphasizing again, that Foucault's concept of knowledge is not of something that we *have*, but something that we *do*. As such, it involves the exposure of power relationships by bringing to the fore marginalized discourses which cannot be heard within the prevailing knowledges. With such exposure comes a recognition that without tackling the decrepit moral and ethical principles on which oppression is based, the separate assignment of legal rights in respect of different aspects of our personhood and cultural identity in *separate* legislatures can be viewed as an exercise in power by the dominant which is aimed at fragmenting its Other. This makes it seem more controllable, as people who are at war with themselves cannot easily gain the strength from a collective 'voice', and 'benefit' fully from the different legislatures. Thus we are conned into believing that disabled people are asexual (Shakespeare *et al.* 1996), or without racial or gender role or identity, by the master/mistress status (Goffman 1968) given to our impairments, for example. Viewing oppression as an archæology means that we can examine the relationships between different dimensions of the Other, different environments and different experiences of oppression in the context of the kind of multidimensional and multi-issue lives that most people live. We retain the concept of oppression as institutionalized in all the environments we are a part of, but we do not separate the experience of oppression from strategies for liberation from it in achieving change, nor do we break what du Gay *et al.* (1997) describe as the ***circuit of culture***, where the five major cultural processes referred to earlier in this chapter are in a constant state of interaction with each other to produce different outcomes.

Shakespeare (1992) points to the insistence of social model theorists that there is no causal relationship between impairment and disability, and this needs to be reflected in the way we think about oppression. As a working model, we might consider Figure 2.1. This model picks up on and develops different conceptualizations of *simultaneous* or **multiple oppression**, as described by Hill (1992), Morris (1992a), Stuart (1992), Gillespie-Sells (1994) and Vernon (1996a, 1996b) in respect of disability, gender, race and sexuality. These, as I suggested above, are dimensions of personhood and cultural identity which people share, and in relation to which they will be perceived as Other if they do not match the archetypal 'norm', 'ideal' person, or prevailing knowledge. None of these dimensions is absolute, however. We are encouraged to think that the female gender is an absolute category in biological terms, but if we begin to view the female in sociological terms we need to look at gender roles, for example. The same is true of sexuality (Herdt 1993; Simon 1996) and race (Tizard and Phoenix 1993; Katz 1996). For this list of characteristics, I have emphasized that childhood must be considered under the heading 'age', since deaf and disabled children often experience

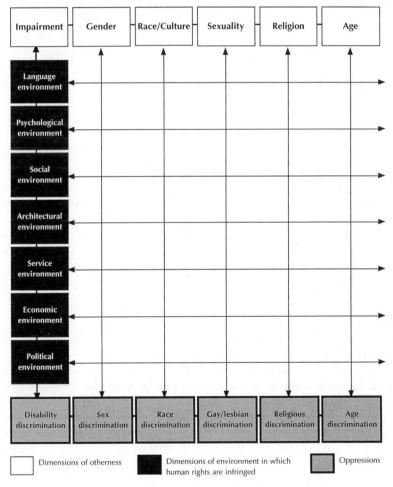

Figure 2.1 An archæology of oppression

oppression in their relationships with adults and yet the concept of children's rights is not articulated nearly as much as the rights of elderly people (Franklin 1995). I would also include Deaf under the heading 'race' since the definition of race within existing legislation is very broad, and incorporates 'colour, race, nationality, or ethnic or national origins' (Race Relations Act 1976 Part 1, Section 3(i)), though at present Deaf people are not legally recognized as constituting a 'nation'. Nevertheless, such recognition would allow Deaf people to view the archæology of their oppression in relation to that of both disabled people and different cultural groups without sacrificing their collective identity, and resorting to the alienation of the Deaf Other.

By a similar process, if we look at documents such as the Universal Declaration on Human Rights or the UN Convention of the Rights of the Child, it is possible to identify a number of interlinked environments, the qualities of which determine our experience of having, or not having rights or personhood – irrespective, for the moment, of legislation. This is important because at present our experience is described only in terms of impairment-specific barriers which can be explained with reference to structural oppression in those environments. Deaf people, for example, are labelled as hearing impaired or linguistically different; they are *in consequence* associated with communication and information barriers of different kinds in exactly the same way that 'non-walkers' or 'nearly-walkers' (Oliver 1996) become associated with 'architectural' barriers. On a materialist level this works, but on another level, it ignores the possibility, for example, that *vision* is a constitutive element of deaf experience (Thoutenhoofd 1997). Descriptions which hinge upon deaf people's lack of hearing rather than on their ability to use vision in themselves become oppressive. Similarly, when *blind* people describe communication and information barriers relative to *visual* impairment, people with learning difficulties question the translatability of society's linguistic exemplars in terms of their language; or when disabled black and ethnic minority people, disabled women and disabled gays and lesbians question the language of dominant metanarratives, this sends ripples of discomfort through those who rely on those theories. The dissenting commentary is often summarily dismissed as being beyond our understanding 'at the moment'. Interconnections between oppressions, and between oppressor and oppressed are, however, part of most deaf and disabled people's lives.

Returning to the proposed model, then, if we experience psychological or intellectual abuse this will diminish our sense of personhood such that we experience what we perceive to be our right to freedom of expression, self-esteem or intrinsic value as being infringed. A systemic approach would allow us to describe how this impinges upon our experience of rights related to other environments, such as the social environment and the service environment, the latter being composed of public services such as education, health and social services. If we experience different aspects of the service environment separately, as is generally the case in legislation targeted at 'special needs' or disability, we may find the different value systems conflict with each other, which makes further inroads on our experience of having rights.

But a systemic view would allow these value systems to be exposed, and the relationships between them reworked. Similarly, if we are Deaf, our parents are Deaf and, as a child we have grown up in a Deaf family and community environment, where sign language is both our home language and the language of community relationships, we might find the separation of race and impairment in legislation impinges on our rights to language, a secure family environment and fulfilling social relationships. Impairment legislation regards our language as a special need, not a home language, and as long as it remains separate, this legislation takes priority. If, however, race and impairment were not separate, but part of a holistic system describing personhood, these tensions would not be experienced, at least not in the same way. Finally, if characteristics of the economic environment mean that we are unemployed, we may be forced to seek cheaper accommodation in an architectural environment which imprisons us in our home because of physical access problems, which makes us more dependent on the service environment. We may feel not only that our right to a decent standard of living and housing are being infringed, but also our right to autonomy.

I must emphasize again that this is a working model, which allows the individual to locate their own oppression and their possible responses to it, and leaves room for the incorporation of further elements. This model is not without its limitations, however, because it creates a different kind of legislative nightmare in seeming to distract from a unifying notion of disability oppression, thus making it difficult to describe it coherently. It does make the point that if we argue, as the social model and, to a lesser extent, the minority group approach do, that oppression is institutionalized, it is nevertheless *experienced* in different ways by different individuals, and an institutionalized response will not always remove the oppression because of these differences and the complex ways in which they interact. I give some important practical examples of this in Chapter 6. The model aims to reconstruct a broader and more inclusive view of, for example, language and communication on the basis of the moral, welfare and liberty rights that all people share. This reconstruction does not exclude specific language and communication oppressions faced by other groups, including Deaf people. It does allow us, though, to envisage a concept of language oppression which is part of the relationship between *all* deaf and disabled people and their environments. Though the connections may not be seen to exist within the experience of some people, we must not forget the other part of Derrida's argument which says that what is apparently absent or invisible is as important as that which is present and observable, which has meaning in the context of earlier comments made about vision and deafness. So oppression and anti-oppression are closely entwined, and one cannot be excluded from discourse on the other; and this is perhaps why Vernon (1996a: 51) argues that 'Black people [and disabled people, by implication] are victimisers as well as being the victims of oppression.'

However, on its own, this model is incomplete because we have not yet covered how cultural processes produce this archæology of oppression. To understand this we must move further into an exploration of the culturally

produced patterns of coded language and coded behaviour which, in interactions between people who do not share the same experience, produce different knowledges; we must also look at the role of language in constructing
and mediating discourses.

Summary

In this chapter, a number of examples are given which illustrate processes
through which essentialist thinking has split deaf and disabled people both
from each other and from understanding their relationships to the dominant
culture. I have discussed the division which has been manufactured between
discourse and social processes, mind and body, and local and national policy.
These processes are presented as compelling reasons both for adding to
existing frameworks such as the social model of disability, and for suggesting
alternative ways in which we think about and describe the meaning of deafness and disability which are based upon the premise that the logic of
'either/or' is itself an intellectual artefact which does not adequately reflect
the characteristics of the world that we live in now. This world might be more
adequately described by a postmodernist paradigm which emphasizes the
'circuit of culture' – in particular, processes of meaning and representation,
pluralism and individuation – and which sees both diversity and the social
resistance it brings as an important means of achieving social change. However, there is a need to avoid simply taking an oppositional stance to essentialism, since such an alternative risks slipping into total relativism, where
there is no 'truth' at all. It is suggested that a more inclusive and rounded
world-view might be achieved by bringing normalcy and Other together
within the same system and to describe the relationships between them in a
systemic, 'both/and' way which conjoins deconstruction and epistemology. A
working model is presented and explored which brings together disabled
people's theories of simultaneous and multiple oppressions. Such theories
break down the boundaries between different dimensions of personhood
and the interlinked environments which comprise our social and cultural
milieux – the qualities of which construct our experience of having or not
having human rights. This model aims to show that the experience of oppression and our different responses to it result from the relationship between
these factors; they cannot be described adequately in terms of absolutisms of
one or the other, since this is precisely how the dominant culture exercises
social control.

 **3**

Meaning what we say and saying what we mean

> 'There's glory for you!'
> 'I don't know what you mean by "glory"' Alice said.
> '... I meant "there's a nice knock-down argument for you!"'
> 'But "glory" doesn't mean "a nice knock-down argument,"' Alice
> objected. 'When *I* use a word,' Humpty Dumpty said in rather a
> scornful tone, 'it means just what I choose it to mean – neither
> more nor less.'
>
> (Lewis Carroll, *Through the Looking-Glass*, 1872)

Introduction

The social and economic world, as we saw in the previous chapter, is increasingly concentrated on the removal of territorial boundaries, networking and globalization, and, in such a world, participatory world-views and shared communication look set to replace the historical tendency towards separation and competition (Reason 1994). This will bring with it a renewed emphasis on language and discourse, as we attempt to share information in many different forms across cultures, nations, time zones – and between narratives of normalcy and narratives of otherness. As Preston (1994: 236) says, 'culture is not a category but a continuum: not a dichotomisation between ourselves and that infamous Other, but a dialogue between self and group'. Culture might be described as a system of shared meanings, though within any culture there will be a huge diversity of meanings associated with different aspects of the world in which we live, and many ways of interpreting and representing them. ***Discourses*** are ways of constructing knowledge – configurations of ideas, images and practices, or discursive formations – which give us ways of talking about, forms of knowledge and conduct associated with a particular issue, social activity, institution or context. It follows that different meanings can only be shared through our common access to language, since language is both the vehicle and the symbol of thoughts, feelings, ideas, beliefs and values and alternative discourses. The view of communication expressed here is one of context-related, functional interaction where thoughts, feelings, ideas, beliefs and values are constantly bouncing between people, constantly being recontextualized and constantly being relocated. The process of communication therefore has an active role in the creation of meaning – a *semantic* role – and in the effects and consequences of particular communications – a *pragmatic* role – which lend themselves to different levels of *discourse analysis*.

I have suggested that language and discourse have not been incorporated into social model theory because they are difficult to explain adequately within a materialist framework. But this may equally be a consequence of seeing discourse in a particular way which marginalizes material, non-human contributors. Michael (1996: 34) suggests, however, that

> At the point of local interactions there are not only individual persons and macrosocial entities present – there are also architectures, furni-tures, technologies, bodies, other organisms. To what extent should these be given voice in the analytic account of such interactions? Do these not too embody morality, furnish resources of acquiescence and resistance . . . and impact upon the situational constitution of persons, identities and worlds? In what measure should we attribute agency to nonhumans, how might we articulate their 'purposes', and how might we go about disentangling the autonomy of their impact from the dis-courses in which they are at once buoyed and constructed?

The mutually constructive semantic and pragmatic roles of communication have also been marginalized from the analysis of deaf discourses except insofar as problematic communication between Deaf and hearing people can be attributed to 'cross-cultural' factors. These analyses tend to focus more on the structural linguistic properties or *syntactics* of sign language (the vocabu-lary, grammar, cohesion and text structure) or, in the case of hearing impaired people, *error analysis* (how the characteristics of hearing impaired people's language *deviate* from the hearing or Deaf 'norms', and so produce socially or culturally unacceptable ways of communicating). The latter studies often limit the functional aspects of communication to the formal description of verbal or signed utterances, and how or whether they are understood. As such, they are of little use *on their own* outside of formal linguistics. Language has a role and capacity in the realm of meaning and representation, in the construction of personal and social identities and the emotions (Parkinson 1995), greater than simple utterances. Language has social power; it accom-plishes things when it is taken up by others in particular ways – 'each speech act makes another appropriate . . . or normatively accountable . . . norms and rules emerging in historical and cultural circumstances operate to structure the things people do' (Harré and Gillett 1994: 33). Language and discourse are both separating and unifying concepts, and whereas separation tends to be concentrated at the level of individual texts, commonality and unification reside at the levels of discursive and social practice.

This emphasizes a framework for discourse analysis which could be thought of as having four main interlinked strands, all of which are impor-tant in understanding the construction and process of oppression:

- *textual* – mapping the specific language used to oppress – the language of disablism or phonocentrism (see for example Rieser and Mason 1991; Corker 1996b);
- *discursive* – patterns and systems of communicative behaviours, the timing of interactions, the construction of identities;
- *social* – ideology, hegemony and power structures, particularly those which are embedded in the dominant culture and define what is normatively accountable;
- *material* – the integration of the physical or non-human characteristics of communicative environments.

The first three of these strands correspond closely to Fairclough's three-dimensional approach to discourse analysis (1992). Hall (1997) integrates the three levels in his view of discourse as being concerned with the effects and consequences of representation, or politics:

> It [discourse] examines not only how language and representation produce meaning, but how the knowledge which a particular discourse produces connects with power, regulates conduct, makes up or constructs identities and subjectivities, and defines the way certain things are represented, thought about, practised or studied. The emphasis . . . is on specific languages or meanings, and how they are deployed at particular times, in particular places.
>
> (Hall 1997: 6)

Anthropological evidence generally supports the idea that culturally embedded discourses create the dominant experience of disability within a given culture, time or social context (Ingstad and Reynolds-Whyte 1995; Barnes 1996b), and that this construction is reinforced by and interpreted through social practices and social structure. For example, Lennard Davis (1995: 1) notes that 'Disability . . . is part of a historically constructed discourse, an ideology of thinking about the body under certain historical circumstances.' Later in the same work (pp. 62, 71), he says that before the late seventeenth and early eighteenth centuries, when society was performance-based, deaf people were not constructed as a group, and there was no significant discourse around deafness. He attributes the subsequent attention paid to deafness in the late eighteenth century as

> part of a general transition from a society that based its cultural production on performances to one that focused its cultural production on texts. In a text-based society, the physical presence of an auditor or an audience is no longer necessary, as it would be in a world based on performances. The cultural narrowness of a society in which spoken language is paramount expands to include all users of language, spoken or not . . . The arbitrary privileging of hearing language over nonspoken language, and the consequent marginalisation of those who do participate in the linguistic majority, emerges as a fact of power . . . because sign language will never actually become a universal language, we must stop

and consider how truly hegemonic and controlling a concept is the notion of writing and speech as a 'hearing' phenomenon.

In this chapter, I develop the argument that we cannot understand or explain deafness in the context of disability oppression within frameworks which sideline discursive practice or confine it to a particular segment of society. This is because unequal access to discourse has significant consequences in terms of disability oppression for the lives of groups of disabled people who are *necessarily* preoccupied with issues of language and communication. In this context, too many people forget, as Davis implies, that the sounds they are so fond of listening to are neither more nor less symbolic of human thought and meaning than the clothes we wear, our facial expressions and body language – or the whistle-talk of the Mazteco, the drum language and smoke signals of Native Americans, the silence of the Athabaskans and the sign language of Deaf people. These sounds only seem to be more symbolic because we live in a phonocentric society: evidenced, for example, by the very high proportion of ascriptive terms which have auditory connotations *and* are in frequent usage in the English language – terms such as 'banging', 'clapping', 'ringing', 'loud' and 'echoing' (Corker 1982). The phonocentric institutions of education, paid work and financial rewards sustain the primacy of cognitive skills at the expense of other attributes such as emotional wisdom, insight and imagination. These same institutions bury the global concepts of communication and language – in particular their function of *reciprocal* interaction which gives them the status of life support systems – under an avalanche of multiple meanings, theories and countless fragmentary investigations into their parts and processes.

In 1964, Ruesh insisted that 'in developing an overall theory of communication, the greatest need at present revolves around the inclusion of communicating persons' (1964: 255): nothing much has changed. As Levine pertinently notes (1981: 11), 'the track along which communication moves in joining individual to milieu is subsumed in the concept of "language," the most ingenious of which, the verbal form, was invented by the same "human link" that seems such an annoyance to theorists'. In this she was echoing George Miller's comment that some communication theorists see the human link in communication systems in much the same way that they regard random noise – 'both are unfortunate disturbances in an otherwise well-behaved system and both should be reduced until they do as little harm as possible' (Miller 1964: 45). When the focus turns to discourse, it becomes clear that deaf people do not constitute the only group who are preoccupied with language and discursive practice – blind and visually impaired people also place emphasis on these issues, for example. I therefore hope to show that in this context, the boundaries between deafness and disability become blurred, and so any framework for thinking about deafness and disability which gives full credence to discourse becomes more inclusive. However, such a framework would also require a very different approach to the mind–body dichotomy, and so I must first return to this.

In the sensory realm

The mind–body dichotomy results in sustained attempts to describe deaf people's experience of oppression *only* in terms of society's construction of physical communication barriers. This may be dangerously simplistic – as simplistic as the suggestion that barriers to participation in society can be removed by the provision of communication aids, whether mechanical or human. In this, as we have seen, deaf people's experience is very similar to that of many blind and visually impaired people. The critical role of language and discourse in relation to sensory impairments, has not, however, been given prominence within social model theory, outside of studies related to disabling imagery and the representation of disabled people in the media (Barnes 1992; Hevey 1992). I have suggested that this is perhaps because a top-down view of the relationship between the individual and society, as framed by the social model of disability, leaves discourse as a side effect of social structure so that it cannot therefore be the focus of social change. Equally, however, bottom-up individualist world-views cannot accommodate any kind of social constructionism, and therefore ignore discourse altogether. As a current example of this we might use the Disability Discrimination Act's definition of impairment, which was the subject of protracted discussion in the Standing Committee. Much of this discussion centred around whether or not the term 'sensory' should be included alongside mental and physical impairment, itself reminiscent of the mind–body split I referred to in the previous chapter. In the end, the Minister's view prevailed:

> The terms physical and mental are intended to be seen in their widest sense and should comprehensively cover all forms of impairment. All the advice I have received suggests that a third category, in addition to physical and mental impairment, might imply that those categories are not all-embracing ... Sensory conditions would generally be covered as physical conditions or, exceptionally, in cases such as hysterical deafness, as mental conditions.
> (Mr W. Hague, House of Commons Debates Standing C'ttee E, col. 71)

This statement expresses the need of legislators to find categories which are 'all-embracing', or to compress human experiences into what post-modernists refer to as totalizing discourses. Whereas these comments refer to impairment, the Act itself is couched in the terminology of the individual model, and so impairment and disability are not discrete. Sensory impairment in governmentspeak generally means physical impairment of the senses in relation to 'normal' sensation, and so it was the Minister's view that the term 'sensory' did not add legal or medical meaning to the definition of impairment (Doyle 1996). Paradoxically, legal or medical meaning does not appear to be concerned with the effects or consequences of the discursive practices which link individuals with their environments, including those which construct our experience of oppression. Even in the context of 'medical' meaning, the casual dismissal of the sensory dimension of experience seems strange, especially when a large number of distinguished psychologists and psychiatrists, particularly those who have emerged from the Jungian school, have for years accepted the distinction between thought, feeling, sensation and intuition, even if priority has been given to the first two.

However, it seems that it would be useful to consider the role of the senses alongside language at the interface between physical and mental, a role which establishes them in many ways as the mediators of discursive practices. I would argue strongly that this gives sensory impairments a completely different configuration to cognitive and intellectual impairments, and makes their relationship to the body less clear. To explain this further, I now turn my attention to the links between discursive practice and identity construction.

Discourse and the construction of identities

Most commentators agree that the strength of personal and collective empowerment emerges from a strong sense of identity, that is, knowing who we are, what this means in different contexts and the boundaries which separate us from or define our sense of belonging to other people, including those we regard as Other. The role of discourse in the construction of deaf and disabled identities would therefore seem to be important for the way in which we analyse social processes and structures, including those which are oppressive. Hall (1996: 4–5) suggests, citing Derrida (1981), Laclau (1990) and Butler (1993), that

> Identities are constructed through, not outside, difference. This entails the radically disturbing recognition that it is only through the relation to the Other, the relation to what is not, to precisely what it lacks, to what has been called its *constitutive outside* that the 'positive' meaning of any term – and thus its 'identity' – can be constructed . . . Throughout their careers, identities can function as points of identification and attachment only because of their capacity to exclude, to leave out, to render 'outside', abjected. Every identity has at its margin, an excess, something more.

Harris (1995) has employed Fairclough's (1992) discourse model in looking at the construction of 'Deaf identity', which she views as a somewhat finite and singular concept, in contrast to Moorhead (1995) and myself (Corker 1996b), who use personal biographies within a participatory paradigm. However, her analysis is ultimately unsatisfactory on a number of levels. She at times appears to confuse discourse with communication and language, since she argues that 'Deaf identity is constructed . . . formed, suppressed and liberated' through the use of sign language (Harris 1995: 18, 27). In isolation, neither sign language nor spoken language *as communicative media* indicate the different layers of meaning which characterize discourse, nor their cultural and social origins and production. This, together with her description of Deaf people as 'functionally linguistic isolates' in the hearing community (p. 177), reduces language to utterances, and seems to support the view that discourse only occurs in interactions among individuals with a shared signalling system. Evidence suggests, however, that deaf children are very capable of 'reading' emotions, differences in attitude and other non-verbal or visual aspects of communication, even if they are unable to understand fully or use the context which would be given by an auditory or more comprehensively visual input. This is a part of deaf children's oppression – their disability. 'The relation to the Other' clearly does have a place in constructing deaf identities, as Diane Kenyon (1994: 136) describes in the context of hearing impairment:

> Whenever I jar up against another human being, it is useless just to tell them I am deaf. I have to hunt for ways of explaining that their method of communication thrusts me into isolation. Although my body and its clothing are in the room of life, I the person am not. My participation is stunted by their immobile lips, hands and attitudes.

There are many different ideas about the process of identity construction, which themselves would take many volumes to describe. These range from those which dissolve the distinction between mind and body (Harré and Gillett 1994) through those which appear to diminish completely the sense of the person as anything other than the discourses of their relationships with their environment (Coupland and Nussbaum 1993), to those which suggest that identity is constructed in a number of discrete phases throughout a person's life (Erikson 1959) and that different outcomes of this process can be described (Marcia 1994). Most of these approaches embrace essentialist perspectives on the relationship between the individual and society which has the effect of removing identity from the circuit of culture described in the previous chapter. Indeed, this is perhaps why some disabled activists and academics are uneasy with the concepts of identity and culture (Barnes 1996b: 49). Further, the different emphases they place on the role of language and discourses in identity production mean that there are some difficulties with their application to the experience of deaf people. However, the most significant obstacle the majority of these approaches pose in the context of the current discussion is in their failure to generate a viable critique which presents an alternative to essentialist descriptions of identity without suppressing narratives of otherness. These criticisms leave me with two main lines of development. The first comes from Grossberg's analysis of identity and difference in cultural studies and its relationship to 'the politics of singularity' (1996: 102) which has been alluded to by some disabled academics. For example, Peters (1996: 215) refers to people acting 'as border-crossers of the personal/political within themselves as well as across communities within which they interact' and relates this to 'the politics of disability identity'. I will explore this further in Chapter 5. The second lies in Ricœur's concept of 'narrative identity'. Focusing on the historical distinction between selfhood and sameness, he argues that this distinction has always been pre-supposed, but never treated thematically. He then suggests (1992: 114–15) that

Narrative theory finds one of its major justifications in the role it plays in the middle ground between the descriptive viewpoint on action, to which we have confined ourselves until now, and the prescriptive viewpoint which will prevail . . . A triad has thus imposed itself on my analysis: describe, narrate, prescribe – each moment of the triad implying a specific relation between the constitution of action and the constitution of the self.

My interpretation of this triad would be that it is suggestive of the physical–sensory–mental distinction, but brings them together to form a relationship. In this context I feel that the distinction does add legal meaning to the definition of impairment, because as long as legislation attempts to squeeze sensory impairment into physical or mental categories, there can be no comprehensive analysis of social, linguistic and attitudinal oppression, and therefore no social change. These forms of oppression are generally thought to be the most prevalent oppressions faced by disabled people as a whole, and the most difficult to dismantle.

The poststructuralist agenda

In Chapter 1, I began to deconstruct the tensions between deaf and disabled people, in part to demonstrate that it is multilayered and, as such, hides issues as much as it reveals them. Deconstruction moves us into a different kind of analysis, and in this context, I now want to explore the contribution that poststructuralism might make to the current discussion. Poststructuralism is an important part of postmodernist philosophy, *so* important in fact that the terms 'poststructuralism' and 'postmodernism' are often used interchangeably. Poststructuralism, however, deals specifically with language and discourse and, as such, is bound up with issues of meaning, representation and identity. Its main premise is that meaning can never be fixed because human discourse is constantly evolving and therefore continually engaged in creating new meanings. Because of the unbreakable links between language and meaning, explanations of the social world lie 'not inside individuals, but out in the linguistic space in which they move with other people' (Burr 1995: 40). Words, signs, pictures, books, jokes and so on change their meaning over time, from context to context and from person to person. Indeed, there is a great deal of evidence for this when we look at how the structure and meaning of language has changed and is still changing. In spite of this change, however, Harré suggests (1981: 9) that there is a tendency to reduce meaning to a simple referential relation between a linguistic term and something actually experienced, usually in a single act of perception: 'the imaginative underpinnings of science are swept away as meaningless, since most theoretical terms like "action" or "complex" or "dialectic" are related directly only to an *imagined* representation of the world'.

Changes in meaning produce diversity and conflict. We might here take the example of 'culture'. The term may be used in a wide sense to describe all aspects characteristic of a particular form of human life, or in a narrow sense to denote only the system of values implicit in it. Unsurprisingly, cultural studies tend to hinge on one meaning *or* the other, depending on what is being investigated and what needs to be established. Thus, understanding culture in the wide sense is a prevalent concern of historical, anthropological and socio-logical studies. The study of culture in the narrow sense lies in the realm of the humanities, where the aim is to interpret and transmit to future generations the system of values in terms of which participants in a particular cultural milieu find meaning and purpose. In either of its interpretations, culture may be thought of as a causal agent that affects the evolutionary process by uniquely human means because it permits the self-conscious evaluation of human possibilities in the light of a framework of values which reflect pre-vailing ideals about what human life ought to be. This leads to yet another dis-tinction between something which signifies or *is* culture (which Deaf people claim is *their* territory – what makes them unique) and something which is *constructed by* culture (which is asserted by social model theorists). However, since it can be demonstrated that there are a number of elements of Deaf cul-ture which are constructed from and through Deaf people's experience of oppression by hearing people, this distinction is not as clear as it may seem.

Similarly, Kim (1995) points out that though the term 'capitalism' is often used in a universal way, in Europe and North America it evolved from within, whereas in Asia, Latin America and Africa it was imposed through coloniza-tion. This difference in the histories of development meant that the cultural response to it also varied, through the growth of different types of moral-political ideologies and their concomitant practices, such as democracy and communism. Fully reciprocal and inclusive communication depends not only on a shared knowledge of the expressive symbolism of a given society, but more particularly on shared familiarity with the habits, values and mores of that culture. Without such familiarity, individuals from different cultures may use the same linguistic term, but they do not necessarily use the same language. At the local level, groups of computer programmers or academics cluster around a specialist language that forms their identity and has the potential to exclude other groups, in much the same way that French speakers might exclude non-French speakers. Social model theorists often refer to the social *creation* of disability, whereas a poststructuralist would use the the term social *construction*. But the difference between the meaning of the two terms is negligible, and so preference for one term over the other can say more about where social model theorists position themselves in relation to poststructuralist discourses.

However, the fact that we apparently use the *same* language does not mean that we share the same meaning. This can be explained by looking at deaf people's use of the deceptively simple term 'discussion'. Hearing people 'dis-cuss' different topics often without thinking about it, and so do many deaf people – when they are with each other. But the minute the suggestion is made that I, as a deaf person, 'discuss' things with hearing people, I begin to ask questions about access, understanding, translatability, first and second languages and so on. So in these terms, the meaning of 'discussion' has many added dimensions for me. If a hearing person imposes *their* meaning on me through social action after I have clarified that we do not mean the same thing by 'discussion', I may feel that I am being treated less favourably in the 'discussion', and because the hearing person's meaning is legitimated in the phonocentric culture, I may also feel disempowered and excluded – less able to contribute to the 'discussion'. The problem can be resolved by 'discussion' – or can it?

The original meaning of the term 'deaf' – 'wholly or partially without hearing' – placed the concept firmly in the auditory sphere. Its common association with the terms 'dumb' or 'mute' established and reinforced phonocentric links between audition and linguistic competence. The meaning of 'deaf' was then broadened to refer to any person who, regardless of whether they could hear or not, ignored, refused to listen to or comply with something or someone, and likewise, 'dumb' became equated with stupidity. Now 'deaf' has two context-specific meanings: the first – hearing impaired – denotes a unifying and inclusive concept of deafness and is used mainly by professionals working with deaf people or in the disability field; the second – Deaf – is used within that group of deaf people who see themselves as a separate linguistic minority group, and their allies. But this, too, is under question, since these terms are in use as conveyors of prejudice. Interestingly, Montgomery (1997: 30–1) points out, with more than a little frustration, that

> The second [complaint] is to do with 'the big D' and what to do when the 'little d' comes at the beginning of a sentence, or in a title where all words start with capitals. My next review will be in swedish which does not use capitals to distinguish proper from improper nouns and hence the swedish deaf community has its solidarity intact and unfragmented by the silly discursive jargon terms which are a nuisance and no-one, including the inventors, knows how to use correctly.

The term 'impairment' has a similar history. Many disabled people reject the term because of its connotations in relation to normalcy, and believe that the term needs to be redefined. For example Crow (1996: 211) says:

> The perception of impairment as personal tragedy is merely a social construction; it is not an inevitable way of thinking about impairment. Recognising the importance of impairment for us does not mean that we have to take on the non-disabled world's ways of interpreting our experience and our bodies. In fact, impairment, at its most basic level, is a purely objective concept which carries no intrinsic meaning. Impairment simply means that aspects of a person's body do not function or they function with difficulty. Frequently this is taken a stage further to imply that the person's body, and ultimately the person, is inferior. However, the first is fact and the second is interpretation.

There are also many examples of disabled people resisting a change of terminology and meaning which seem to be based upon a desire to retain the links between disability oppression and impairment. The following example is interesting, because the challenge is issued by a deaf person:

> Terminology was an equally important and contentious issue. The words we use make us think about meaning and the impact of our actions on, and our attitudes to other people. There were two groups of disabled people on the strategy group who could not agree with each other on terminology. While people from GMCDP (Greater Manchester Coalition of Disabled People) preferred to use the term 'impairment' . . . the profoundly deaf members of the group felt the word 'impairment' has a negative meaning and should be rejected. They preferred to talk in terms of 'difference'. They emphasised cultural and language differences rather than the existence of an impairment. However, 'difference' was unacceptable to GMCDP members because it was regarded as too general and did not classify the functional range which is the basis on which oppressive societal and individual attitudes are formed.
>
> (Emanuel and Ackroyd 1996: 181)

This particular situation was resolved by accepting 'impairment' as the majority view and recording 'difference' as the minority view, which is an example of why I have some uneasiness with the terms 'Deaf' and 'impaired' because each signifies a power relationship to the Other, depending on the context in which they are used, and each is exclusive of the Other. Hence in this example, the 'resolution' is only effective as a reinforcement of an existing majority balance of power. However, conflict often happens because, as in situations like this one, new meanings do not simply replace old meanings, they can also withdraw into themselves. Meanings tend to exist alongside each other and interact with each other; in addition to their definitive role, they also delineate the boundaries between things and people, their relationships to other things and other people. The process of defining is bound up in issues of social identity, and therefore, with action which is taken – political or otherwise. The term 'impaired' as applied to Deaf people tends to change their concept of 'normalcy' and is rejected; the term 'different', as applied to disabled people, neutralizes their political power. Similarly, the advent of **cochlear implants** and the increasing possibility of **genetic engineering** have changed the meaning of 'hearing aids'. Because implantation is viewed by some Deaf people as a modern-day equivalent of eugenics, and genetic engineering to 'root out' the deaf gene would mean the extinction of the Deaf community, hearing aids are now increasingly being seen as the lesser evil, associated with alleviation and choice. Jenny Corbett (1996) notes that it is particularly important to look at how and why we select particular meanings because this has implications for the ownership of the dominant discourse and therefore for discursive practice. She says (pp. 32–3, 101):

> Language reflects conceptions of reality, or truth. As such, I feel the term 'special need' is no longer useful or constructive. To me, it is reflective of professional ownership where medical and educational definitions

dominate the discourse. It jars uncomfortably with the discourses in the disability movement where new languages and metaphors are emerging in a creative burst of pride and assertion . . . if we are able to 'move through' identities, we can also adopt a similar approach to the use of special language. Maybe if there are more 'nomads' filling the central arena the plurality of discourses will make all language special. Thus 'special' becomes normality.

'Nomad', in this context, is drawn from the work of Bauman (1992), who makes a distinction between the 'pilgrims' of modernism (who structure their journeys through life within the framework of some grand design or the pursuit of an ultimate goal) and the nomads of postmodernism and post-structuralism (who remain ambiguous and changing in their identity).

Discourse and power

However, some meanings persist when words or signs become attached to them and so may appear 'fixed' in that relationship (Saussure 1974). The vast majority of people, including government and the judiciary, still define deaf-ness as impaired hearing, use the term 'deaf' in its wider sense and, along with many deaf and disabled people themselves, do not make a distinction between impairment and disability. Language, then, is not a system of signs with fixed meanings with which everyone agrees, but a site of variation, con-tention and potential conflict. As such, language is about power relations, because discourses compete with each other on many different levels and in many different contexts. The meaning of the phrase 'Does s/he take sugar?' will convey different power relations when addressed to children, adults with limited or no direct experience with children or disabled people, parents of disabled children and disabled people themselves (Burr 1995). Also the dom-inant culture continues to exercise power through the legitimation of the term 'disabling' in the context of disabling unexploded bombs, for example, but is unable to accommodate its use in the context of disabling people.

The poststructuralist view of power, as defined by Foucault, is that it is held by those who are able to draw upon discourses which allow their actions to be represented in the light of 'knowledges' currently prevailing in society – knowledge is power over others *and* the power to define others (Foucault 1972, 1979). Thus the *availability* of different discourses is critical to under-standing meaning in context, and to power, because 'knowledge' refers to the particular construction that has received the stamp of 'truth' or 'normalcy'. In Western society, as we have seen, this is individual, liberal humanist dis-course, which is central to our present social and economic organization and which is used to mystify us in legislation. The individual construction of dis-ability is legitimated within this discourse, and so brings with it the potential for acting in one way rather than another and for marginalizing alternative ways of acting, such as those framed by the social model of disability or the linguistic minority construction of deafness. This is clearly expressed throughout the work of many deaf and disabled academics and activists I refer to in this book. But, significantly, it also forms the subtext of others' work. For example, after an initial solitary reference to the 'social construction' of disability (p. 172), without citing the origins of this approach in the disability world or its relationship to the social model, Lane (1995) then proceeds to reinforce the idea that the linguistic minority construction is different to the disability construction, *through continuous reference to the individual construction of disability* and the attribution of negative value to it. This is a dominant theme of Lane's work, which though it has been significant in strengthening our understanding of the DEAF-WORLD, has done little to further the cause of deaf people who do not 'fit' the ideal, particularly in their relationships with disabled people:

> An embarrassment for the medical model of cultural deafness heretofore was that this 'pathology' had no medical treatment. With cochlear implants, however, the medical specialty of otology has been expanding its traditional clientele beyond adventitiously deafened hearing people who seek treatment, *for whom an infirmity model is appropriate*, to include members of the Deaf community, for whom it is not.
>
> (Lane 1992: 206, my italics)

Hearing impaired people, and particularly deafened people, are often trapped between different discourses of tragedy from which there is no escape and from which they cannot develop alternative discourses because of the marginalizing effects of negative value judgements. In a sense, then, Lane selects particular discourses on deafness and disability which are not directly comparable. In doing so, he successfully emphasizes his main premise that Deaf people are not disabled by drawing upon disablist discourses; he thus justifies Deaf people's claim to the right to coexist as a minority group which advocates special measures, a share of available resources and, in Britain, a high degree of dependency on the dominant culture for its livelihood (Kyle 1991).

But this brings us to another important element of poststructuralism, which stems from Derrida's concept of *différance*, which emphasizes that a particular discourse only has meaning in relation to other discourses – the identity of something is as much a function of what it *is not* as what it *is*. So, to describe oneself as Deaf means that one is not hearing (or deaf), but it also means that being Deaf is defined *in relation to* hearingness, impairment or even vision – the changing meanings of the term 'deaf' described above signify different relationships to hearing and different kinds of linguistic and cultural representation. This is why Lennard Davis (1995: 1) says that on the one hand, 'One is either disabled or not', and on the other that 'normalcy and disability are part of the same system' (p. 2). These two perspectives epitomize the struggle between *structuralism* and poststructuralism, which, like normalcy and disability, exist alongside each other. However, when Davis, as a hearing person with Deaf parents (p. xix) says of his wish to be hearing that 'what I was fleeing was not deafness *per se*, but the deafness constructed by the hearing world', and this flight led him to the understanding 'that deafness was a category of oppression' – a path which Lane (1992) describes as making an 'extrapolative leap' of the imagination – his meaning is somewhat different to that which is implicit in disabled people's use of social model discourse to locate disability in society. The effect of the conflict between linguistic minority discourse and medical discourse for deaf people, as we have seen, is ultimately fragmentation; this, in turn, produces further categories and further conflict. The process is circular. For hearing people, on the other hand, the effect is to manufacture a division between the 'positive, proud Deaf person' (whom they revere and see as a legitimate area for 'academic' and 'sociocultural' study) and the 'negative, impaired deaf person' (whom they pity or reject in line with Western society's 'individualistic' discourse). Thus their positions and their power within *both* discourses are maintained. This echoes Derrida's (1978) belief that the widespread use of the language of Otherness in anthropological discourse to describe the West's encounter with non-Western cultures, or with anything which is 'other than' the dominant beliefs and values of Western culture, tends to keep the dominant discourse intact. As we will see in Chapter 6, this has particular implications for working roles and relationships between deaf and hearing people.

The application of a poststructuralist framework suggests further examples of the way in which the dominant culture maintains its power in relation to the Other. As individuals, we are constantly subject to an interplay of different discourses, each with its own structure of rights, obligations and possibilities for action, and each carrying identity and power implications. The restructuring of meaning depends to a very large extent not only on how people 'position' themselves in relation to alternative discourses, but also on whether all discourses are available and accessible to all people. Class, age, gender, ethnic origin, sexuality and disability can all be linked to restrictions on the kind of person we can claim to be, and this is as true within our communities as it is within the dominant culture. The poststructuralist view of development is one of a process of becoming more and more sophisticated in one's ability to produce accounts by using the linguistic and accounting rules of one's culture. Harré (1981) sees this ability as developing, at least in part, through the social interaction between young children and the adults around them. This again emphasizes that language is not just a descriptive tool – we use it and do things with it to achieve certain effects, and so language itself is a means of exercising political expediency. For example, consider the dialogues presented in Boxes 3.1, 3.2 and 3.3, all of which are transcriptions of nursery or primary school interactions between a teacher and a class, where the focus becomes concentrated on a particular child or children. Who has the power in each of these dialogues and why?

It is only in the dialogue in Box 3.1 that the children, Terry and Sean, seem powerful. They take control by temporarily locating themselves as male and their teacher as female within a 'nonsense' discourse on sexuality which makes their teacher relatively powerless, and, when placed in the context of

Box 3.1 from Walkerdine (1981)

The sequence begins when Annie takes a piece of Lego to add on to a construction that she is building. Terry tries to take it away from her to use himself and she resists. He says:

Terry: You're a stupid cunt, Annie.

The teacher tells him to stop and Sean tries to mess up another child's construction. The teacher tells him to stop. Then Sean says:

Sean: Get out of it Miss Baxter paxter.
Terry: Get out of it knickers Miss Baxter.
Sean: Get out of it Miss Baxter paxter.
Terry: Get out of it Miss Baxter the knickers paxter knickers, bum.
Sean: Knickers, shit, bum.
Teacher: Sean, that's enough, you're being silly.
Sean: Miss Baxter, knickers, show your knickers.
Terry: Miss Baxter, show your bum off.
       (They giggle)
Teacher: I think you're being very silly.
Terry: Shit Miss Baxter, shit Miss Baxter.
Sean: Miss Baxter, show your knickers your bum off.
Sean: Take all your clothes off, your bra off.
Terry: Yeah, and take your bum off, take your wee-wee off, take your clothes off, your mouth off.
Sean: Take your teeth out, take your head off, take your hair off, take your bum off. Miss Baxter the paxter knickers taxter.
Teacher: Sean, go and find something else to do, please.

the dominant discourse of nursery education at that time, makes it difficult for her to resist the position that is being offered. If we compare that situation in the other dialogues we get a different picture. In the dialogue in Box 3.2, the children are forced into a submissive role by the racist attitudes of their teacher and other pupils in such a way that they seem to 'fit' the stereotype being promoted. Aftab, for example, is described as 'shy' when perhaps he feels 'ashamed' of the position he is being forced into, whereas Rehana has to face constant denial of her own cultural experience which reduces her, for the most part, to single-syllable responses. In the dialogue in Box 3.3, Katherine, the deaf child, neither understands nor is understood by the teacher, and the teacher's power in this situation is reinforced by the communication she has with the other children. Katherine may seem to be the focus of the teacher's attention, but what opportunity is she getting to 'develop' outside of the teacher's frame of reference, and how can she know whether there are alternative discourses which she might draw from? Moreover, what is the point of

---

Box 3.2   from Gill *et al.* (1992)

Teacher:	Last time we talked a little about the different languages we speak at home and in school, and we made a list on the board, and I said that we would talk about this book that I found in the library (*Holds the book up to the class*). Rehana and Aftab might be able to help me. It is an unusual book. Can you tell me why? (*Holds book up for class to inspect*)
White girl:	It's got funny writing
Teacher:	It's written in two languages. English and . . . can you tell me Rehana?
White boy:	Jamaican
Rehana:	(*Shyly*) Urdu
Teacher:	Is that how you say it? Urdeo? *Rehana laughs, embarrassed. White pupils snigger.*
Teacher:	(*To Rehana*) Say it again
Rehana:	Urdu
Teacher:	Urdeo *Asian pupils laugh, embarrassed*
Teacher:	Say it again
Rehana:	Urdu
Teacher:	(*Mimicking Rehana but showing signs of defect in the pronunciation, laughs*) Urdeo
Teacher:	(*Laughingly*) How do you say it Aftab? *Aftab holds his head down, refuses to respond*
Teacher:	Can we write it on the board? . . . . . (*To Asian boy*) Can you read that? (*Boy bows his head*) I think he's shy, that's fair enough. Well I can't read it. I might even have it upside down, I don't know. (*To Asian girl*) Can you tell us about 'Urdeo', is it written like that (*pointing left to right*) or written like that (*pointing right to left*)?
Rehana:	No, that way (*pointing right to left*)
White pupil:	Backwards
Teacher:	It's written from right to left?
Rehana:	Yes
Teacher:	No, its not backwards. It's English that's written backwards . . .

---

her communicating the 'right' answers if the teacher (and the other children) are unable to understand her?

Using this kind of developmental framework we can ask further questions about the apparent gulf between knowledge of social model discourse in the Deaf community, and Deaf people's well-documented experience of dis-

---

Box 3.3 from Gregory and Bishop (1989)

The class are discussing the conventions of maternity hospitals to label babies as 'Baby + Surname'. None of the other children have had difficulty with this concept. Then Katherine, a deaf child, is asked.

Teacher:	What would you have been called Katherine?
Katherine:	I don't know
Teacher:	What's your second name?
Katherine:	???? (indecipherable utterance)
Teacher:	Baby Ash . . . ?
Katherine:	Ash
Teacher:	What's your second name? What comes after Katherine?
Katherine:	(no response)
Teacher:	Baby who?
Katherine:	Ash
Teacher:	Ash De. Come on
Katherine	Ash De
Teacher:	Ash De. I'll give you Ash De. Ash who? What's your second name? Katherine Ash De?
Another child:	Down
Katherine:	Ash De
Teacher:	Ashdown isn't it? So you would have been 'Baby Ashdown'.
Katherine:	(laughs)
Teacher:	Ssh can you all be very quiet whilst we listen to Katherine. Quickly, good, that's much better
Katherine:	(indecipherable – very soft voice)
Teacher:	Katherine can you talk a bit louder 'cos I know you've got a much louder voice than that haven't you?
Katherine:	Yes
Teacher:	Yes. Talk a bit louder so that we can all hear you
Katherine:	(three sentences that the teacher does not understand)
Teacher:	Do you want to go and fetch your little book so I can read to everybody what you did? It's on my . . .
Katherine:	(six word utterance not comprehensible)

ability as social oppression. For example, consider Christopher Reid's (1994: 19) comment:

> When they use an interpreter, how do Deaf people know that the interpreter's voice-over of their signing is correct? Have they ever wondered, but could not know for sure, whether poor interpreting voice-over was to blame when communications with a hearing person did not go well?

Does it worry these Deaf people that an interpreter may do a poor voice-over at an important meeting, such as a job interview?

This is an important example, because it demonstrates another way in which hearing people maintain their power within both discourses, but it has different implications for the form that this power takes. There has been much evidence to suggest that signed discourses and spoken discourses are not fully translatable because signed discourses originate in the visual-spatial realm and spoken discourses in the oral-aural realm. This means that translating from English to French, for example, is a completely different exercise to translating from English to BSL (British Sign Language). There is also a great deal of evidence of the huge barriers experienced by many deaf children to learning a language which gives primacy to the oral-aural realm, and of the problems of transmission of culturally relevant linguistic and accounting rules when most adults in a deaf child's immediate social world are effectively from an 'alien' (hearing) culture. If a deaf child learns his/her first language primarily through the visual-spatial mode, this will serve them well in social situations *with other sign language users*. However, if a Deaf person is subsequently unable to learn the language of the dominant culture fully, and cannot therefore draw upon a range of alternative discourses, the skills of the interpreter in the above situation will be irrelevant *because* language is not just about words or signs, it is about their meaning in a whole variety of contexts, and because the interpreter functions at the interface. A fair proportion of this meaning, as I have suggested, may not be translatable – for example, hearing idioms and their Deaf equivalent, ***non-manual signs***. But if a Deaf person has only *one* meaning for a particular term within their linguistic repertoire and, especially, if this meaning is part of the dominant discourse and so imbued with cultural value judgements, it is this meaning which will be understood, irrespective of whether the translation is accurate (Corker 1994a). I will come back to issues of translation and interpretation in Chapter 6.

Cybernetic models and network metaphors

Coleman and DePaulo (1991: 62) have shown that 'mis-communication and problematic talk' are created in interaction between disabled and non-disabled people, and are therefore to some degree issues for *all* disabled people and their Others. They are moreover usually additional to the impairment, which may manifest itself in major disruptions to the flow or synchrony in communication. In social model theory, this view identifies communication dysfunction in terms of disability:

> Displays of problematic talk in interactions between disabled and able-bodied individuals can occur at several levels. Highly salient modifications in speech are common, but miscommunications occur in other channels or modes as well e.g. facial expressions, eye contact, kinesics,

interpersonal distance [and] the selection of an inappropriate communicative register or style from the many available types . . . disabled and
able-bodied interactions lack agreement about the meaning of communicative behaviour or about what constitutes appropriate communicative
behaviour.

(Coleman and DePaulo 1991: 62)

These observations form a useful lead-in to the areas of discursive and
social practice – the discursive production and social context of meaning –
where I have found **cybernetic** models of communication to be useful in
schematizing the construction of patterns of shared experiences (Watzlawick *et al.* 1967; Dallos 1991), including our common experience of
oppression as it is linked to discourse. However, it is important to emphasize
that patterns of interaction are not causal – one does not cause the other or
vice versa – because the interaction itself is set in a wider context which has
both *epochal* and *institutional* dimensions; each of these dimensions can be
attributed properties of contextuality, agency and effectivity in ways which
serve in current interactions (Michael 1996). So when, for example, we think
about interaction between Deaf and disabled people, we must correspond-
ingly consider the non-disabled and hearing values (the Others) culturally
embedded in the context in which they interact, and which thus themselves
become 'actors' in the interaction. Discursive practice itself, including attitudes and perceptions, both constructs and is a composite result of the
embeddedness within overlapping networks across social, political and economic domains. This is what Michael (1996) describes as **actor-network
theory**.

Earlier in this chapter it was pointed out that in any situation where we
come together we will have different knowledges which result from our
ability to draw from and position ourselves in relation to alternative discourses. How the process of communication develops then depends to a large
extent on what discourses are used, where we position ourselves, and
whether these discourses are legitimated in the dominant culture. The structure of the interaction is constituted and reconstituted by the process of communication. So if we take Figure 3.1 as a simple example, it is possible to
examine how particular knowledges reinforce each other to construct a
shared experience because these knowledges become what Dallos (1991)
calls 'the dynamic equilibrium' of the interaction, which, in this case, keeps
oppressor and oppressed in their given roles.

Both parties in the interaction in Figure 3.1 are acting in legitimated ways
of behaving and feeling, because oppression *and the expected response to it* are
institutionalized; they therefore place broad constraints on the types of relationships which are possible between oppressor and oppressed. Further, the
differences in power between each of the parties in the interaction constrain
the dynamics and even the moment-to-moment flow of the interaction, as
does the introduction of a third party (for example sign language interpreters), and culturally produced values and expectations (for example

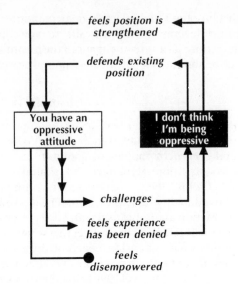

Figure 3.1 Communication behaviour

associated with time). Many deaf people point out that the different way in which communication has to be managed when deaf people are present in a hearing group, and the consequences of breakdowns in technological equipment such as *loop systems* and *Palantype*, place extra time constraints which are usually not allowed for – because there is no time! French (1992: 98) agrees that the lack of time can have 'far-reaching consequences', because 'disabled people tend to experience a general shortage of time in their lives, partly because the world is not designed with them in mind, and partly because of the limitations imposed by their impairments'.

I will return to these issues in Chapter 6. However, they illustrate precisely why manifest oppression cannot be reduced to individual experiences, as it is in legislation; it may, however, be *experienced* in qualitatively different ways by different individuals through the extent to which and how they conform or resist. Going back to Foucault's notions of power and resistance as an effect of discourse, to construe the world in terms of oppressor and oppressed can be said to produce one particular 'knowledge', which brings with it a power inequality between those groups. There are differences in the knowledges that each party has available to influence the other: the Foucaultian solution would be to open up alternative discourses which destabilize the oppressive equilibrium by refocusing interaction on the struggle between oppressor and oppressed. But it is more likely that these discourses will be taken up by the oppressed than by the oppressor, because 'discursive practices are ideologically invested in so far as they incorporate significations which contribute to sustaining or restructuring power relations' (Fairclough 1992: 91).

At the same time, as I suggested in the introduction to this chapter, there is a danger that we focus on discursive practice in a way that assumes that all the actors are human. However, most deaf and disabled people live in environments where non-human 'actors' such as technology, architecture, lighting, information transfer (or informatics), and disability-specific aids and equipment such as hearing aids and wheelchairs form part of the network: 'We are never faced with objects or social relations, we are faced with chains which are associations of humans and nonhumans. No-one has ever seen a social relationship by itself . . . nor a technical relation' (Latour 1991: 110).

These became cultural artefacts with their associated embedded discourses such as discourses on cure ('hearing aids mean you can hear so they are a cure for deafness'), discourses on support ('the computer to enable the disabled person to do the job'), discourses on access ('a *minicom* will solve the problem of access') and so on. If we consider Figure 3.2, for example, it can be demonstrated that not only do groups of people tend to draw upon particular patterns of communication networks which become institutionalized – Figure 3.2 shows only four of the most commonly used ones – but each pattern has different implications for a deaf or disabled person. Different networks have different inbuilt capacities for intentional or unintentional modification of information, and for information transmission rates which may or may not match the input-processing and output-generating capacities of individual actors in the network (Stohl 1995). For the deaf or disabled actor, the nature of the information received may also depend on where they are located in the network in relation to the initiator of the message and to various kinds of technology. Moving the technologies to different locations where they 'act' more effectively can substantially change the picture, with the asset or the risk that the whole network will change also to accommodate the actor's new role. This is the subject of another book, but I will explain further this particular example within the context of Chapter 6.

Summary

This chapter began with an explanation of the various terms, analytical tools and frameworks which have become associated with the twentieth century's 'turn to culture'. The construction of deafness and disability happens through the historical creation of shared systems of meaning or discourses, which may or may not become culturally embedded, and language and communication are seen as mediators of this process. It is suggested that current dialogues and theory marginalize the role of discourse: top-down views leave it as a side-effect so that it cannot be the focus of social change, and individualist, bottom-up views do not accommodate discourse at all. Any framework for looking at discourse needs to adopt an integrated approach to different levels of discourse analysis, together with a deeper understanding of the structural and functional dimensions of communication, since culture itself can be reified if it is separated from the discursive practices and social networks which reproduce and, more importantly, change it. However, a

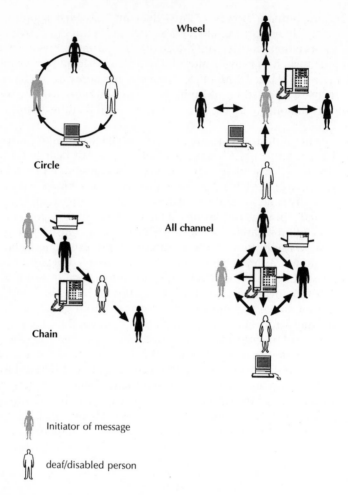

Figure 3.2 Patterns of information transfer

focus on discourse need not mean the exclusion of the material, since different aspects of the physical and economic environments are as much 'actors' in the networks which construct oppression as people are.

The marginalization of discourse has particular consequences for deaf people's inclusion in social model theory, along with that of other groups of disabled people for whom textual, discursive and social practice is inextricably linked to both impairment and disability. Through analysis of the connections between the sensory realm (which alongside language, occupies the middle ground and mediates between mind and body) and concepts such as narrative identity, it is argued that as long as discourse is marginalized, there can be no deconstruction of linguistic, social or attitudinal oppression, and therefore only limited social change.

Following up the notion that discourse has the capacity to unify deaf and disabled people as much as to fragment, the chapter goes on to explore issues of identity, meaning and representation within a poststructuralist framework. At the textual level, an evolution of meaning in deaf and disability discourses can be demonstrated; this produces conflict because different meanings coexist, each signifying a power relationship to the other. There is then competition for ownership of the dominant discourse. Those who hold power are those who are able to draw upon legitimated discourses. For this reason, it is important to look at the subtext of discourses – what is *not* present as well as what is present, and *how* legitimation is achieved. Power can be dismantled by opening up alternative discourses, but there is inequality of access to these and to the process of their construction. Thus the same discursive practices can result in the fragmentation of oppressed groups and the strengthening of the position of the oppressor in relation to all discourses. Different schematic frameworks are then introduced – cybernetic models of communication and actor-network theory – which enable us to deconstruct the process of oppression in a way which incorporates the role of the social, political, economic and material.

In a climate of cooperation, finding common ground between deaf and disabled people through a thorough examination of discourse is essential if we are to be effective in demanding speaking rights or 'warranting voice' (Gergen 1989); it will also help us understand the way in which power is owned and exercised, the nature of our participation, choice and agency in political and social processes, the distribution of resources and services, and the way in which policy is developed. It is to these issues that the second part of this book now turns in an attempt to relate some of the theoretical frameworks we have explored to life, as it is experienced by deaf people.

 **4**

Books without pictures

'What is the use of a book', thought Alice, 'without pictures or
conversations?'
(Lewis Carroll, *Alice's Adventures in Wonderland*, 1866)

'Thinking again?' the Duchess asked, with another dig of her
sharp little chin.
'I've a right to think,' said Alice sharply, for she was beginning to
feel a little worried.
'Just about as much right,' said the Duchess, 'as pigs have to fly.'
(Lewis Carroll, *Alice's Adventures in Wonderland*, 1866)

Introduction

Thus far, I have concentrated on developing a number of ways in which we
can bring deaf and disability discourses within the same theoretical frame of
reference. My main premise has been that this should be the social model of
disability reconceptualized within a postmodernist, poststructuralist framework which gives equal credence to both discursive practice and materialism. I have suggested two examples of networking theories – the first based
on theories of simultaneous and multiple oppressions and the second on
actor-network theory – which, in application, may allow us to achieve this.
The value of these working models can only be understood, however, if there
is a move away from essentialist ways of thinking to one which views the
individual *and* society as the unit of consideration and the arena in which discursive practice is culturally formulated and produced. This chapter is the
first of three which aim to explore those characteristics of a hostile and
unadaptive society which impinge especially upon deaf people's lives to
create their experiences of oppression. These *dimensions of oppression* are the
particular conceptualizations that Western society has of:

- social justice and equality
- needs and rights
- care and control
- access and support.

These are not the only dimensions to oppression but they are of critical significance. This chapter focuses on issues of needs, rights, equality and justice, with particular reference to educating deaf children. It argues, in particular, that the functional categories of hearing impairment are a hopelessly inadequate tool in predicting deaf people's potential as producers and consumers in the circuit of culture. Nor can they explain deaf people's experience of disability oppression, since they distract from the widespread evidence, too numerous to cite in this volume, that individuals' language development and learning is more closely correlated to the accessibility and the quality of their language environments. This, as has been illustrated, applies to all disabled people to some degree. By extension, if we are genuinely committed to removing language oppression from the lives of deaf people, we should recognize that assessing or measuring hearing impairment *by itself* will not achieve our goal. Without the parallel assessment of visual and spatial skills and the appropriateness of particular social and educational environments in which individual deaf children live, for example, such assessment is not an adequate predictor of development in the sense in which it was described in the previous chapter. Therefore it is not the 'right' to hear or even the 'right' to speak which should be enshrined in legislation in the form of welfare rights, but the 'right' to language in the form of liberty and human rights. There has to be a move from viewing language as a 'special need' of the privileged few to a location within a properly formulated discourse of human rights and social justice. This belief is based on the evidence of previous chapters and demonstrates that language oppression means to be without the shared meanings of culture, without identity and without social network support. It is to be a non-person for whom power, choice and participation are meaningless.

Perspectives on social justice

I want to begin with an analysis of social justice as it impinges on the lives of deaf people because, in its clear links to the moral and ethical framework of our society, it is very much a contemporary issue – not least in the demands that the National Curriculum should be set within 'a clear moral framework' – and the increasingly heated debates between religious and political leaders over the definition of morality and who has responsibility for deciding how morality should function in our society. Theories of social justice are well documented in the literature, so this is by no means a new subject, but the way in which social justice is conceptualized within special education, for example, needs to be made more explicit. The main differences between theories of social justice focus on what is conceived as 'fair' or morally and ethically justifiable, by whom and for which particular social groups. Specific concerns are:

- *distributive justice* – the ethical appropriateness of which recipients get which benefits and burdens;

- *retributive justice* – the ethical appropriateness of punishment for wrong-doing;
- *corrective justice* – the ethical appropriateness of compensating with some good because of a loss or appropriating some good because of a gain.

Most legislation in relation to 'special needs' and disability tends to include elements of all of these. For example, the Disability Discrimination Act 1995 is essentially about a balance between prohibition (retributive justice), justifiable discrimination (distributive justice) and reasonable adjustment (corrective justice) (Ruebain 1996). Similarly the Education Act 1981 is concerned with a balance between special provision (corrective justice), appeals procedures (a watered down version of retributive justice in England, though in Scotland, the powers given are much stronger) and special needs (distributive justice). However, technically, the operative word in both cases should be *tension*, as opposed to balance, because the principles of social justice are somewhat muddled in relation to deaf people. The three forms of justice simply end up contradicting each other in terms of what is fair and morally and ethically justifiable.

To understand why this is, I want to turn to the theory of John Rawls (1971) since, in some aspects, its principles appear to be closest to those of the social model of disability. Rawls's theory is derived from the observation that all characteristics are environmentally determined from a moral perspective according to prevailing societal norms and standards. Therefore the principle function of social justice in Rawls's view, expressed by Mithaug (1996: 31), is:

> to adjudicate balance between one person's freedom as power and another person's freedom as right . . . On the one hand, individuals experience capacity and opportunity to choose and enact choice in pursuit of personal needs and interests, and on the other hand, groups of actors experience protection from denial or infringement of their capacity and opportunity for experiencing comparable levels of self-determination . . . *Freedom as power* and *opportunity rights* entitling the expression of that power are locked in interdependent relations that demand boundaries that both separate and join Person and Other.

Uncontrolled freedom of a few people leads to the accumulated loss of freedom of many others; this more than anything contributes to inequality, because it allows morally arbitrary and culturally and historically inconsistent social processes to distribute prospects for self-determination unequally among a network of actors. This may be explained further with reference to Section 2(2) and 2(3) of the Education Act 1981 as amended by the Education Reform Act 1988 (my italics):

> (2)   Where a local education authority arrange special educational provision for a child for whom they maintain a statement under Section 7 of this Act it shall be the duty of the authority, *if the conditions mentioned in subsection (3) below are satisfied,* to secure that he is educated in an ordinary school.

(3)   The conditions are that account has been taken in accordance with Section 7, of the views of the child's parent and that educating the child in an ordinary school is compatible with –
(a)   his receiving the special educational provision that he requires;
(b)   the provision of efficient education for the children with whom he will be educated; and
(c)   the efficient use of resources.

In terms of Rawls's theory, the Act therefore makes *special* provision for individual deaf children 'to experience capacity and opportunity to choose and enact choice in pursuit of their *special* personal needs and interests', as determined by the views of the child's parents and the 'expert' judgement of professionals who assess these needs. It also *protects* children who do *not* have learning difficulties 'from denial or infringement of their capacity and opportunity for experiencing comparable levels of self-determination'. The question then becomes, 'Does special provision create the capacity and opportunity to choose or provide for deaf children to enact choice in pursuit of their personal needs and interests?' The answer to this has to be negative, on two counts. Firstly, the Act does not provide for the statutory participation of children in the assessment process or decision-making, and is extremely guarded in its view of contact between children with and without learning difficulties:

(7)   Where a child who has special educational needs is being educated in an ordinary school maintained by a local authority or in a grant maintained school it shall be the duty of those concerned with making special educational provision for that child to secure, *so far as it is both compatible with the objectives mentioned in paragraphs (a) to (c) of subsection (3) above and reasonably practicable*, that the child engages in the activities of the school together with children who do not have special educational needs.

Secondly, there is non-statutory guidance which suggests that 'wherever possible . . . the feelings and perceptions of the child concerned should be taken into account, and older children and young persons should be able to share in the discussions on their needs and any proposed provision' (Circular 22/89, para. 17). But if an 'older' deaf child does not have a language to engage in participation and discussion which is understood by those who claim 'responsibility' for ensuring that future-orientated decisions are carried through, will it then be construed that they are incompetent to participate in decision-making and therefore that they do not have an awareness of their own 'personal needs and interests'? Moreover, what about younger children, who seem to be labelled as incompetent *per se*. It must be remembered that the possession of welfare rights to, for example, education, health or a minimum standard of living, require only that the right-holder possess '*interests* which can be preserved, protected and promoted' (Archard 1993: 65). There are moves to increase children's involvement in the Education (Special Educational Needs) Bill currently passing through Parliament, which 'aims to give children a full and independent voice in appeal proceedings by taking appeals away from the SEN Tribunal and hearing them in the High Court instead'. But it is of note that the aim of such change is to restrict *tribunals*, which are said to be 'susceptible to organised campaigning by certain pressure groups' (*Disability Now*, March 1997: 4). Many of the tribunals I attended in my role of parent advocate for just such a 'pressure group' in the 1980s were nothing less than intimidating for the child's parents, let alone the child; without my presence, I did wonder how parents would fare. Formal legal situations, as much current research shows, are equally intimidating, if not more so, so it remains to be seen whether such changes will achieve the stated aims.

There have been a spate of 'alternative' policies about deaf education in recent years, none of which amounts to anything more than policy statements because they contradict the law as it stands. They nevertheless form the basis of an interesting comparison. We might expect, for example, that because the DEAF-WORLD is apparently so diametrically opposed to the hearing world, the policy statements emerging from Deaf organizations, such as the British Deaf Association's (BDA) *Education Policy* (1996), would contain some strong challenges to the 1981 Education Act (please see note at the end of this chapter). Indeed, it does in some predictable areas such as the retention of the special school option, the 'right to be treated as equal but different', and the right to belong to and participate in the cultural heritage of the Deaf community. The first of these principles needs to be highlighted at this point because we will remember that the Deaf community's belief in segregated education marks one important distinction between the community and the disability movement. Ladd (1996: 121) explains what he believes to be the community's view:

> At the centrepiece of it is our schools. All this has been achieved despite the disgusting work of oralists, our schools are where we are socialised into the culture. Integration threatens to destroy these centres of achievement, quite apart from the damage caused by thrusting lone deaf kids into mainstream schools with no access to what teachers are saying, no easy access to the rest of the school's activities, no deaf adults, the total lack of a peer group, etc. etc. The irony is that 80% of deaf kids are integrated, with no little thanks to disabled people; we are the ones sent into the Valley of Undeaf, not they.

This uses the outdated language of **integration**, though it seems that this belief extends to the practice of **inclusion** since, as we saw in Chapter 1, Deaf people 'do not wish mainstream society to restructure so [they] can be *part* of it' (Ladd and John 1991: 14). The disability movement, on the other hand, has traditionally viewed segregated education as a fundamental abuse of disabled people's human rights. I will come back to these issues in Chapter 7. However, in other ways, the BDA policy is not that much different from the Education Act 1981 in terms of its implications for justice and equality. For example (BDA 1996: 2, my italics), it states:

Deaf people have the right to a quality education throughout their lives, which accepts who they are linguistically, culturally and socially, which builds positive self-esteem and which *sets no limit to their learning* [though inside the document this latter statement is replaced with '*maximises their potential for learning*' which implies something very different, as we will see below] ... This document refers to all deaf children whatever the preferred language may be, signed or spoken, with a hearing loss which has a significant effect on their education, across the range of ability, home language, family circumstances etc.

Later in the document, however, in relation to provision and placement, there is the following:

The BDA asserts that bilingual education is the most appropriate form of education for the majority of deaf children and that this should be offered from the start. Some children will be monolingual in either BSL or English, and this is acceptable *if it is in the child's best interests in the view of the parents, the LEA and the Deaf Community.*

(BDA 1996: 7, emphasis added)

Robert Murphy (1987) uses concepts of **liminality** and impurity to portray the state of **ambiguous personhood**. This suggests that when utilitarian measures of distributive justice are employed, liminality and impurity are a mark of difference, and so needs have to be conceived of in terms of 'social integration' and 'purity' if one is to 'become' a person, whichever normative framework – Deaf or hearing – is adopted. I will come back to the question of personhood below. But for the moment, I am wary about defining 'inclusive education', for example, because at the roots of the inclusion principle is the idea that deaf children are accepted *as they are*. There are many ways of being deaf which do not necessarily reflect the labels which are commonly ascribed to this experience. As we have seen, different labels such as Deaf and hearing impaired have different connotations which often form the underpinnings of discrimination targeted at those who do not conform to these normative views.

Both the Education Act 1981 and the BDA Education Policy seem to be saying, however, that the advocacy of children's rights is antipathetic to adults' rights and diminishes adults''genuine' rights claims (Heartfield 1993: 13). In these circumstances, children's rights are simply demands for protection by adults, which leads naturally to questions of who decides who we are and what our potential is, and what does it mean when something is said to be 'in the child's best interests'?

Children's rights to resources and protection are promoted far more than their autonomy rights, although some conventions enshrine children's rights to freedom of expression, of thought, conscience and religion, and of association. Resources and protection tend to be justified in terms of children's best interests usually as defined by adults, in contrast to rights as chosen and claimed by right-holders. Young people are often more concerned about their right, as they see it, to stay out late with their friends, than about their best interests as perceived by their parents to be safe at home. Experts' advice about child care which used to be framed in terms of 'what is right for children' is being rewritten as 'your child's right to', for instance, music lessons. If the child does not want or need these, such advice plays fashionable rights language and distorts its meaning. Rights can be claimed in the wrong context. When adults define children's rights, *rights language can be more oppressive than other terminology if it suggests freedom and choice when these are actually missing.*

(Alderson 1993: 33, my italics)

In both the above BDA policy examples, there are clear question marks about deaf children's autonomy rights – the child does not appear to have a say in the matter, and this is based on the assumption that adults can competently assess what is in the child's best present and future interests. Children's claims to *liberty* rights – the freedom to self-determine and to participate in decision-making, for example – have always been fiercely contested by philosophers like John Stuart Mill (1969), who argue that 'such rights require the capacities for reason, rationality and autonomy and that therefore children are excluded from their possession – along with people who are mentally ill or brain damaged' (Franklin 1995: 12). However, there are numerous examples of adults being no more competent to make decisions than children are. Adults repeatedly behave in certain ways and do certain things which children have been taught are wrong or ill-advised (Dworkin 1977). Obvious examples might be smoking, drinking, verbal abuse and the oppression of those who are disadvantaged in some way – indeed, for role models, we need only to look to the chambers of government. Archard has looked at the question of 'future orientated consent' in terms of a 'caretaker argument' (1993: 51–7). The suggestion is that 'the caretaker chooses for the child in the person of the adult which the child is not yet but will eventually be' (p. 53), which essentially means that adult choices may be linked with 'self-justifying' rather than 'future-orientated' consent. Alderson (1993: 167) continues with a graphic description of how adult judgements are used to persuade disabled children to consent to 'treatment' (in this particular case, to surgery):

Impartial discussion is inevitably qualified by medical uncertainty, choice of words, pressures of the illness or disability being treated, and attempts to respect but also to protect anxious children. So persuasion overlaps broadly with reason at one end and force at the other. Yet at some point, persuasion moves from informed optimism to deliberate distortion. Adults who gave high ages of competence [at which children could consent to treatment] tended to dismiss coercion as necessary firmness – 'Kids only play up'; 'They're only frightened', – as if fear is irrational and therefore unimportant: 'They've got to learn to put up with it for their own good'; 'There isn't time to hang about until they're ready'. The most powerful way to justify coercion is to deny that children can reason, and to align reason with force; children's resistance is then seen as mindless 'self-destruction', to be overridden by rational adults.

Being 'impressionable' suggests, further, that children are not always able to distinguish between 'real' feelings and feelings which they are expected to feel, and this contributes to the tendency for cognitive activity and rational thought to take precedence over feeling and emotion. But recent research into the role of emotions in children's lives suggests that we may be under-estimating the importance that emotions have. Harris (1994) suggests that young children grasp that people's emotional reactions differ depending on the beliefs and desires that they have about a situation, and that by the age of 6, children grasp that the emotion displayed on the face may not correspond to the emotion that is really felt. Further, Parkinson (1995) describes emo-tions as residing in encounters between people, and expressed in gesture, movement, talk and silence, rather than as internalized, individual and intrapsychic entities. This moves issues of language and competence into an area which is accessible to deaf children.

When freedom as power determines who deserves what control over what resources, individuals with power deserve their power only by virtue of having it. Such people discourage those lacking capacity and opportunity from attempting to enhance their own resources to pursue their own ends by reinforcing the existing distribution of advantage and disadvantage in society. It is this paradigm which is at the heart of the whole special education industry. I remember vividly being told by an ex-colleague in deaf education that I mustn't start creating more educational opportunities for deaf people because if I did, it would 'open the floodgates'; I also recall the view of another, that deaf children only 'had a right to be educated to the average' (Corker 1989a: 9): these are examples of such reinforcement. But it goes much further than this. Everything is channelled into reinforcing the deaf-ness as impairment paradigm. Hearing *loss* is measured (according to both the government and the BDA), not visual and spatial acuity; psychological tests compare the deaf child against a hearing population – again the normative principle. On the surface, this reinforcement provides compelling evidence for the view expressed in Chapter 2 that the answers we get depend on the questions we ask. If we ask about hearing impairment we get answers about impaired hearing, and very few surprises. But all this continues in spite of the evidence provided by the largest single compilation of data describing deaf people's intelligence (Braden 1994), which notes the substantial similarities in range between deaf and hearing people. The relationship between deaf-ness and intelligence depresses verbal IQ and does not affect nonverbal IQ; moreover, deaf children with deaf parents have performance IQs that are above the mean for hearing people. In the light of such evidence, it is arguable whether the three objectives given in Section 3 of the 1981 Act ensure that balance is adjudicated 'between one person's freedom as power and another person's freedom as right'. The power held by adults in determining who each deaf child *is* and, therefore, who they *will be* and which path they will take to get there creates a situation where the 'treatment' matches the *label*, and as such education is not needs-related at all. This does not bode well for informed personal and social identity choices, nor the ability of 'special' education to facilitate their formation (Corker 1996b). If we really endorse the inclusion principle, application of the poststructuralist framework proposed in Chapter 3 suggests that this principle needs to be accompanied by the right *not* to be labelled. I will return to this particular issue in the following chapter.

Special needs and human rights

Within current legislation on 'special needs' and disability, there is a clear tendency towards treating deaf children unequally in *distributive* matters because of the impairment paradigm. Deafness is specified as a difference (it is 'special'); I would argue that this difference is used to distinguish deaf children *as persons who can justifiably be treated unequally*. To treat persons unequally with respect to the distribution of important benefits and burdens, *in the absence of a justification*, is a paradigm of injustice. Thus, what can be called injustice clearly depends on what we mean by benefits and burdens and, on defining these things, whether we feel that deafness (or disability) is actually a justifiable reason for unequal treatment. A large variety of criteria have been proposed for ethically just distributions, such as relation to contribution, effort, need, desert, or according to the history of how a certain distribution came about. The one that stands out in the context of the present argument is *needs*, which is itself linked with issues of welfare and benevolence. *Utilitarianism* – the universal theory of benevolence which refuses any necessary connection between feeling and right action – provides one of the most compelling explanations of distributive justice, but seems incapable of discharging the justificatory burden. This is partially because justice and benevolence have an uneasy relationship with each other:

- Benevolence is said to depend on the agent's feeling concern for others, while the demands of justice are recognized by reason. As such, benevolence is inadequate to meet the demands of morality because it is neither impartial, nor ultimately, open to rational assessment.
- Justice, because it is by definition concerned with what is strictly *due* to others, marks the boundaries we are morally *obliged* to uphold, while benevolence consists in morally desirable, but in the final analysis, *optional* actions. However, this reflects the largely unargued assertion that justice is of overriding moral importance.

My understanding of the term 'benefit' is that it is something which is helpful or advantageous in some way, whereas a burden is something which is an oppressive duty or obligation. This gives us a curious paradox because, on the one hand, we might say that the provision of benefits to deaf children is justifiable as long as this doesn't impose an oppressive burden on the provider or the majority. On the other, it seems to be the case that imposing an oppressive burden on deaf children is justifiable because it is in their best interests or to their benefit. This is a bit like asking another question which arises from the previous section:'Why do children without learning difficul-ties/disabilities need protection from the claims to "rights" of those who have learning difficulties/disabilities, and is this protection therefore morally and ethically justifiable?' The answer to this question depends on how we define 'difference', and, therefore, what it means to be a person.

When we talk about needs in deaf education, we mean 'special educational needs' – that is, the needs which deaf children have which are *different* from those of other children. In their association with impairment, it is con-tentious as to whether 'special' needs embrace *educational* objectives, because emphasizing difference in this way disregards the needs, and therefore the rights, that *all* children share as a consequence of being human; it ignores that education is an important, though largely implicit satisfier of those shared needs. Moreover, in view of the discussion above, it could perhaps also be said that such an emphasis could lead to shared needs *not* being satisfied. In terms of the impairment paradigm, deaf children are not seen as normal, and making them normal becomes more important than allowing them to be human and facilitating their learning by whatever means. This has significant implications for their personhood, as Ingstad and Reynolds-Whyte (1995: 4, 10) illustrate:

> impairment raises moral and metaphysical problems about personhood, responsibility and the meaning of differences . . . how do biological impairments relate to personhood and to culturally defined differences among persons? Are people with impairments impaired people? Are they valued differently than other members of society?

Personhood, in their view, refers to the evaluation of others, so where a person's worth is conceived in terms of individual abilities and achievements as it is within the culture of education – the *egocentric concept of personhood* (Geertz 1973; Schweder and Bourne 1982) – we would expect impairment to diminish personhood.

I think it can be argued quite convincingly that when we refer to human needs, the terms 'needs' and 'rights' become interchangeable because all people can legitimately claim a moral entitlement to certain things. There are some commentators who are wary of using any kind of needs-based para-digm, but this is perhaps because of the difference principle. It seems indis-putable that human beings objectively and universally have physical needs such as air, water, food, shelter and social needs, whatever cultural wants, desires or preferences they happen to have. Objective human needs can plau-sibly be defined more abstractly as the necessary conditions for flourishing or well-being through the exercise of essential human capacities: in brief, phys-ical and psychological health, and freedom or autonomy (Doyal and Gough 1991). Because a person cannot enjoy well-being in conditions of poverty or oppression, well-being is also a political notion, and so must be explicated in the interdependence of the moral and the political. I have no quibble with these lists of needs. Indeed, I have referred to them consistently in my earlier work (see for example Corker 1990, 1994a and 1996a). But I think there is one major omission from both these lists, and that, unsurprisingly, is language.

A critique of language education

Because language can be seen both as a prerequisite for health and autonomy and as the primary means through which these basic needs are satisfied, it attains the status of a basic need in itself. Doyal and Gough (1991: 182) acknowledge that 'the acquisition of language . . . is widely recognised as the most crucial cognitive skill enabling individuals to impose order and understanding on their world', and that 'the cognitive dimension of autonomy expands in relation to linguistic efficiency'. But I don't think that they fully embrace the implications of language defined as a special need and how this subsumes language as a right, nor do they quite meet the urgency of Hoffman's (1989: 124) point that

> Linguistic dispossession is a sufficient motivation for violence, for it is close to the dispossession of one's own self. Blind [*sic*] rage, helpless rage, is a rage that has no words – rage that overwhelms one in darkness. And if one is perpetually without words, if one exists in the entropy of inarticulateness, that condition itself is bound to be an enraging frustration . . . If all therapy is speaking therapy – a talking one – then perhaps all neurosis is a speech disease.

Most deaf children have hearing parents; they are consequently in an integrated deaf-hearing social environment from birth (Corker 1989c) which presents them with a largely inaccessible and alien language environment. No one disputes the latter point, but the former is often ignored. The solution for most 'caretakers', who in this instance are professional 'experts' since parents are initially seen as incompetent to make decisions, is to change the child so that he/she becomes more like the parents. This, in most cases, is exactly what most parents want, not always because of their experience of vulnerability in having a child who is different, but because parents very often prefer to mould children in their own image. In such circumstances, the child must eventually come to acknowledge, according to Archard (1993), the correctness of the decision made on their behalf, including decisions which are personally painful for them. With deaf children, this is achieved by reinforcing denial both of deafness and of deaf people. In the context of deaf education, it means that the form of language education that most deaf children receive and is legitimated by the majority culture, is through **auditory-oral approaches** which aim to teach speech through making the maximum use of the deaf child's residual hearing. Lynas (1994) says that professionals who subscribe to this approach do not claim that normalcy can be restored, and that their aim is to provide an 'adequate analogue of the message received by people with normal hearing' through the use of technology and particular approaches to teaching (p. 7). Whatever the validity of this counterclaim, it is something of a contradiction in terms to say on the one hand that one is aiming for 'an analogue of the message received by people with normal hearing' while believing that normalcy cannot be restored. If it cannot be restored then why is it necessary to try, and on what basis is normalcy decided anyway?

In view of this contradiction, it is when she uses the term 'oralist' to refer to anyone who subscribes to the auditory-oral approach, that I find my main point of departure from her argument. I do not think that oralism and the auditory-oral approach can be linked in this way, nor should they be. Oralism, for many deaf people, is the phonocentric philosophy and practice of education combined with what Montgomery (1996: 84) calls dactylo-phobia (which loosely translates as a fear or rejection of sign language). It aims to make pretend-hearing children out of deaf children on the premise that they will be more able to participate in mainstream life, and is religiously vehement in its insistence that the pursuit of the goal of speech is paramount in achieving this outcome. Little is said about whether speech achieved in this way is intelligible or not, and, as was highlighted in the previous chapter, even some specialist teachers of deaf children are unable to understand them. Moreover, the Deaf community is full of Deaf adults who discover that the speech they had drilled into them from birth is unintelligible to most hearing people when they start out in mainstream life after they leave school. In such circumstances, teaching speech does not achieve its stated aims and can be regarded as a form of oppression, particularly when children are sub-jected to it without their consent. It is not an approach to education. Oralists can be distinguished from people who use an auditory-oral approach by their constant reference to the supposed inadequacy of sign language and how its sustained use stunts the development of spoken language. As an example, I recall a situation – not an isolated situation, I must emphasize – when visiting a class within special provision for deaf children. The teacher was late for the class, so I began engaging with the children using a mixture of speech and sign (I had been told this school used **total communication**) and we became involved in an animated conversation. Then the class teacher arrived and the children immediately stopped signing – not quickly enough, however, as the teacher turned to me and said 'Don't use *that* stuff in here – *we* use **cued speech** in this classroom!' Educationally, both oralism and the auditory-oral approach *when used in isolation*, are indicators of the impairment paradigm.

Now, most professionals agree that skill and fluency in a primary language, which serves as a basis for acquisition in adolescence and beyond, has to be learnt before the age of about 15 years, and that this is biologically deter-mined by changes in the nerve cells in the brain – **neuronal plasticity** (Bochner and Albertini 1988). Auditory-oral approaches do not make a dis-tinction between the articulation of speech and the learning of a language which happens to have a spoken form. Language articulation might be described as a physical skill which is quite distinct from learning the cognitive and intellectual basis of language. We can quite legitimately say, then, that learning English language is a necessary prerequisite for acquiring spoken English, but learning speech, for many deaf children, is of no use at all for acquiring language. English language, as one of the five most widely used living world languages, has different forms of production; speech is only one of them – the most inaccessible or difficult for most deaf children. So what might be more comfortable and easier? People often ask me this question implicitly when they want to know how I learnt English *language*. My answer is unequivocal – from books. This is still my primary means of acquiring knowledge, and though I can **speech read** after a fashion, frankly I find the exercise boring and exhausting, because, as Gregory and Bishop (1989) demonstrated very well in the previous chapter, people change their communicative style and content when they talk to me in a way which insults my intelligence. Learning from the written word does have disadvantages, however. Firstly, we live in a phonocentric age – indeed, I think the millennium will see the rapid growth of a new wave of the performance-based societies described by Davis (1995) – and this is reflected in the way the school curriculum is structured and delivered increasingly through interactive groupwork. In spite of the advent of new technology, if young people have the choice between the written word and the spoken word/sign, most will choose the latter – boys more so than girls, according to informal interactions I have had with young people, and Deaf people more so than hearing, since sign does not have a written form beyond a code which is indecipherable to all but professionals, unless video is considered to be 'written'. Understanding the visual symbolism of the written word and how to teach it is therefore generally of very low priority in education, although there are ways in which computer technology can make the written word more visual. Secondly, there is the question of cultural transmission which is something that happens through social interaction, through being *in* a culture, and yet it is not something which can be readily articulated in the written word beyond surface descriptions of traditions, rules of behaviour and customs. So, for example, I have often felt that the main gap in my knowledge is how to behave with different hearing people in a hearing world; the fact that hearing people are unable to teach me this easily or to learn my way is a very large part of how I am disabled.

The problem of cultural transmission is also an issue for Deaf community perspectives on language learning, though it is a problem that is not always addressed as fully as it might be. The solution to the difficulties of deaf children with hearing parents, for the Deaf community, is to change the language environment, which appears to align them more closely with social model theory. This means teaching hearing parents sign language. However, sign language curricula are not designed with parents in mind. They do not teach parenting skills in sign language, nor do they educate parents in interactive skills which are appropriate for use with deaf children at different stages in their development. This, incidentally, does not mean the paternalistic child-talk that many deaf and disabled children are subjected to. Sign language cur-

ricula are primarily aimed at people who might become sign language interpreters working with Deaf adults. It should also be pointed out that the
teaching of sign language to deaf adults who have missed out on sign language in compulsory education is based on a model of teaching sign language
as a second or foreign language to *hearing* people. Deaf people who are not
already native users of sign language often find themselves learning sign language in a learning environment which reflects all the worst characteristics
of integrated education. Deaf people who are native users, on the other
hand, have the facility of working in Deaf-only groups which aim to for-
malize their skill with qualifications and enable them to teach sign language
professionally, which seems to be a great deal more concerned with the political aims of the Deaf community than the reality of language as a means of
access to a variety of social networks, information and to life.

Acquiring any new language is a cognitive-intellectual activity which
involves a particular process of learning. Skill in learning sign language will
largely depend on learning ability and continuous cultural immersion in the
Deaf community because, like most languages, BSL is constantly evolving
(*British Deaf News*, January 1997), probably at a much faster rate than other
more established languages because its use has been suppressed for so long.
Hearing parents must learn this language if they wish to support a deaf child
who shows an inclination towards signing, but this is a very different kind of
support to the practical or physical support required by some disabled children and which is based on practical skills already acquired to some degree,
though which perhaps need adapting. For example, most non-disabled
people are capable of lifting, subject to their own physical constraints such as
age and size. They know what lifting means and can learn how to lift something or someone in a particular way. I do not want to diminish practical
tasks, but I do want to emphasize the difference strongly.

Somewhere between these two approaches is bilingual education – what
Llwellyn-Jones (1991) describes, drawing on Fitouri (1983), as 'learning and
using two languages (of which one is the mother-tongue) irrespective of
level of achievement in the languages at any given point in time'. Whereas in
principle, bilingual education might seem to be the logical means of gaining
both a structured approach to language education which does not introduce
bias and which maximizes opportunity for *choosing* and using two languages,
in the present climate, bilingual education faces a number of obstacles, some
of which also apply to monolingual education through sign language. The
first is the prevalence of institutional racism in Britain which means that
non-Eurocentric or non-traditional minority languages are not for the most
part integrated into education. The five most widely used living world
languages, out of more than 4000, are English, Spanish, Russian, Chinese
and Hindi (Crystal 1987). Yet school language curricula are heavily biased
towards European languages such as French, German and Italian, and most
would not include Chinese and Hindi, rarely Russian, unless they are
targeted at students who are mother-tongue users of these languages. Secondly, British Sign Language (BSL) is not an officially recognized language in

government circles, but a 'special need', which mitigates against a structured approach to sign language education, even for children who are growing up in a Deaf family environment. Children do not *choose* to use sign language, they are assessed in order to make decisions about whether they *need* to use it, as we have seen. The battery of tests they undergo are not designed to test skills which are relevant to sign language acquisition and use, and so will almost certainly produce the outcome that there is no *linguistic* basis for children to be learning sign language. If the child has enough residual hearing, they will not, as a rule, be assessed as needing sign language because they will be seen as having the potential to communicate 'in the hearing way'. These two obstacles have, historically, had a large part to play in the suppression of sign languages.

If the goal of education is to enable communicative choice and freedom in social participation, it is shortsighted and arrogant to suppose that deaf children will want to communicate *only* with hearing people. Moreover, manipulating language in this way, particularly at the political level, creates an artificial division between Deaf and hearing impaired people and, it must be said, between the 'successes' and the 'failures' of the system. It is still the case that only the 'most profoundly' hearing impaired children – those who are most likely to 'fail' – *need* sign language. This does nothing for the legitimation of sign language as a language, and so the circle is complete. Further, because like most languages, learning BSL needs immersion in a signing environment, it is practically impossible to achieve this in a mainsteam environment without contradicting the terms of Section 3 of the Education Act 1981. So if deaf children are to receive effective sign language education, which can achieve the goals given above, this must happen in the environment of the special school. For most, it means separation from their family for long periods of time, which in turn, creates a division between family and school and has implications for both parental and child motivation. The family cannot be viewed as a microcosm of the individual–society unit which has at its roots the logic of both/and; this takes us further away from the possibility of looking at how family relationships can be strengthened and the family environment be made less risk-laden for the child. I have suggested elsewhere (Corker 1994c) that it may sometimes be more appropriate to consider the development of a category 'family at risk' which identifies and monitors the situation in families where hearing parents are struggling with including their deaf child in the family environment, for a variety of reasons: it is often such families which later produce deaf children who are 'at risk'.

The 'radical' Deaf community view is that the cultural growth encouraged in special schools is more important for the deaf child's future than preserving his/her birth family heritage and parental nurturance. However, this view seems to assume that all hearing parents are potential perpetrators of emotional and psychological abuse of deaf children, and ignores the power of 'expertise'. Quite apart from the fact that the majority of special schools for deaf children focus on auditory-oral approaches to language learning, segregated education through sign language also potentially separates deaf children from mixed, multicommunicative environments, outside of formal teaching, where there is the opportunity to see languages interacting and to learn about the translatability of languages. This does not seem to be very different from separate monolingual education in sign language. In the previous chapter, I expressed concern about the difficulty of translating between two languages which have completely different cognitive and sensory bases. It is this difficulty which makes bilingualism in English and BSL quite different from an educational perspective. The most compelling evidence for this comes from the headache it creates for the National Curriculum assessment process. The BDA's Education Policy, for example, says that 'end of key stage assessment . . . should be conducted through the pupil's preferred language' (with the hidden assumption that for most deaf children to whom the policy refers this will be BSL) and that 'BSL cannot be assessed by translating English assessment techniques into sign' (1996: 6). But it does not give the corollary: English, for example, cannot be assessed by translating BSL assessment techniques into English, when translation is dependent on people who – whether Deaf or hearing – are not fully bilingual. Hearing users of sign as a second or foreign language, rather than Deaf native users of sign language, are more likely to be fully bilingual because of the legacy of deaf education. English, in the wisdom of language planners implicitly acting in accordance with the goal of standardization of the dominant language, is a core subject in the National Curriculum. The problem is exacerbated in the adult Deaf population by the lack of contact between the two languages which is free from the normative undertones of phonocentric or Deafcentric philosophies. Nevertheless, perhaps a distinction does need to be made between those who are *being* educated and those who are *doing* the educating, because in terms of the latter competence in the two parts of the bilingual equation *is* important if *educational* goals are to be met.

Anti-oppressive environments and equal opportunities for learning

If hearing parents are to be persuaded into a language learning contract, a great deal of commitment is required by professionals who come into contact with them. At the moment, as a rule, that commitment is enshrined in phonocentric beliefs and values which collude with those of most hearing parents, or with the political goals of the Deaf community. Both of these are, to use Archard's terminology, often 'self-justifying' rather than an expression of deaf children's rights. Only legislation on language rights can make any long-term difference, as countries such as Sweden have found, because of the power enshrined in the binary in terms of what is perceived to be moral and ethical. Without it, changes will remain local and lack real coordination. However, there is one remaining issue which has taken a back seat in discussion and that is the *motivation* to learn. Learning a language is dependent on the age at which it is learnt, as we have seen, but also on the conditions for learning, a willingness to learn, previous experience of the language, previous learning achievements and probably the presence of any factors which manufacture social disadvantage. This is true for all learners.

The current legal situation is that the learning environment must, wherever possible, be a mainstream environment. There are no legal requirements about the mainstream location of the 'special' learning environment, nor about what constitutes an optimum climate within which children of all ages and abilities can flourish. It is, however, worth noting that the first GCSE 'league tables' for England and Wales published in *The Guardian* newspaper (22 November 1994), showed that a high percentage of schools which housed provision for deaf children, whether special provision or mainstream provision, performed below the national average in each of the grade categories (Figure 4.1). Now there are many professionals who will doubtless suggest – and indeed *have* suggested – that the diminished grades reflect the presence of 'special needs' pupils, an assertion which is extremely offensive. It might be more appropriate to suggest that deaf children are not being exposed to educational or social environments which stimulate and encourage a wide range of learning activities and high academic standards, so their opportunities and motivation to succeed are substantially lessened. This links to notions presented earlier in this chapter about the links between benevolence and optimal actions. As succinctly expressed by Mithaug (1996: 50),

> Equal opportunity theory bases its optimal prospects principle on a theory of the group that explains how social conditions evolve toward the advantage of some and the disadvantage of others and, as a consequence, justify constraints on personal freedom to ensure optimal prospects of self-determination for all . . . this addresses directly questions of social justice.

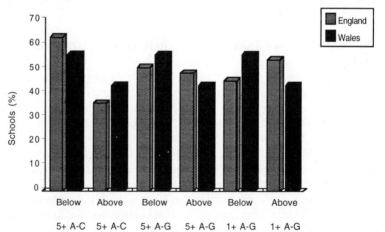

Figure 4.1 GCSE performance of schools which have mainstream provision for hearing impaired children (units) as compared with national average grades

The distinction between human needs and special needs creates unequal prospects which can then lead directly to different motivations to learn. There must be attention paid to the characteristics of the school community which promote the satisfaction of human needs if learning is to be non-restrictive. To explain this further, I want to elaborate on the systemic analogy introduced in Chapter 2. In France, there is a phrase *education perma-nence*. While the literal translation is 'lifelong education', a colloquial version exists which translates, I am told, as 'spreading the muck'. Now muck can be of two kinds. It can be the kind that we tread in at inconvenient times – perhaps the kind that hits the fan. Or it can be a source of general nourishment and fertilization which stimulates a liberal growth in the area where it is spread, and surprises us with different outcomes. Further, spreading the muck widely and indiscriminately provides the foundation for a potential ecosystem which creates more opportunities for surprise and has more opportunities to become self-supporting because it has had that good start in life. But if we confine the muck to flowerpots, we would possibly only ever get a single surprise, if we are lucky, because there are all sorts of other variables such as over- or, in this case, under-watering, the wrong quantity and type of fertilizer, and so on.

Returning to education, I do not want to imply in my reference to surprises that we leave everything to chance or to the times when adults happen to feel benevolent; nor do I wish to suggest that deaf children do *not* have learning difficulties. What the above analogy tells me is that it is possible to conceptualize a set of 'optimum prospects' and 'optimum conditions' for learning which are of relevance to all children, and which are based on a **sociocentric concept of personhood**. The starting point for building such an environment, an example of which is given in Figure 4.2, is one which is firmly grounded in children's rights, which as I have said, closely approximate objective concepts of human needs. It supports optimum conditions and opportunities for every child based on the principles of social justice and equality and allows all children to participate in its construction without becoming embroiled in self-defeating power struggles. As such it embraces Mithaug's concept of a theory of equal opportunity which 'implies two ends. One is to promote equal distributions of self-determination prospects among *all* members of society and the other is to optimise prospects for self-determination for *all* members of society' (Mithaug 1996: 38), along with the attractions of 'pluralism' and 'complex equality', as presented by Michael Walzer (1983) in his book *Spheres of Justice*. Children through their interactions with each other and with adults collectively create innumerable learning discourses and distribute them in accordance with many criteria, the appropriateness of which changes historically and varies with the local community concerned. Presumptions based on difference and outcome make it virtually impossible to distinguish those children who have *learning* difficulties directly related to impairment and which may require intervention, from those who have difficulties with learning as a direct consequence of being disabled by an education system that fails to provide a range of approaches to teaching and learning and other

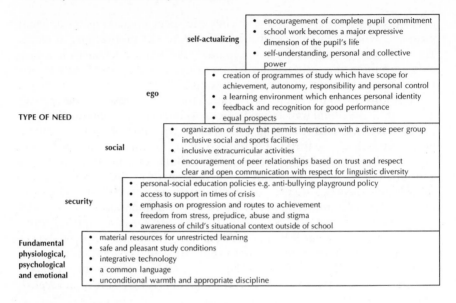

Figure 4.2 Need satisfaction: the school environment and peer relationships

opportunities through which natural competencies can be optimally developed. All efforts at change tend to be focused on individual children because of the equation which is made between learning difficulty and disability. This makes it difficult to achieve manifest change at the level of the system or to achieve what the Tomlinson Report *Inclusive Learning* (Further Education Funding Council 1996) describes as 'a common, unifying and inclusive language' at the level of policy.

Figure 4.2 contains aspects of all the frameworks proposed in the first part of this book, and though it is presented in steps, this is to emphasize developmental progression that aims to maximize access to the life choices coming from shared meaning through undirected and unbiased exploration of alternative discourses. Language remains the key to unlocking these discourses, and without experientially relevant language books will remain 'books without pictures'. Only education which builds in an entitlement to this kind of environment as its primary goal is education 'for all'. The difficulties with the current system will persist as long as children with learning difficulties and disabled children are grouped together within a bureaucratic nightmare of 'special' legislation and provision which is designed and implemented by administrators and policy-makers who do not understand the difference. They will also persist as long as language is used as a political tool to wedge deaf children between the two sides of a cruel paradox – How can I be Deaf *and* be 'like' my hearing parents whom I love? – which, for many, will be unresolvable because of the pressure to adopt one way *or* the other.

Summary

This chapter has explored the concepts of social justice and equality as they are conceptualized within the legal and service frameworks of special education. Using a comparative analysis of the Education Act 1981, which represents the dominant impairment paradigm and the British Deaf Association's Education Policy, which is proposed as an alternative based on minority group principles, it is suggested that both policies dictate the prospects for deaf children's self-determination in a way which reinforces existing distribution of the advantaged and disadvantaged in society. In the 1981 Act, the tension between distributive, retributive and corrective justice produces a bias towards utilitarian policy based on benevolence, which has always had an uneasy relationship to justice because benevolence is watered-down entitlement that is concerned with what is morally desirable – in this case, what is needed, and therefore with optional action. In such circumstances, deaf children are seen as being in an ambiguous state of personhood, described in terms of social liminality and impurity; it therefore becomes morally or ethically justifiable to restore them to the condition of social integration and purity. However, because deaf children are also regarded as incompetent to self-determine their needs and interests, the justificatory burden is discharged by adults who 'know' what is in the child's 'best interests', and who therefore have the power to determine the child's future identity. This means that deaf children only have the right to protection from adults, whether Deaf or hearing, and there is a danger within the current normative and politically charged framework that adults, who have power, will see their 'caretaker' role in self-justificatory terms. Children's liberty rights are confused with welfare rights, and this in itself provides the justification for their having different needs. Making deaf children 'normal', in whichever way, is more important than allowing them to be human – objective human needs/rights, as something that all people have, are not satisfied by the difference principle. There then follows a critique of the needs base of special education, of language teaching and learning, and of educational environments in relation to optimal prospects for learning, all of which continue to reinforce this principle. It is concluded that the special needs framework is hopelessly inadequate for predicting or determining ethically just distributions which work directly against social justice and equality for deaf children in education. Presumptions about the nature of difference and consequential outcomes make it difficult to separate impairment from disability; thus change cannot be effected at anything other than the local level because everything is reduced to the level of the individual.

Author's disclaimer

I am listed as a consultant in the development of education policy for the BDA. I accept that the document from which I have quoted is BDA policy.

However, I was *not* part of the group which produced the final policy as published. For professional and political reasons, I do not feel comfortable being associated with parts of this document.

 **5**

The power of well-being

> 'Who are *you*?' said the Caterpillar.
> This was not an encouraging opening for a conversation. Alice replied, rather shyly, 'I – I hardly know, sir, just at present – at least I know who I *was* when I got up this morning, but I think I must have changed several times since then.'
> 'What do you mean by that?' said the Caterpillar sternly. 'Explain yourself!'
> 'I can't explain *myself*, I'm afraid, sir,' said Alice, 'because I'm not myself, you see.'
> 'I don't see,' said the Caterpillar.
> (Lewis Carroll, *Alice's Adventures in Wonderland*, 1866)

Introduction

The previous chapter included some discussion on needs discourses, suggesting that in certain circumstances, it was possible to conceive of objectively defined human needs such as psychological and physical health, and autonomy, as embracing some form of entitlement which gives them the status of rights. The focus of the discussion was on autonomy, particularly in the context of special education and children's rights to self-determination, and the confusion between liberty rights and welfare rights. This chapter moves to explore notions of 'care' and well-being, in the context of different service cultures, as these notions are linked to different concepts of personhood, identity and the relationship between person and Other. This area is notoriously difficult within the framework of social model theory because it cannot be adequately addressed without reference to health, illness and, in particular, psychological oppression; once we attempt to close the mind–body gap, it can seem to threaten the materialist base of the model. Nevertheless, the interaction between the distribution of well-being and the use of disciplinary power – the power which, it must be remembered, is most effective when we don't know it is being exercised, and which manifests itself largely in the form of internalized oppression – is one of the most pernicious ways in which deaf people are subjected to the mind-games of social control. This is because what is at stake – well-being – is something so much a given that most of us take it for granted. When we don't have it, the consequences can be devastating. There are always going to be deaf and disabled people who are vulnerable, and those who cave in under the avalanche of institutionalized oppression. An expectation that they should help themselves can be commensurate with the kind of 'pull yourself together' attitude which creates the oppression. As Jenny Corbett (1989: 146) says,

> The basics of self-help, which are second nature to the able-bodied, might be an intolerable chore to some people with disabilities. Why should they bother with them? A narrow focus upon basic skills impedes the quality of life and inhibits self-expression.

As deaf and disabled people, we may personally find some forms of caring patronizing, even offensive – probably with good reason – but this does not remove the wider responsibility to effect changes in 'cultures of healing' so that the help which is on offer is not intrusive, is controlled by deaf and disabled people's organic experiences rather than the positional views of 'experts', and does not add to the momentum of the avalanche.

Well-being is intricately bound up with our ideas about what constitutes human happiness and the sort of life that it is good to lead – it is said to be both a condition for the good life and what the good life achieves. However, the meaning of the term 'the good life' is ambiguous, shifting between the morally good life – what is morally or ethically justifiable – and the sort of life most people aspire to, in which personal comfort and enjoyment play a large part. It seems that the ambiguity can at least be taken as an indication of how unclear we find the connection between being morally good and possessing wealth, health and happiness, and the other components of well-being. Some philosophers have nevertheless objected to the suggested dichotomy expressed by this ambiguity, feeling that well-being spans both moral-political and non-moral aspects of life. Though the description of well-being is inevitably complex, it should be possible to specify the primary conditions of well-being and the sociocultural and political processes which will facilitate its development in much the same way that we can specify the dimensions of institutionalized oppression and the sociocultural processes which create it. This is more easily said than done, however, because the question of the distribution of well-being lends itself more readily to utilitarian constructions of health, welfare and illness. Since it is difficult to justify inequalities of well-being even when it seems possible to justify inequalities of socio-economic goods, it is assumed that the question will be best answered by some principle of equality which gives priority to policies whose end is to make well-off those who are badly off in terms of well-being. Equally, one can be prevented from answering this question by engaging in the kind of radical relativism which insists that different people have different concepts of well-being anyway, and this in itself justifies unequal distribution. This becomes oppressive when both the concept of well-being and the response to those who are perceived as being badly off in terms of well-being are controlled by those who have well-being, and imposed on those who do not know what it means.

Deaf well-being

It was suggested in Chapter 1 that 'notions of Deaf identity, culture and community' have been constructed to enable us to clarify the 'different rights of
Deaf people'. However, defining these notions seems to be somewhat problematic:

> Who are these Deaf people? Padden addresses the question directly
> (1989: 8) with the following definitional conclusions: Deaf people can be
> born Deaf by virtue of having Deaf parents; they identify with other Deaf
> people; they behave like Deaf people. The problem with this, it seems to
> me, is that the three criteria are all founded upon some notion of the
> meaning of the word *Deaf*. We can't appreciate the explanation of what
> Deaf means until we know what Deaf means.
>
> (Turner 1994: 105–6)

Turner then goes on to relate this to Fairclough's (1993: 50) comment that
'the problem of, and indeed crisis of, authenticity in social identity [is] associated perhaps with the unprecedented scale of cultural engineering', and asks:
'How do you distinguish the "authentic" from the "engineered"?' (Turner
1994: 109). By extension, these notions will remain somewhat ethereal, and
therefore powerful, as long as a division can be manufactured between those
who *live* them and those who *explain* them, which is reminiscent of Foucault's
perception of knowledge as being 'power over others *and* the power to define
others'. Continuing with this question of cultural engineering, it can be construed that if the concepts of personhood and well-being were subjected to
the same engineering process – to paraphrase Turner (1994), we can't appre-
ciate what being a person or having well-being mean until we know what
personhood and well-being mean – we have moved into the arena of engineered social control. Particular identities can be manufactured which reinforce the existing power structure simply because they are seen to be
'desirable', if inexplicable, and because those who embrace these identities
are enticed by the promise of greater well-being in having them. This is especially easy to achieve when the engineers have the knowledge granted by
both the dominant discourse (which affirms the position taken), and alternative discourses (which remain hidden and inaccessible).

I want to take up as the basis for discussion of this point, the analysis which
began in Chapter 3 and which I will here develop further in relation to
oppressed identities: the different ways in which identity might be manufactured which embrace contrasting views of personhood. The impairment
paradigm means that we see the impairment and not the person, or, as
Murphy *et al.* (1988: 239) say, 'We are treated to the paradox of nobody
"seeing" the one person in the room of whom they are most acutely, and
uncomfortably aware.' This frequently produces a huge discrepancy between
the *actual self* – how the disabled person perceives themself – and the *ideal self*
– the self that is constructed by sociocultural norms. In making an equation
between a person's worth and their individual abilities and achievements,

the impairment paradigm is synonymous with diminished personhood (Ingstad and Reynolds-Whyte 1995). Such a view of personhood implies that we have only two intervention choices: we 'either "cure" the individual condition . . . or provide a system of care' (Bayliss and Thacker 1995: 156). To set the 'pure identity' up within a framework of 'care' as a model to which people might aspire may actually diminish their sense of well-being, firstly because they lose the capacity for multiple realizations, and secondly, because the equation between 'care' and misguided expectations risks manufacturing a pretend-person – a false consciousness – who is unlikely to feel human in a way which is valued and meaningful (Corker 1989c). Clegg (1989), drawing on the work of Laclau (1983), says that the category of false consciousness is tenable only if the person has a fixed, true identity which she or he is capable of realizing.

However, there is a somewhat different paradigm which rejects the idea of 'purity' as untenable. This is based on Kenneth Gergen's (1996: 132) view of 'the happy, healthy, human being' as someone who 'wears many masks', which poses a challenge to the traditional doctrine that well-being requires a coherent sense of identity. Gergen proposes instead that every person carries the potential of many selves – which might together be conceptualized in postmodernist terms as the *individuated self* – which are capable of being realized in different social settings and through self and Other:

> The second model emphasizes the impossibility of such fully constituted, separate and distinct identities. It denies the existence of authentic and originary identities based on a universally shared origin or experience. Identities are always relational and incomplete, in process. Any identity depends on its difference from, its negation of the former. As Hall (1991: 21) puts it 'Identity is a structured representation which only achieves its positive through the narrow eye of the negative. It has to go through the eye of the needle of the other before it can construct itself.' Identity is always a temporary and unstable effect of relations which define identities by marking differences.
>
> (Grossberg 1996: 89)

Grossberg develops this model further in the context of cultural studies and, in particular, the relationship between the marginalized other (which he calls the **subaltern**) and the dominant culture. He suggests that the model itself is subject to a number of different interpretations which have together theorized 'the problem of identity'. He describes these interpretations in terms of:

- *différance*, where the marginalized other is constitutive of and necessary for the dominant culture, for example we could say that without the oppressed *and* the oppressor there can be no oppression;
- *fragmentation*, which emphasizes the multiplicity of identities and of positions within any apparent identity, for example deaf and disabled people who are also from black and ethnic minorities;

- *hybridity and border existences*, which incorporate images of groups of people:
  - who define the *in-between space*, for example, bisexuals, mixed race people and deafened people,
  - who exist *on the border* between different worlds, but effectively do not belong anywhere, which is equivalent to Turner's (1967) concept of liminality, and might include hearing children of Deaf parents, for example (Preston 1994);
  - who lead a nomadic existence and are constantly engaged in 'the mobility, uncertainty and multiplicity' of *border-crossing*, which is closer to Murphy's (1987) concept of ambiguous personhood described in the previous chapter;
- *diaspora*, which consists of transnationality, movement and a political struggle to define a distinctive community, for example Deaf people (Clifford 1994).

When framed by essentialist notions of identity, whatever the origin of these notions, all of these 'images' are either pathologized or marginalized. For example, there is a tendency to look at the experience of black Deaf people in terms of 'which comes first – black *or* Deaf?' Within a service culture, particularly within one which aims to enhance well-being, where Deaf is given master/mistress status, black may be marginalized in such a way that a fragmented identity is actually maintained, which, in Gergen's terms, would work *against* the development of well-being. Hence, though the deconstruction of identity dynamics complicates ideas about purity and fixity, it clearly has implications for the way in which personhood and well-being are conceptualized, and also, as we will see in Chapter 7, for deaf and disabled people's political struggles within essentialist service cultures.

I now want to continue with an examination of the implications of reducing complex notions of language, power and identity to essences or 'pure' forms which then become inextricably linked to the state of well-being. Further, since recent research on identity suggests that the most mature identities are those which are the result of exploring alternatives within the social environment as part of the developmental process (see Corker 1996b), it is important to consider what happens to well-being when *available* alternatives are grounded in the logic of essentialism and prejudice.

The difference principle and cultures of care

Helping interventions which form the basis of service cultures might be described in terms of three broad approaches, which Lang (1995), with particular reference to education, has described in terms of their purpose, aims and type of response. These are:

- reactive or responsive
- proactive
- developmental.

The first is curative, remedial and 'top-down', the second is preventive and 'bottom-up' whereas the third is focused on the enhancement of social development and personal effectiveness. Lang notes that there is a tendency for a strong emphasis on the first category – that is, wait until the problem arises and then cure or remedy it. As adults, hearing people experiencing 'problems' generally find themselves in a bottom-up, growth-creating helping model where the first helping intervention is self-determined, and based on the person's perception, accurate or otherwise, of their 'problem' and the possible 'solution'. They have access to the huge literature on counselling, for example, which can help them to decide which approach, how to fund it, how to choose one from the enormous number of professionally trained counsellors – most of whom provide independent, confidential community-based services. The literature can also advise on the large numbers of courses linked to a more developmental approach, such as training in assertiveness and interpersonal skills, and on 'the talking cure' itself – the language of counselling. Though counselling is always a matter of trial and error, if the first attempt is unsuccessful, it is not difficult to find someone else. Psychiatric units, segregated hospitalization and so on are generally a last resort, unless clinical signs of mental illness are present. Hearing impaired people may have access to information, but frequently fall at the last barrier because the counsellor lacks deaf awareness, has a stereotyped view of deaf people one way *or* the other and is unable to communicate in a way which is easily understood. The only option is then to take the same route as Deaf people, who are caught up in a top-down reactive model which treads a fine line between the assessment of Other (hearing impairment) and the assessment of person (Deaf) – again, the difference principle. The system frequently pressurizes them, sometimes against their will, into the 'hard cure' as the first port of call for help – in this case 'specialist mental health services' or psychiatric units for Deaf people staffed by 'experts' who are, on the whole, medically trained. There will be some Deaf people who are mentally ill and require aggressive intervention, but, with the emphasis on Other, the way in which mental health services for Deaf people have been promoted as the universal panacea – appropriate for all 'problems' – must be questioned. The same is true, to a certain extent, in the mental health services available to hearing people, but hearing people, for the most part, are deemed 'competent' to choose the type of intervention they require. Robert Fancher (1995: 308–9) describes 'biological psychiatry's confusion of tongues' in his hard-hitting but fascinating book *Cultures of Healing*:

> We can specify just what mental health care is supposed to help us with and what it is supposed to help us toward. The basic concept of mental health care is that some distress results from failures in essential functions of being a person. Mental health care aims to restore (or compensate for) the deficit. We might want to say to the mental health professions, 'It is not your job generally to relieve distress. Some distress has causes other than mental illness, and you have not been given

license to address these. Your job is to identify essential human functions and their failures and to figure out how to correct them.' We can say 'We did not agree to your role in providing a general palliative for the sufferings of individuals. We agreed to your existence because you offered to fulfil a certain task.' We can demand that the mental health professions do both more and less than relieve distress. They could identify genuine mental disorders and treat those, and they should stop pretending that everything that offers relief from distress reflects some set of truths about mental illness and health.

In these circumstances, we might compare the relationship between deaf people and the 'helping' professions to that between the pharmaceutical industry and women, who are convinced of their need for hormone replacement therapy or tranquillizers in ways which play on women's emotions and perceptions of what is desirable in a woman – in the eyes of men. We know how often women have been led to believe that the expression of their emotions is either 'wrong', 'due to pre-menstrual tension' or 'hormones', and should therefore be 'controlled'. But hearing women have access to a range of information which can provide them with alternative ways of looking at themselves which does not play upon the idea of women as 'the weaker sex'. Because many deaf people have been taught to accept what they are told, particularly if the information is given to them by 'all-knowing' hearing professionals, and they do not have access to alternative discourses since this knowledge is held by the same professionals, they are easily manipulated into compliance by the promise of 'well-being'. This encourages complacency about a particular concept of 'mental health', and the acceptance of what is being offered without question or analysis (Corker 1995b). We have enough tension in our lives from the fact that lay perceptions accompanying the labels 'mentally ill' and 'mental health problems' can collude with a professional's view that a deaf person with 'problems', or even without them, is powerless to solve problems without 'help', and so these labels can become a very effective and disempowering deterrent for deaf people's choice and participation in service cultures.

This kind of service culture constructs deaf well-being differently to hearing well-being; it frequently suggests that we don't know what 'deaf wellness' is, distributing deaf well-being on the basis of the particular construction being promoted. Thus services which are aimed at improving deaf well-being should be 'different'. Kyle (1996: 79), for example, with reference to 'mental health' services, says that

A mental health team needs to be clear in its deaf–hearing relations, where it places its emphasis and how it seeks to understand the real deaf factors in this area. As such there has to be a commitment to a clear description of deaf wellness. Our tradition of seeking the norm requires a better understanding and involvement in the deaf community. Creating a view of what are well deaf people and the process by which they reached this point, is vital not only to the assessment of mental health but also to the rehabilitation and therapeutic process. Such a goal can be negotiated.

We might note the reference to 'assessment of mental health' and the 're-habilitation and therapeutic process', which signify that the impairment paradigm is being used. Kyle's allusion to 'the *real* deaf factors' and 'a *clear* description of deaf wellness' when combined with statements such as 'seeking *the norm*' and '*creating* a view' further suggests that the aim of re-habilitation is to restore deaf people to some unspecified and probably Deaf 'norm'. We therefore need to think about deaf well-being in different terms and to view the concept of well-being as something that *can* be described in clear, essentialist terms. As we have seen, the Deaf view which comes from 'a better understanding and involvement in the deaf community' (Kyle does not use the term 'Deaf', but his comments refer to the linguistic minority group) is likely to reflect the Deaf 'norm' which will be promoted as an alternative to the impairment paradigm. The process of constructing parti-cular states of well-being is often a product of service culture, but the corol-lary is also true that a particular state of being deaf can create a new service culture with a modified value system which, given certain circumstances, undermines the effectiveness and appropriateness of 'care'. There is some evidence, for example, that within specialist mental health services for Deaf people, the 'cure' for ambiguous personhood or Other, which is believed to be at the root of some deaf clients' 'problems', is to achieve a state of *Deaf* 'purity', and the service model can become concentrated on the idea that improved well-being will be reached by achieving this 'pure' state. Attempts to define well-being within a preconceived dichotomy will itself produce normative concepts along the lines of 'Deaf people experience well-being when, *and only when*, they are in the Deaf community and communicating through sign language' or 'hearing impaired people experience well-being when they learn how to cope with the problems of being hearing impaired and take advantage of all the opportunities which are open to them in main-stream life'. But these are not statements about well-being itself. Though they focus, in Kyle's terms, on 'the process' by which people 'reach the point of well-being', they do not actually describe the *state* of well-being. At best, such notions of 'purity' problematize the experience of oppression; at worst, they ignore it, because those who are unable to reach this state are pathologized. This relates back to Grossman's models of *différance* and hybridity discussed earlier in this chapter, since the groups characterized by these models most often become trapped within the Deaf–hearing dichotomy.

The tenuous links between a particular identity and well-being are also inherent in provision of other welfare-based services which aim to promote well-being, though they seem to be applied in a rather *ad hoc* fashion. It has long been the tradition within social services departments, for example, to categorize deaf people as deaf-with-speech or deaf-without-speech. The first category loosely corresponds to hearing impaired people and the latter to Deaf sign language users. These categories were developed in an attempt to overcome the problems created by unnecessary bureaucracy and to assist in the prioritizing of services. However, it is generally to the client's advantage if they are placed in the second category. On the basis of my experience of working with deaf people in London and the Home Counties, and conversations I have had with deaf people around Britain, it seems that Deaf sign language users are considerably more likely to get housing association flats, disability living and working allowance, special aids and equipment, personal visits and communication support for visiting their GP, a solicitor, Citizen's Advice Bureau and so on. I am not in the business of arguing the ethical principles behind this situation; however, categorizing people and distributing resources on the basis of these categories does, in my view, need to be examined more closely. There are many people in the second category who *choose* not to use speech, for a variety of reasons (which include political reasons) and in a variety of contexts; for many in the first category, speech achieves nothing because, at the end of the day, society believes that because they can speak, they can hear, and this is the basis of their oppression. We will return to this issue in the following chapter, but for the moment, I think I could confidently say that there is a huge gulf in terms of well-being between an isolated, unemployed deafened adult whose long-term relationship has disintegrated and a Deaf adult who has regular employment teaching sign language, has an active social life in the Deaf community and a stable relationship; I would have no difficulty in prioritizing service provision which aims to promote well-being if these facts were known to me. However, if the bias of the service we work within leans towards deaf people without speech and/or our professional values dictate what is in the best interests of people who are deaf-with-speech, we might be forced to decide priorities on the basis of these things rather than decide who genuinely had the most need for available services. In such circumstances, decisions might have nothing to do with the client's well-being, or even with the provision of 'care'.

Value-added helping?

In terms of the 'both/and' model presented in Chapter 2, it becomes particularly important to look to the relationship between the 'client' and different 'caring' or 'helping' service cultures for the process of construction. In this context, Ken Davis (1990: 6) warns us about the nature of this word 'client':

> Hearing some of these people explaining the terminology can be equally interesting. For example, they may say that 'client' is a nice easy word, which avoids the anonymity of 'person' or 'disabled person'. Or that you can't use 'person with a physical impairment' because the phrase is too long! Or that 'client' gives a disabled person some dignity, some status. That one is particularly pleasing, as it conveys the idea of equality wrapped up in more recent connotations which assign customer status to both patron and client. A very neat professional sleight of speech,

suggesting equivalence in choice and control, even though they know and we know that the reality is very different.

Terms such as 'care' and 'help', which I use here interchangeably, can also be usefully deconstructed along the lines discussed in Chapter 3; the terminology used tends to reflect the ethos of the service culture and the professional attitudes and values of those who staff it. So, for example, 'helping' professionals working in medical contexts tend to use terms such as patient, diagnosis, forensics, clinical depression and treatment (Denmark 1994), whereas **person-centred counsellors** might use terms such as empathy, genuineness, unconditional regard, safe environment, empowerment and personal growth (Corker 1994a). 'Helping' is itself a multifaceted activity which includes advice, guidance, the use of listening skills, the use of counselling skills and the practice of professional counselling, psychotherapy and psychiatry. Though the term 'counselling' is often used to describe all of these activities, and their functions may overlap, the British Association for Counselling (BAC) is of the view that they need to be distinguished from each other if the client is to be able to match themselves to the service culture. But there are also terms which have become very ambiguous in their meaning because of the way they are used in different service cultures. 'Empathy', for example, has become a very fashionable term, but for some, empathy is just another word for enculturalization, invasion, or the abuse of power, and nothing to do with trying to understand what the client feels from their perspective or understanding the client's structure of meaning *as it is* (Rowe 1995).

The term 'confidentiality' has a similar history. Deaf people contextualize confidentiality in a particular way because most have grown up in an environment where it has usually not been respected – indeed, it could be said that this is why 'openness' has come to be a cornerstone of Deaf community life, and there is a tendency for everyone to know everyone else's affairs whatever the costs. Counsellors understand confidentiality as a conscious activity through which they seek to preserve a safe environment in which clients can build a trusting relationship. Confidentiality is assured solely out of respect for clients and their well-being; in the counselling context it is *absolutely* guaranteed unless the client has given permission for disclosure. Thus there can be a conflict of meanings, and additional difficulties with professional practice when a counsellor is working with a Deaf client (Corker 1994a). Sign language interpreters, on the other hand, might view confidentiality as not disclosing information which has come to them in an interpreting assignment, but this seems to be more about avoiding compromising situations than about the well-being of the client. This can be associated with the more serious problem that if confidentiality is associated in Deaf people's minds with professionalism (because in the absence of access to alternative meanings of confidentiality, *one* meaning of the term is applied to all contexts), there can be an expectation, for example, that all 'professionals' when asked to keep something confidential, will automatically do so. Both sign language interpreters and counsellors have codes of professional practice which include confidentiality, but I think it would be fair to say that they embrace different principles, aims and levels of confidentiality since on the one hand (interpreting), the code is referred to as a code of *practice* and on the other (counselling), it is a code of *ethics*. Another example is the term 'client-centred', which is used either to describe practice which is focused on the client (or more usually, their Other) and which is therefore closer to client manipulation, or practice which is focused on client empowerment, client-led, resourced and orientated (Corker 1995b). There are numerous examples of how value systems come to be reflected in particular language. Consider the following:

> Recent work on the problems faced by sufferers from Alzheimer's disease has shown that part of their difficulty with other people is simply a matter of the timing of the speech ... If you ask people, even the medical specialists who are dealing with the Alzheimers patient, they will nearly always tell you that the sufferer has a mental defect, which is displayed in defective speech. Alzheimers patients are then spoken to as if they are simple minded or mere infants . . . Conversations between the Alzheimers patients and caretakers in places like day-care centres frequently fail because the interlocutor is irresistibly drawn to fill in the time gaps with what it seems the Alzheimers patient should have then said next, not waiting for the sufferer to say it for themselves. The result is often unsatisfactory for both speakers. If one's speech is patterned by the conversation time of ordinary intercourse, which is usually fairly close to clock time, one cannot converse easily with an Alzheimers patient.
>
> (Harré and Gillett 1994: 31)

This description could be usefully related back to the dialogue given in Box 3.3, but what is interesting is that the authors seem unaware that by using terms such as 'sufferer' and referring to Alzheimer's patients' 'difficulty with other people' is part of the creation of the very process which they then criticize.

I am well aware of the difficulties of advocating care in our use of language, but sometimes we confuse terminology with meaning. If the meaning or the practice remains oppressive, attempts to change the language in which it is couched will achieve nothing. The recognition of this is critical for our understanding of counselling and therapy in the context of the difference principle, particularly in the light of some deaf and disabled people and their allies' suspicions of these activities. For example, Zarb (1995: 4) says that

> Therapeutic research such as studies on rehabilitation, counselling, or medical treatments concerns itself with evaluating the best ways of helping disabled people to come to terms with their impairments – either physically or emotionally – or with trying to evaluate ways in which some of the effects of impairments can be partially alleviated.

This view clearly places one helping activity – counselling – at the rehabilitation end of a range of helping activities. At this end of the spectrum, intervention (which might include some forms of counselling) may involve attempts to rehabilitate deaf people to some arbitrary 'norm' (Alderson 1993; Oliver 1996), sometimes accompanied by 'solutions' to 'problems' which involve denial of their experience. For example, a deaf client who has been abused in childhood might be told that it is 'in their best interests' to forget it. At the other end, however, counselling practice can embrace a commitment to environmental and social change as the main route to equality, social justice, client self-empowerment and human rights. The same deaf client might be supported by the counsellor in making a report to the police about their abuse and in taking the perpetrators to court, thus liberating the client from past abuse and preventing the perpetrators from inflicting more damage. There are many combinations and permutations of these polarized perspectives, and I think we need to be very careful about summarily dismissing them under one heading in our attempts to negate the individual model of disability:

> Most psychotherapists [are now] acknowledging a more equal relationship between client and counsellor. The humanistic approach has also been influential in undermining the medical emphasis upon labelling, symptoms, and illness categories. Thus, the direction of ideas is both ways. What we are left with is a number of social enterprises which reflect both differences and similarities.
>
> (Woolfe *et al.* 1993: 10)

How 'help' is experienced by deaf people will be dependent on the form this social enterprise takes, or in Fairclough's (1992: 43–9) terms, on the content of the interaction, the relations between the participants and the roles which they are occupying. Helping, therapy and rehabilitation are all social processes and as such can facilitate different kinds of social construction (Gergen and Kaye 1992). The wider rules of everyday communication can be used to control the specific infringements by, for example, an uncooperative client who does not follow 'the rules' of helper/helped or deaf/hearing discourse. Thus even the lack of apparent conflict can be cause for suspicion:

> the perceptions of either the powerful or the powerless may be a distortion of the power which provides the basis for their interaction. Therefore, any apparent consensus within the profession, between professions or between professionals and the users of their services must be taken as the object of enquiry as much as the observed conflict . . . What professionals do and do not do, what they see as properly their concern and not their concern must be examined in relation to the structural positions of those professionals.
>
> (Hugman 1991: 33)

Going back to the description of the process of 'helping' which might be found in medical contexts, for example, there may well be the activity that counsellors would call counselling. But there will also be a large number of nurses, clinical psychologists, occupational therapists and social workers who are trained in counselling skills but whose *primary* training is in a health service occupation – that is, the orientation of their primary training is clinical or medical. Counselling, *in the context of the Health Service*, is allied with a health service philosophy which sometimes misconstrues the historical origins of the relationship between psychoanalysis and medical practice, for example:

> Such questions are linked to the three threads of lay, traditional and scientific medical treatments and to the dilemma of where counselling fits into the dominant paradigm of the medical model. It is also linked to the past and to the roots of counselling and psychotherapy. Although Freud was medically trained and construed himself as scientific, his education, typical of his time, also included philosophy and literature. It was not Freud's intention that psychoanalysis be welded to medical practice . . .
>
> (East 1995: 50)

As we have seen, however, forging relationships between counselling and medical practice may result in a particular emphasis on how a deaf person's 'problem' is discovered, how it is described, how it is dealt with and who deals with it:

> While 'medical context' suggests the different locations and institutions in which counselling is seen to take place, we prefer to define it in terms of all settings where the medical 'ethos' is seen to dominate – i.e. where there is a primary expectation of prescriptive solutions to physical problems (either by medicine or surgery), although there may be some recognition that psychological problems interact with the physical . . . The relationship of counselling to psychiatry, the adoption of doctors of the pastoral role previously practised by the churches, and the inclination of counsellors to adopt aspects of the well-defined medical process of referral, assessment, and formulation, all serve to narrow the gap between counselling and medical forms of helping. Thus, when counselling takes place within a medical setting, often in conjunction with medical personnel, one might imagine that counsellors would have difficulty in maintaining a distinct role.
>
> (Abel Smith *et al.* 1993: 122)

This 'ethos', together with the 'counsellor's difficulty in maintaining a distinct role' may lead in some cases to a situation where even the most experienced counsellor is forced to contradict some of the primary aims *of counselling*. A further example can be found within education where there are two dominant models of teaching and learning – the transmission model which is directive and sees students as recipients of education delivered by teachers, and the self-empowerment model which is collaborative and facilitative and sees students as participants in the processes of teaching and learning. Counselling clearly leans towards the self-empowerment model but it might find itself isolated in a school ethos which is based on the transmission model. The history of helping activities was founded in the medical model of psychiatry; as our understanding of helping processes has increased, in particular within the sociocultural context, so too has our awareness of the limitations of this model and the need to develop alternatives. At the same time, different approaches to helping assume dominance of different elements of well-being in what, for some people, can be a 'cause and effect' waterfall. For others, this can be a bad case of 'putting the cart before the horse'. We might recall Derrida's argument that Western ideology privileges the position of the mind over the body and reason over emotion, for example, and this influences the value base of the helping culture.

Van Deurzen-Smith (1988: 1) has suggested that all approaches to counselling find their origins and the way in which they are practised in 'a set of ideas and beliefs about life, about the world, and about people ... Clients can only benefit from an approach in so far as they feel able to go along with its basic assumptions.' When counselling deaf people, ideas and beliefs about deafness, the quality of life that a deaf person has and the value we place on it, and the relationship between deafness and personhood become operational. Of particular importance is whether professional values, ideas and beliefs reflect those of individual deaf people who are being 'helped'. Drawing upon a description of different schools of thought in counselling and therapy proposed by McLeod (1993), Figure 5.1 looks at the different perceptions of the deaf or disabled person which may be insidious in the value systems, attitudes and language of practitioners from each of these areas. It can be read in a number of ways, because the left of the figure could refer to professionals who may be in possession of 'specialist expertise' about deaf people and/or have limited understanding of how such knowledge can translate into counselling practice and outcomes of the helping process, or it could refer to the deaf person's perception of him- or herself. The right of the figure sets out the value systems inherent in four dominant approaches to counselling practised by professionals who may have a high level of professional training, experience and expertise in this approach, but lack knowledge and understanding of different ways of viewing deaf people and may actively resist the value bases of alternative approaches. If we cross-reference the two sides of the figure, we can see that some methodological approaches to counselling are consistent with a particular perception of the deaf person's difference. So for example, behaviourist and cognitive approaches are, in different ways, closer to the medical/legal perception of deafness. It might be construed from this that considerable power is vested in the counsellor to determine how the client can be rehabilitated to a 'normal' condition.

Psychoanalytic approaches are more ambiguous in that though there is an element which could collude with the image of deaf people as incompetent, much will depend on whether the deaf person's perception of him- or herself is at variance with how the counsellor thinks a deaf person ought to or can be. If the counsellor holds any unconscious or conscious assumptions that deaf people cannot be competent, they may focus the counselling relationship on adjustment to accepting an 'incompetent reality', which is assumed to be fixed. However, if they have some understanding that both deafness and

Perceptions of deafness/disability

Helper values

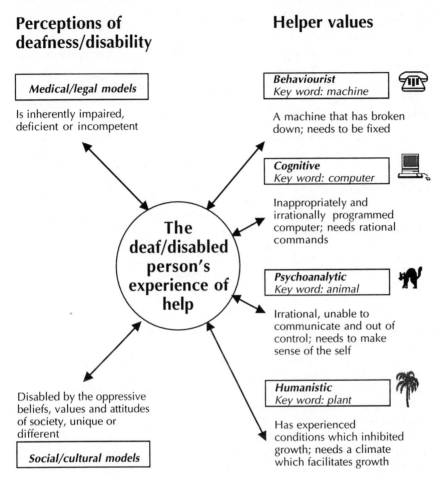

Figure 5.1 The deconstruction of helping

competence can be socially constructed, such negative assumptions are less likely to guide the way in which the counselling relationship develops. With humanistic approaches, on the other hand, an awareness of barriers which inhibit personal growth places them closer to sociocultural perceptions of deaf people, and a more equal relationship in which power is shared or given over completely to the client so that it is closer to being client-centred.

This cross-referencing assumes that belief and value systems are consistent, but of course they may not always be. Humanistic counsellors, for example, are not always immune to the insidiousness of the impairment paradigm. Indeed, it has been suggested that *all* individual counselling, precisely because of its focus on individual self-empowerment, falls under the remit of this paradigm. However, the relationship between self-empowerment and the collective empowerment embraced by the social model is ultimately circular, and the outcomes of counselling for some deaf people will mean both acceptance of and pride in being unique and different. The cross-referencing also assumes that the professional roles occupied by the practitioners are separate with clear boundaries. As implied above, however, this is rarely the case, particularly with those professionals to the left of the figure who are encouraged to carry out multiple tasks in a multi-role environment. The notion of 'special needs expertise' can easily cloud ways in which 'experts' help, as described by Dave Mearns and Brian Thorne (1988: 6):

> Experts are expected to dispense their expertise, to recommend what should be done, to offer authoritative guidance or even to issue orders. Clearly, there are some areas of human experience where such expertise is essential and appropriate. Unfortunately, all too many of those who seek the help of counsellors have spent much of their lives surrounded by people who, with devastating inappropriateness, have appointed themselves experts in the conduct of other people's lives. As a result, such clients are in despair at their inability to fulfil the expectations of others, whether parents, teachers, colleagues or so-called friends, and have no sense of self-respect or personal worth.

The power of well-being

It was suggested at the start of this chapter that the interaction between the distribution of well-being and the use of disciplinary power, along with what Hugman (1991: 33) drawing on Lukes (1974) describes as 'the manipulation of bias ... the form of power relating to latent conflict of interests', is one of the most pernicious ways in which deaf people are subjected to the mind-games of social control because it works through the placing of conditions on the state of well-being. In Chapter 3, we noted that the dominant culture creates inequalities which mean that not everyone in society is able to 'warrant voice' or be engaged in decision-making about their lives. Discourse, in such circumstances, is aimed at preserving existing inequalities and dominant values. Habermas (1977) believed that power is produced within social relationships and exercised through

> the manipulation and/or distortion of communication, in which different groups have a different say in the construction of what passes for consensus and in which communication is directed . . . not towards reaching agreement [but] towards the achievement of ends of those whose interests it expresses, becoming the dominant way of thinking about issues.
>
> (Hugman 1991: 35)

Rojek *et al.* (1988), using discourse analysis, demonstrate that help is provided by the caring professions through knowledge and language, but that they also define the objectives of caring in the form of a general concept of the client/patient; in this way 'their theories and practices together create an idealised concept of the service user which stands between actual professionals and actual service users' (Hugman 1991: 36). Deconstructing the relationships between helper and helped is one way in which power structures can be both exposed and demolished. But this is not always a way which can be meaningfully employed by deaf people, because disciplinary power manufactures and reinforces low self-worth and dependency to such an extent that they may lack the capacity to act (Lukes 1974; Corker 1993a). A life without 'care' becomes inconceivable because problems, their solutions, and therefore the person's sense of well-being, are externalized and always in the hands of 'caring' professionals or 'society'. This is what Rotter (1966) refers to as an externalized locus of control rephrased in terms of postmodernist notions of power, and it is further reinforced by the lack of trust in immediate social networks, itself a product of past experiences of 'care'. For some deaf people, the conceptual barrier and/or the language barrier may mean that they are unable to comprehend the implications of this situation sufficiently to decide whether to participate in it or not. This places an enormous burden of responsibility on those who try to reconstruct notions of 'care' in terms of empowerment, because for many deaf people who come to the realization that the truths they have been persuaded to believe are not *their* truths, the realization comes too late for change. In this scenario, the 'carers' will always have the last word on what constitutes consensus, and this generates new meaning for reward, coercion, legitimacy, reference, expertise and social redress.

Summary

This chapter has highlighted vulnerable deaf people who, it is argued, are particularly susceptible to social control through oppressive 'care' which engineers different perceptions of well-being, deaf identity and personhood. The impairment paradigm is synonymous with ambiguous or diminished personhood and moulds the helping process into a quest for a 'pure' identity through a top-down 'hard cure' that places emphasis on the destruction of the Other. The postmodernist perception of identity as an individuated self which 'bears many masks', on the other hand, underpins bottom-up helping processes which are empowering, participatory, growth producing and person-centred. These 'cultures of healing' can be presented as a universal panacea which deters deaf people's choice and participation in the helping process because deaf well-being or hearing-well-being become the goals of the process. The corollary of this, however, is that a particular state of deafness can create a new service culture with a modified value system which may undermine the effectiveness of 'care'. By deconstructing the process of helping it is possible to see that prevailing languages can be both a useful pointer to differences in ethos and value, and ambiguous creators of confusion of meaning across activities which have very different philosophical bases. These issues are explored in the context of counselling as an example of a helping activity which itself has many masks in relation to work with deaf people. How help is experienced by deaf people depends on the content of the interaction with helpers, the relationships between participants in the helping process and the roles they occupy. To analyse this further we explored the practice of counselling in medical contexts and the different value bases of counselling which embrace different perceptions of the person. Finally, the role of discourse analysis in the deconstruction of power structures between helper and helped was examined, leading to the conclusion that the experience of care and therefore the possibility of social change depends on the access that we, as deaf people, have to the processes of consensus, choice and participation in the creation of our well-being.

 **6**

Running twice as fast

> 'Now *here* you see, it takes all the running *you* can do to keep in
> the same place. If you want to get somewhere else, you must run at
> least twice as fast as that!'
>
> (Lewis Carroll, *Through the Looking Glass*, 1872)

Introduction

There is no doubt that one important dimension of adult well-being is moti-
vating and satisfying work, and, in this respect, deaf and disabled people are
no different from the rest of the population.Yet evidence suggests that within
the deaf population of Britain there is a high incidence of unemployment,
underemployment and 'non-employment'. The latter is a measure of economic activity and indicates the number of people who withdraw from the
labour market and onto benefits, for example, often because they are unable
to get jobs. Statistics are notoriously varied, unreliable and incomparable
because they use different classification systems, most of which are based on
diseases, illness and clinical conditions, or the impairment paradigm. But, as
an example, Honey *et al.* (1993), using the Labour Force Survey, found that
there were 130,504 people with 'difficulty in hearing', which represents 0.4
per cent of the working age population and 2.8 per cent of the disabled population, 17.1 per cent of whom had their economic activity limited through
unemployment, and 42.7 per cent by non-employment. Many employing
organizations are more likely to balk at the employment of deaf people than
at the employment of someone who has epilepsy, mental illness, or is a
wheelchair user, for example. This research also found that, of 'employers
who experienced difficulty with disabled people in employment', the second
largest number (12.3 per cent) cited problems in relation to 'hearing difficulty', and that these problems were primarily in the areas of communication
(87.5 per cent), job ability (27.6 per cent) and the effect on other staff (16.7
per cent). Predictably though, the authors also estimated using Social and
Community Planning Research data, that 20 per cent of the deaf population
were economically active, but we have no measure of whether these people
are in jobs which are commensurate with their qualifications, skills, experience and abilities. However, research on the experiences of deaf people in

employment or looking for employment suggests that they are more likely to find employment in low-level, manual work (Montgomery and Laidlaw 1993; Montgomery 1996), and to be prevented from taking up education and training opportunities which might improve job and promotion prospects (see for example Taylor and Bishop 1991; Corker 1994b).

This scenario is only part of the overall picture, however, a picture which must be contextualized further by changes in the world of work and in legislation, specifically the Disability Discrimination Act 1995 (DDA). For most employers in the private and public sectors, the primary recruitment pool is the 18 to 24 age bracket. As we approach the millennium, the size of this pool is reducing demographically and in terms of the number of people who have the necessary skills and qualifications for recruitment. An employer still has to recruit, however, if they are to avoid overloading existing employees and provide for the continuing flux of innovation and ideas which keeps the organization healthy. We are therefore fast reaching a point where demographic shifts mean that diversification of the workforce must be achieved by drawing from non-traditional recruitment pools. This in turn means changes in working patterns and work environments already under pressure from rapid technological change and industrial restructuring which have altered the characteristics of staff who are needed (Bones 1994). Emerging work environments are likely to be information-based and operating in a global economy, and there are already signs of changes in work patterns to meet this challenge. For example, there is a growth in ***intrapreneurialism***, or 'corporate venturing' whereby 'venture capital is provided by the company to a set of its employees for them to set up a business on their own' (Wilson and Rosenfeld 1990: 451); there are also attempts to re-create 'community' within organizational theory and practice (Gergen 1992). Atterhed (1985) has suggested that for intrapreneurialism to succeed in the long term will require a major change in the value base of organizational culture along the lines suggested in Box 6.1. There is also a rise in the visibility of a new category of worker – the ***knowledge worker*** (Drucker 1977; Sisson 1989) – who has specific knowledges, and the ability to apply these knowledges to particular situations, and who prefers more open operating environments, resents traditional styles of control and restrictive working practice and aspires to the growth and personal satisfaction which can be derived from challenging tasks.

These changes, on the surface, seem to suggest work environments and work patterns which are less restrictive as a whole and which aim to respond to the postmodernist realities of pluralism and individuation. But, set against this, from the perspectives of deaf people, assumptions around hearingness, mobility, time structures, knowledge and communicative ability, for example, are 'fundamental to the reproduction of power in most organizations' (Hearn and Parkin 1993: 154), as are the way in which they produce and collude with discourses about access and support which are now enshrined in legislation.

Box 6.1 Changing organizational cultures

Corporate cultural values	Intrapreneurial culture values
control	trust
meddling	protection
boss	mentor
instructions	visions
planning	flexibility
orders	viewpoints
alienation	participation
fragmentation	wholeness
rules	customers

The Disability Discrimination Act – legislating for change?

I have already made it clear that I regard the Disability Discrimination Act 1995, in its muddled combination of prohibition, justifiable discrimination and reasonable adjustment, to be one of the most ill-conceived pieces of legislation which has ever reached the statute books in relation to deaf and disabled people. As such, I am not sure that it will facilitate disabled people's involvement in what could be exciting times of change. This is not the place to explain the details of this legislation – for this, the reader is referred to the growing number of texts on the subject, for example Doyle (1996) and Gooding (1996). But I do want to spend some time looking at some of the more glaring anomalies and issues it raises for deaf people. I also want to be clear that my involvement in researching this area was born out of my own experience of victimization in the workplace which has been recorded elsewhere (Corker 1993b). At the time, I was unable to publish this account under my own name because of possible repercussions for those who were close to me and continued to work in that employing organization. However, times have changed and that organization has changed, and I now feel more able to be open. What has not changed, however, are the feelings of anger and injustice, the panic attacks, the occasional nightmares about persecution and the frustration that I was not able to stop the same thing happening to others subsequently because my mental health was so badly affected. What has not changed, also, is that I have a gap in my employment record which is not easy to explain in an unemotive way, and which remains the cause of questions used covertly as an excuse for justifying why I might be difficult to employ. The 'powers that be' have been remarkably successful in defining the course my life should take, and yet to them, I am just a statistic who, like many others, I suspect, will not appear on any of the lists mentioned above. Having absorbed the available information on the DDA to date, I am not confident that the Act would have helped me if it had been on the statute books seven years ago. So the issue of compensation, which civil rights legislation for all deaf and disabled people would be more than enough to satisfy, is still outstanding.

Doyle (1996: vii) acknowledges that the DDA is not the legislation that many disabled people and their advocates want to see, and that

> The key to the Act's success will be how the protected class of disabled person is defined and refined by regulations and by judicial interpretation. The lack of strategic reinforcement agency or disability rights commission is also probably a telling criterion of the Act's progress and achievements.

The DDA defines deafness in terms of a barely disguised impairment paradigm which, though it 'establishes a new definition of "disabled person" does not reflect any fundamentally new understanding of disability' (Gooding 1996: 9). This is yet another example of the impotence of a cosmetic change in terminology when old meanings remain in force. I have already outlined my reservations about the Act's reduction of deaf and disabled people's experience into the dualist categories of 'physical and mental impairment', but if we look further at the way in which these categories have been broken down in relation to deaf people, a number of further difficulties arise. The *Draft Guidance on Matters to be Taken into Account in the Definition of Disability*, published in April 1996, for example, refers to the 'ability to understand some-one *speaking normally* in his or her native language', while taking into account 'any effects on speech patterns or which impede the acquisition or processing of one's native language'. The emphasis on *speaking* normally means, ostensibly, that if a Deaf person describes themselves as a member of a linguistic minority group and competes for a job with a hearing impaired person who can match the definition as stated, and the Deaf person is given the job, the hearing impaired person may have redress under the DDA. The same may also apply to jobs which are advertised for Deaf people only (Douglas Silas, David Levene and Co. Solicitors, London, personal communication). Still under the heading 'Speech, hearing and eyesight', but in connection to the definition of 'substantial adverse effect on normal day-to-day activities', the draft Guidance says that it *would* be reasonable to regard as a substantial effect 'the inability to give clear instructions orally to colleagues or providers of a service' or 'the inability to ask specific questions to clarify instructions', but it would not be reasonable to regard as a substantial effect the 'inability to converse in a language which is not the speaker's native language'. So, since 'native language' is not defined, if a Deaf person insisted that sign language was their native language and was unable, or unwilling to converse in English, does this mean that it would not be reasonable to regard this as a substantial effect? The Act, in its emphasis on categorization and its denial of diversity within the disabled community has the potential to perpetuate further fragmentation and alienation.

In other ways, of course, the DDA does recognize diversity, as interpreters are included in Section 6(3) as examples of a means by which reasonable adjustment can be achieved, and in Section 21(4) as an example of 'an auxiliary aid or service'. Moreover interpreters and the agencies who supply them also come under the Act's definition of 'services' in Section 19(3) of the Act as 'access to and means of communication' and 'access to and use of information services', something I will return to below. In the area of goods and services, and in relation to the issues raised in the previous chapter, health authorities are in law able to contract out services. So if a deaf person was referred against their will by a GP working for one health authority to a service provider within another health authority when a similar service existed within the first health authority, and that deaf person felt that they had been treated unfairly by the providers of the service in the second health authority, who becomes liable if it can be proved that a hearing person would not have been treated in the same way? Because so much depends on the 'burden of proof', what would happen if 'professional experts' were then asked to justify the decision to designate the client as having 'mental health problems' sufficient to warrant this referral? Would the deaf person be able to prove otherwise, and would the time taken for legal proceedings add to the deaf person's 'mental health problems' such that they became 'mentally ill', and therefore justified the original decision?

Comparing the DDA with other anti-discrimination legislation reveals further substantial flaws, which demonstrate that disability is being treated differently and unfairly when compared to sex and race, for example. Unlike the Sex Discrimination Acts 1975 and 1986 (SDA), which does not require the complainant to prove their sex or gender, or the Race Relations Act 1976 (RRA), which has a very broad definition of 'race' which is not the subject of special guidance for clarification purposes, the deaf person *does* have to prove that they are deaf especially if they wear hearing aids, the way they describe their deafness *does* have to match the legal definition, and they *do* have to demonstrate that their deafness has 'a substantial adverse effect on day-to-day activities'. Moreover, the SDA and the RRA cross-reference each other so that it is technically possible to make a claim under both Acts if one is a black woman for example. The DDA is not cross-referenced to the SDA and the RRA, and there are some areas of institutional oppression which have yet to be covered by legislation – sexuality and age being notable examples. Quite apart from the fact that this upholds the dominant culture's view of disabled people as asexual and genderless and of impairment as occupying 'master/mistress' status (Shakespeare 1996; Shakespeare *et al.* 1996), what happens if one is a black, deaf woman, or more importantly, a deaf gay man or lesbian? In the latter case, would they have to prove that it was *not* their sexuality which was the reason for their being treated unfairly before they could bring a case on the grounds of *disability* discrimination under the DDA?

Further, there are a number of exceptions from the definition of disability such as hay fever, which *may* be taken into account where it aggravates the effect of another impairment such as hearing impairment (though again this has to be proved), but may not be taken into account if there is an observable and potentially debilitating effect resulting from hay fever alone. Another exclusion is 'addiction to or dependency on nicotine, tobacco, any drug or other substance (other than those medically subscribed)'. But what happens if the addiction originally arose as a result of accumulated stress from past legal disability oppression, or is linked to 'justifiable' discrimination in current employment? These examples all result directly from the need for legislators to work with clear and definable categories.

The case for Genuine Occupational Qualification

A further major weakness in the DDA, in my view, is the absence of reference to deafness and disability as a Genuine Occupational Qualification (GOQ) (see Corker 1995a for further analysis). Again this emphasizes the difference between the DDA and the SDA and RRA, both of which contain relevant clauses. This means that a job cannot be reserved specially for or allocated to a deaf person, even if it can be demonstrated that deafness means that that person could do the job better than a hearing person because of their deaf experience. As a case in point, we might refer back to the dialogue in Box 3.3, where the hearing teacher of the deaf was unable to understand the deaf child. Quite apart from existing regulations which restrict the training and employment of deaf and disabled people as teachers, it is still legal under the DDA to appoint such a teacher, or for that matter, any teacher who is difficult to speech-read or cannot use sign language, for example, in preference to a deaf person who is a skilled and flexible communicator but does not have the required teaching qualification because of past discrimination. Likewise, even some deaf organizations are now insisting that posts at managerial level require an MBA qualification and several years of experience in a managerial role, when large numbers of highly experienced deaf people have been prevented from training for MBA and from starting on the path to gaining sufficient managerial experience.

The first rung on the ladder can be remarkably elusive, and is sometimes made more elusive by an assumed division between the concept of 'the professional' and that of the 'deaf person':

> Deaf people have fewer qualifications – and as a result gain less extensive work experiences. Deaf people entering any work setting are seldom as well prepared as hearing people. From this point of view deaf people brought in to work with professionals in any team may not bring with them the personal resources to function effectively on their own. This is often the crux of the matter. Work situations for deaf people, however enlightened, frequently, for economic reasons, offer an uncertain contract for a single person. Deaf people work as individuals within professional teams.

> (Kyle 1996: 75–6)

I will come back to this below in relation to 'role models'. However, perhaps this situation arises because of the difficulty that hearing people have in seeing the benefits and value of specific subjective knowledges when they are focused on their own, supposedly 'objective' expertise. We could consider the definition of 'reasonable adjustment' further in this context. Most deaf people have many years of experience of being deaf and of using various kinds of specialist equipment and technology, yet the dominant culture still tends to believe that it knows the deaf person's needs better. The Minister confirmed that examples of reasonable adjustments which might be made in the case of a deaf person would include the provision of 'a sign language interpreter' or 'minicom facilities' (Doyle 1996: 67). In Chapter 3, I pointed out that aids and equipment have their own associated discourses of access and support and so they can be regarded as actors in the social and information networks of organizations in their own right. We could describe this in terms of *sociotechnology* or a human–machine system of mutually interdependent parts where aspects of both parts will affect performance. The Act, as I have noted, emphasizes *the provision* of aids and equipment as reasonable adjustments of the work environment in anticipation of potential access problems. There is a danger, first, that provision is just that – it does not overcome the access problem at all nor does it actually assist the person in doing their job without other changes in working patterns. But this does not stop people from assuming that a particular provision is the universal solution for all people with a specific impairment; in some ways, the Act perpetuates this. Going back to the example I introduced in Chapter 3 in relation to time, Sally French (1992: 97) continues:

> as a visually impaired person with greatly reduced working speeds, I was reluctant to burden myself with the additional paperwork which the task of 'chair' would entail. There was a short and baffled silence, until two of the committee members asked, almost simultaneously, what could be done to 'support' or 'enable' me to achieve this task? I told them, with a growing sense of guilt, that although I had access to all the support I knew to be available – tape reading services, special computers, large print, personal readers – it did not solve the problem, indeed that many of these services were considerably slower and less efficient than my own protracted working speeds.

But the fact that the employer *has* provided the means of reasonable adjustment may make them complacent if they believe that the act of provision will remove the disability. For example, let us suppose that a deaf person and a hearing person are employed to do the same job which involves contact with members of the public by telephone. The employer provides a minicom and a fax machine on a separate telephone line which is allocated to the deaf person, and advertises these numbers alongside the voice telephone number allocated to the hearing person plus a note to the effect that if voice callers wish to contact the deaf person, they should use the National Telephone Relay Service, *Typetalk*. So, members of the public know that there is a deaf person employed by the organization and that they have a choice between contacting the deaf person and contacting the hearing person. Fax machines, minicoms and Typetalk are a real boon for deaf people – but they have their downside for hearing people. Most standard textbooks on organizational communication and the sociology of work provide descriptions of different kinds of communication in terms of advantages and disadvantages (see for example Smither 1988). The written communication needed for fax machines, for example:

- can be time-consuming;
- can be expensive;
- tends to be more formal and distant;
- can cause problems of interpretation;
- reduces the possibility of instant feedback;
- once dispatched, it is difficult to modify the message;
- does not allow for exchange of opinion, views or attitudes except over a period of time;
- may require a journey to the source of the fax machine.

Similarly, the efficiency of minicoms depends on the speed of typing and, in some cases on the ability to understand Deaf typing nuances; Typetalk involves a third party which, though confidentiality is assured, puts a lot of people off. After a few weeks, the hearing employee in our example feels overworked because all the phone calls are going to her. She notices that, on a regular basis, the deaf employee is often sitting at his desk 'doing nothing', and becomes resentful. She eventually makes a complaint to her manager who, after an investigation, moves the deaf person to a different, lower status job on the grounds of 'poor performance'. Now, the employer could argue that they had made reasonable adjustments through the provision of special aids and equipment, but the deaf person *may not realize* that the hearing person is getting all the phone calls, nor why. Without sensitive deaf awareness training from an experienced insider perspective, it is unlikely that either the deaf person or the employer would have the wherewithal to see their way around this situation, let alone to recognize the reasons for the 'poor performance'. If the deaf person makes a claim under the DDA it is possible, nevertheless, that the demotion will be found to be justifiable, especially if there are no deaf people on the tribunal panel. It might be useful to think of this in relation to the growth of knowledge workers described above, and also to consider its relevance for the need to look at disability oppression at the institutional level. Whereas I do not think it is appropriate to ghettoize deaf people into deaf sector jobs, nor is it always appropriate to create a job which matches the disability, such as happened in the past when blind people were channelled into telephonist roles, I do think that deaf people represent an enormous resource on deafness and deaf issues and that it is appropriate that this is accredited in the mainstream context. Without the GOQ facility, positive action which might give some redress for past discriminations is illegal, which means, for example, that a hearing person can be appointed to provide deaf awareness training. In my experience, this means that a great deal of important information will be missing from training opportunities which could, in both the short and the long term, save employers' resources and time.

Organizational culture in context

To explore this point further, it is important to remember that good communications are essential to the efficient operation of any organization and vital to the motivation and fulfilment of those who commit their working lives to it. Deaf and disabled people are actors in this process, even if we are often reduced to the level of our functional impairments. The DDA does not describe the processes of oppression, nor, in my view is it relevant to these processes, because it perpetuates the view that oppression is impairment-related – that deaf people experience oppression at work, for example, because they are deaf and so reasonable adjustment means accommodating the deaf person's needs. This does not fully take on board that oppression is socially created in the relationships between different actors and the organizational environment, which itself has been described as 'a cultural jungle' (Aldrich 1992), and which may have been functioning from an oppressive base a long time before the deaf person arrived. Such organizations are described, albeit in a slightly different context, as 'learning disabled' (Senge 1990) and do not bode well for the long-term prospects of the economy, but those who lead them are often unable to see the impairment. An example of such an organization might be a deaf sector organization where most of the staff, particularly those at senior levels, are hearing. Whichever way we look at it, this means that the organization will do things the hearing way and any deaf people entering the organization, again particularly at senior level, will find an implicit expectation on them to continue in the hearing tradition, and to perform all the tasks which hearing people feel are necessary in the hearing way. If a deaf person in such a position is not supported by a structure which includes sufficient numbers of deaf people to demonstrate that the hearing way is only one way, not always the best way, they will become isolated within such a culture. In such circumstances, aggressive recruitment practice because of fear of prosecution, tokenism or reasonable adjustment will achieve nothing because the organizational structure and the culture will work against all of these measures.

This is one reason why attempts to translate the strategies of the Deaf President Now! (DPN) campaign to install the first Deaf President of Gallaudet University in Washington DC into similar campaigns in Britain seem misguided. Gallaudet University is a deaf university. A high proportion of the staff are deaf themselves or at the very least, hearing people who are deaf aware; sign language and English are both in frequent use. DPN was a localized campaign which employed disruptive tactics successfully in its focus on a single, morally persuasive issue in a relatively small, contained institution set in a well-developed and supportive political/cultural climate with a tradition of and respect for civil rights (Christiansen and Barnarrt 1995). The university already had particular values in place in relation to both deaf–hearing relationships and deaf education at all levels except governance. It had considerable outside support from communities, government officials and the media. Moreover, there was more than one possible appropriately qualified deaf candidate in the running for the presidency. Campaigns in Britain to date, far from being localized and concentrated on a single issue, have focused on the massive human services industry. This is a symptom of our *lack* of civil rights, because it has a deeply entrenched culture which is nothing like that of either Gallaudet or the USA. Thus, one dominant outcome of British campaigns has been that enormous pressures have been brought to bear on a few individual deaf people to succeed within an oppressive political and cultural climate. More obvious parallels to Gallaudet – such as the somewhat glaring anomaly that the majority of university Deaf studies departments across Britain are led by hearing academics, award proportionally more doctorates to hearing people (doctorates being an important criterion for university teaching and research posts) and conduct research where deaf people are often confined to the role of assistant and have limited say in the final outcomes – have not thus far been the focus of deaf people's campaigns. By way of comparison, it would be unheard of to have a man responsible for a women's studies department, and the two main disability studies departments in Britain are both headed by disabled people. This is another example of why the experience of oppression must be contextualized.

Deaf people's oppression at work can be best understood and challenged at the level of their interaction with the communication and information structures and functions of the organizational culture, since it is here that their identity as 'communication disabled' is likely to be most threatening, and most revealing. Historically, organizational cultures have their own embedded structures of meaning that constitute what organizational members value and to which they subscribe (Frost *et al.* 1985; Turner 1990). The postmodernist view of organizations would then be that

> Organizations exist through individual actors. Actors, singly or in groups, can crack the facade of the 'competition', the 'government pressures' or the 'economy' and interpret them, sometimes even re-form them. Organizations are in environments, but environments are also in organizations – an intriguing conundrum. In other words the social structures which influence organizations are human creations but at the same time part of the process of creating new structures and meanings …As action – doing work, speaking, collaborating, negotiating – unfolds over time, interpretations and meanings also evolve which coalesce into a system of taken-for-granted rules and structures, and a sense of 'the organization'.
>
> (Fineman 1993:11)

This implies that organizational cultures are potentially unpredictable and chaotic, which they almost certainly would be without the 'negotiated order'

(Strauss 1978) that is achieved through communication, or the continual adjustments to situations through local agreements, deals, compromises and trade-offs of strategic political activity and the social construction of worker identity. Fineman (1993: 12–13) continues:

> To express our individuality we have to rely on the language, manners and gestures that are already 'there', defined by others and in terms of the roles they expect us to play. But exactly what role we are to play, and how, in various organizational encounters, is not always clear. There is risk involved. In the politics of negotiated order there are enemies as well as friends 'out there', and there is the ever present fear that a valued working order may collapse – if we get it wrong.

As was suggested in an earlier example, this implies that an outsider entering an organization for the first time will have to learn how to become part of the negotiated order to which Fineman refers. A deaf person entering this cultural jungle is not just an outsider – s/he is Other – an Other who brings with them observably different sets of communication rules and structures which are critical for their optimal functioning. These rules and structures may actually bring collective benefits to the organization through enabling more effective communication if applied more widely. As a simple example, a **speech-to-text reporter** employed to support a deaf person can provide a verbatim transcript of meetings which can be used as the basis for producing minutes and removes the need for secretarial support. When this form of support is used *alongside* a sign language interpreter, the transcript can also provide a check for the accuracy of the voice-over. Both of these functions support hearing people as much as the deaf person to whom the support is 'assigned'. But paradoxically, the deaf person's rules and structures become aligned with hearing perceptions of Other, and the provision is seen to be problematic because it is only conceptualized in terms of the deaf person's 'special' needs and not as part of the framework of organizational functions as a whole. Together they can be seen as a threat to the negotiated order, especially if that order is itself faulty, because deaf people's necessary involvement with communication means that the organization's communicative function is also highlighted. Most organizational cultures have their own inbuilt barriers to effective communication such as those associated with:

- serial communication or the tendency not to communicate directly;
- status differences;
- social conformity (which includes work styles and informal rules, and patterns of interpersonal relationships);
- emotional labour, or 'the way in which roles and tasks exert overt and covert control over emotional displays' (Putnam and Mumby 1993: 37);
- spatial distance;
- defensiveness which can be both a result of threat to self-image and intolerance of different points of view;
- rumour transmission and the organizational grapevine.

Time and time again, I am faced with people, both hearing and deaf, who berate the way meetings are run, complain about group dynamics, communication systems, and about the failure to arrive at clear decisions or get rapid responses which answer the questions posed, and these are all indications of dysfunctional communication *which have nothing to do with impairment*. Within a dysfunctional culture, these barriers are not simply appendages to work, they constitute and contribute to the evolution of processes through which workers create their work environment. Communication flow and communication networks may subsequently be built on these barriers, but because communication is exactly the kind of taken-for-granted activity that Fineman refers to, the dysfunction will not necessarily be visible and may not therefore be acknowledged as the source of difficulties.

For example, all organizations have a grapevine, but in some, this will be the only means by which information is passed. The grapevine may itself have a number of different patterns (Figure 6.1), and it could be anticipated that each of these will have different implications for deaf people entering the system. In *monochannel* and *cluster* grapevines, there is a chance that the deaf person will receive the relevant message as long as the source of the information, and the holder of the grapevine power, decides that this should happen. *Gossip* grapevines are informal organizational networks notorious for distorting the message and for playing people off against each other because a slightly different version of the message may be given to each of the participants. They can therefore become the channel for backstabbing and other forms of harassment, victimization and indirect discrimination. *Random* systems also tend to be informal, but they do not operate on a need-to-know basis at all, distributing information to the 'select few' and leaving the rest to chance. If the deaf person is the outsider in this kind of grapevine – and most deaf people in the mainstream sector will be to some degree – it is unlikely that they will get the information.

Grapevines as a whole mean that a few people have considerable power in making decisions about and influencing what deaf people need to know – what information is given, and when and how they find out – and this is a large part of deaf people's oppression in organizational settings. However, it may only be when a deaf person, or any other outsider who symbolizes 'communication barriers' enters the culture that the inefficiency and inaccuracy of the grapevine as an information system becomes obvious. What begins as symbol can quickly become cause; outsiders who are also Other are more likely to be made the scapegoats for any dysfunction that subsequently emerges, even if it has always been present. Organizations are frequently so deep in denial of their own communication barriers that they may fail to notice that the dysfunction remains even after the deaf person has left.

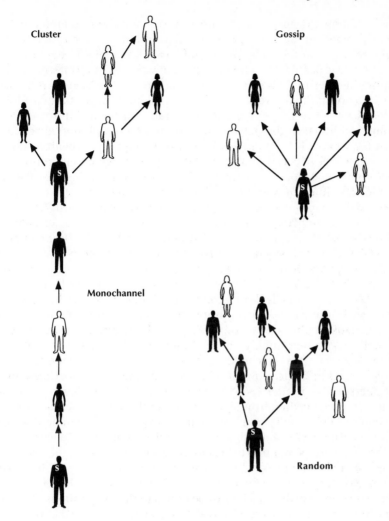

s source of information

Figure 6.1 Information grapevines

Access to misinformation

Similarly, all organizations have multidimensional patterns of communication flow and feedback which might be schematized as shown in Figure 6.2. Each step of the communication process holds the potential for information distortion. If a sign language interpreter enters the picture at some point in the network, this is not going to remove embedded distortion; it may well create additional distortion if the Deaf person and the interpreter are not properly matched or have particular perceptions of their role in the communication process. It is, for example, a common misconception on the part of hearing people that a Deaf person can work with *any* interpreter. But because the interpreter is seen to be an 'auxiliary' to the Deaf person rather than an actor in the network as a whole – and often works to their profession's rules than to those of the organization – this added distortion may become subsumed in the network distortion, and so will not be acknowledged for what it is. Sociolinguists and psycholinguists recognize that the quality and style of social contacts and the type of language environment in which communication occurs frequently determine and influence language behaviour in different ways and with different people. Thus, for example, a woman who is faced with an all-male interview panel may use different language if she were being interviewed by women or if she were engaging in ordinary social conversation. A move towards describing the Deaf community in terms of its diversity rather than its uniformity, can be extended to language use among Deaf people. For example, language contacts mean that very few deaf people are monolingual and many Deaf people do not use 'pure' BSL or 'pure' English, but a combination of both. Maxwell *et al.* (1991) have pointed out that research, in its concentration on error analysis, has failed to look at the interaction which occurs between vocal and visual channels in so-called 'impure' forms, which provides evidence for **bimodal communication** (BC) – communication which occurs simultaneously through and is influenced by both the vocal and the visual. BC, from a functional perspective, is often seen by the user to combine the best of both languages to give maximum access, because each can compensate for the deficiency of the other in terms of the user's expression and understanding, and not because BSL or English are in themselves inherently deficient.

However, there are political expectations in some sections of the Deaf community of language 'purity' which mean that mixed forms can be the subject of derogatory abuse. Sign language interpretation is, within the terms of the DDA, a 'service', which as such must be linked to the expectations of service users. But at present it is a service which is heavily entrenched in the translation of one language to another in accordance with these political expectations. The 'best' sign language interpreters are those who come closest to the Deaf way (in the cultural sense) of transmitting and receiving information, not those who are skilled and flexible translators of information in a form which is accessible to the deaf service user (communication support workers, or CSWs). Whereas I think it is important for sign language to be given the same credibility as any other language because there is no doubt that it is a language in every sense of the word, this raises difficult questions about the function, and sometimes the effectiveness of sign language interpreting as an 'auxiliary aid'. Many deaf (and hearing) people working in mainstream settings still see sign language in its role as providing access to information *in a hearing environment,* as opposed to its role as a native language and a transmitter of cultural information in a Deaf environment. The two roles are quite

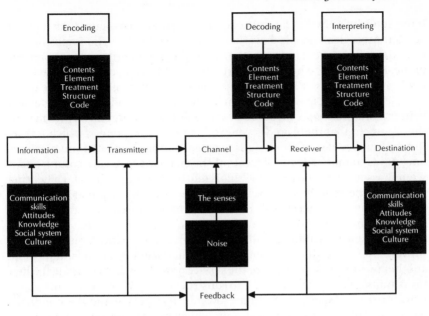

Figure 6.2 Composite communications model

distinct, and this distinction leads to further questions about exactly what is it that we require access to. Information? Or information which conveys the meaning structure of a particular language, which can be either BSL or English? For example, consider English-dominant deaf people with a particular preference for human contact in communication. Some may not like staring at a speech-to-text reporter's screen because of the difficulty of gauging the non-verbal elements of communication from this, nor may they be happy with speech reading because of the limited information which can come through speech reading alone, as a result of the potential confusions of similar lip patterns. In situations where it is not possible to have a written transcript of proceedings in advance, a sign language interpreter may be preferable, but in order to make sense of the information, there must be access to the meaning structure of English. This means that focus is on the face and there is expectation of English lip patterns, but the signed support supplements information which might be missed through speech reading alone. Now, BSL uses English lip patterns sparingly because technically it is not possible to speak English and use BSL at the same time. Added to this BSL has its own mouth patterns which are nothing to do with English, and which can confuse if one is not fully aware of them. Many deaf people report being used to political repercussions of making interpreting preferences known and the irritation this brings.

The main problems arise, however, when there is no control over provision, as might happen, for example, when attending a meeting, course or conference where the bookings are made by the organizers, or when the interpreter assumes they know the communication needs better than the deaf person. Most deaf people have become accustomed to the imposition of essentialist language standardization in situations where it may not be appropriate. For example, when BSL interpreters and voice-over are provided, this implies that full access, insofar as this is possible, will be granted to the privileged few Deaf people who are fluent in BSL and who understand the subject matter, *and to hearing people.* Some Deaf people may counter this criticism with the argument that there are very few skilled BSL interpreters, which is true. But the number of students in sign language training drops off dramatically as one moves to more advanced levels of the sign language curriculum, and it seems possible that a large part of this is due to the limits to how far a hearing person can become Deaf. However, it is important to grasp that a poor BSL interpreter does not necessarily make a good BC interpreter. A common argument used in favour of using a strict bilingual approach is that translation raises the same difficulties as with any foreign language interpreting service. However, it is one thing to aim for 'pure' languages as an ideal and quite another to insist that the client or the service provider matches the ideal when the conditions are not yet in place to construct it fully. We have to think about British culture, especially attitudes towards deaf people and the dominant perspective of equality of opportunity which are entrenched in the culture, the market economy and legislation. We can protest about those attitudes and perspectives and work to change them, but actually changing them takes longer. That too is used as part of our oppression – we are told to be patient. The period of change will continue to generate a lot of people who do not match the ideal through no fault of their own, but it might nevertheless make a significant contribution to our levels of access and support.

A conference or course on deaf issues is likely to attract a variety of deaf people in the same way that a conference devoted to women's issues attracts a variety of women. Assuming for the moment that there are no deaf women at the women's conference, but there are Bengali-speaking women, what is the role of the Bengali interpreter from the service users' perspective? Ostensibly, it is to translate accurately the presentations of speakers into the language of listeners and to facilitate interaction. But implicitly, it is also to enhance equality of opportunity. If the speaker's presentation is simple, the translation will be simple; if the speaker's presentation is complex, so too will be the translation. Barriers to access will occur only when the interpreter does not fully grasp the information content, when the listener does not understand the information content, or perhaps, when the listener does not agree with the information content. We would not expect the interpreter to translate presentations into Urdu or Hindi for Bengali-speaking delegates, and expect those delegates to muddle through with their limited or non-existent Urdu or Hindi. At any course or conference where there are deaf people the first difference we may find is that the deaf delegates will be varied in their level of skill and fluency in *both* BSL and English, and possibly also that they may be unfamiliar with the conceptual content of the presentations. They may also be attending the conference for different reasons. When the conference languages are BSL and English, those deaf people who, when they are communicating comfortably and easily would use BC, and who *are* familiar with the content of the presentations, might find themselves in a situation similar to Bengali delegates who had only limited Urdu or Hindi and were expected to 'make do' with an Urdu or Hindi translator.

Some of this arises from another common difficulty that can be faced by English-dominant deaf people: *how* information is translated, as the following example illustrates. The setting is an equal opportunities meeting where a draft policy is being discussed. There are four deaf people at the meeting and only one is a BSL user. The interpreter is a BSL interpreter, who has been booked by the organization without consultation with the deaf users. The topic under discussion is whether the organization in question can afford to include a statement which prevents discrimination on the grounds of sexual orientation. One hearing person gets very angry, starts to rage about paedophiles because he thinks, wrongly, that paedophilia is confined to the gay and lesbian community, and then calls that particular statement 'the nigger in the woodpile' [*sic*]. Now, if we know the expression *in English*, we would understand that the term 'nigger in the woodpile' is racist. As there were black and Asian people present at the meeting, the result was uproar – but the four deaf people sat back with blank faces, apparently not comprehending what all the fuss was about. However the Deaf person and the other deaf people were unaware *for different reasons*. Why? Because the interpreter had signed THE ODD ONE OUT, and although this *is* an innocuous translation of what 'nigger in the woodpile' means in the context, it does not include the racist element. The interpreter may have assumed that the deaf people present would not understand the English idiom, or they may have been too shocked by the use of the term to be able to translate it accurately, but, on this particular occasion, the simplified translation amounted to misinformation.

Examples such as these illustrate why the provision of a particular interpreter cannot be a universal solution for all deaf people and why it is crucial that assumptions are not made about what the interpreter can actually achieve. In this sense an interpreter is not so very different from a minicom or fax machine which is assumed to solve 'the access problem', but which instead creates an apparent performance problem which can be used by others to justify the discrimination.

The myth of the deaf role model

This discussion should not be construed as a suggestion that all interpreters will be perceived or function in this way, nor that technology is always limited in its ability to assist access. It aims to illustrate how easily enculturated discourses on access and support can undermine the intentions of anti-discrimination legislation which has no teeth. It also aims to show how piecemeal legislation such as the DDA completely misses the point about deafness at work, namely that mainstream organizational theory and culture is premised on hearing discourses which demand that deaf people are expected to adjust to the 'organizational' norm. As with other disabled people, women, black people, gays and lesbians and so on, the presupposition is that *they do not belong there*.

> Organizations can be viewed from the bottom, the middle or the top, from the inside and from the outside. Those who view from the outside may not be organizational members but may often be consumers of organizations, such as children or patients or clients of services. They usually have policy made for them and have often been viewed as outside organization theory and politics. This is especially evident with issues of disability.
>
> (Hearn and Parkin 1993: 161)

This ignores the fundamental nature of divisions between person and Other, and also the relationship between the personal and the political, public and the private, production and reproduction (Hearn 1987). For example, the pressure on deaf people to be 'objective' in organizational life stems from the objectification of deafness which locates it only in the personal and private spheres. So in the political and public spheres, there is an expectation that deafness is hidden. But this places particular pressures on Deaf people working in deaf organizations, for example, who are more likely to experience cultural overlap in all of these spheres and the subsequent pressures of carry-over between work and private life (Corker 1995a). It also drives a wedge between the concept of the 'deaf role model' as compared to that of 'model employee':

> positive images can also create role stress in employment. Some deaf and disabled people, for example, relate how their professional skills and knowledge and personal experience and expertise have become less important than how they conduct themselves as deaf or disabled people, or how successful they are in being deaf or disabled *role models*. Being a role model, therefore, is not just about being a model employee in a particular role, but also about being a 'model deaf or disabled person', the image of the model deaf or disabled person being subject to the positive stereotyping of 'courageous and exceptional' and 'ability not disability' images. The model Deaf or disabled person is the one who smiles through all number of trauma, overcomes every barrier placed in their path with tact and diplomacy, and copes with a minimum of support without complaint. Many of my deaf and disabled colleagues have summed this up as 'be super-human, shut up, put up, don't rock the boat and, for heaven's sake, *never* mention equal opportunities!' Employer expectations associated with performance in a particular job or a particular task, when framed by this model, can be inflated because these expectations are more in respect of the deaf or disabled role model than in terms of the employee's performance in relation to the tasks that are expected of them.
>
> (Corker 1994b: 6)

These divisions challenge the notion of hearing 'objectivity'. In the paper from which the above quotation is taken, I sought to highlight how hearing people deny their oppression of deaf people in working relationships. This article was written from the inside looking out, which is probably the best way of describing organic experience, and from the perspective of a number of deaf people who had experienced oppression in the workplace. In 1996, Jim Kyle, a well-known hearing researcher of Deaf issues, referred to my earlier publication within one of his own analyses of different types of deaf people who can be found in the workplace. He says that I describe a particular type and the corresponding work situation 'in terms of tokenism. However, although the situation she describes is similar, I believe the motivation in mental health work is probably different' (Kyle 1996: 14). My point, here, was that my own writing reflected where I and other deaf people who had described this situation to me were coming from – it was the perspective of deaf people who had experienced such a situation as tokenism because our considerable abilities and achievements were often devalued or considered secondary to those of hearing people, regardless of our position in the organization. An equation was then made which placed achievement in an inverse proportion to our support needs – the more we had achieved, the less support we needed. This equation did not balance because firstly, it totally ignored the often unsupported struggles that we had gone through to achieve in the first place, and secondly, new jobs represent new situations and new people – in short, different environments which carry with them their own inbuilt support requirements. In suggesting that 'the motivation' for such an equation 'in mental health work . . . is different', Kyle acknowledges this. But, because his is the view of an outsider, the supposed shift of environment to a different workplace in order to justify his own perspective could be construed as denial of the 'facts' of oppression as seen by deaf people.

Deafness and disability are not just issues or images, metaphors, paradigms or 'problems'; they have always been part of cultural life and have only become translated into these things because deaf and disabled people have resisted and pushed for change. Deafness and disability are still mostly talked about in the context of work, organization and organization theory in terms of hearing and non-disability. Paradoxically the way in which deafness and disability are defined by their Other parallels the dominant equation of deafness and disability with impairment; this avoids viewing hearing and non-disabled people, and their systems and cultures, as dysfunctional. Thus organization, whether social or employment-related, creates and re-creates oppression. Given the contribution which organizations like the Confederation of British Industry have made to governmental preference for the DDA rather than full civil rights legislation, and the continuing nervousness of employers about employing disabled people (Honey *et al.* 1993), experience suggests that most employers are more likely to spend money in determining ways to use the loopholes in the legislation than to spend it on making reasonable adjustment or on examining the oppressive fabric of structures and cultures.

Summary

In a changing world of work and organization where workforce diversification is becoming increasingly important for the survival of organizations, it is important to locate deafness and disability *in* new discourses of organization rather than outside. However, this chapter has explored how past oppression has resulted in high levels of unemployment, underemployment and non-employment in the deaf population which can only be redressed, it is argued, through affirmative action. It is suggested that the Disability Discrimination Act 1995, with its muddled combination of prohibition, justifiable discrimination and reasonable adjustment, cannot achieve this. When compared to the Race Relations Act and the Sex Discrimination Acts, it is clear that disability has been treated differently, particularly in the omission of disability as a genuine occupational qualification and the severance of legislative links between disability, race and gender. This means that specific discourses on the construction of deafness and disability and access and support continue to be fundamental to the reproduction of power in organizations and to be perceived as a threat to negotiated order. Further, the DDA, in its emphasis on impairment categories, creates potential competition among deaf people since they are under pressure to match the stated definition; it does not remove 'the burden of proof' from the hands of disability 'experts'.

However, ignorance of the benefits and value of specific knowledges to organizational life can result when 'objective' expertise is the main focus. In the absence of such knowledges, there will be prevalent assumptions that a particular provision is the universal solution to the access and support issues raised by a specific impairment. Nevertheless, technology and other forms of access and support have inbuilt advantages and disadvantages which will be constructed differently by deaf and hearing people, for example. In the end it is the culturally embedded construction which still determines patterns of use, access and support. Therefore deaf people's oppression in employment situations can best be understood and challenged at the level of our inter-action with the communication and information structures and functions of organizational culture. If provision does not match the person and if the person is not in control of the provision, access becomes perceived as access to misinformation, which obscures organizational dysfunction. In some circumstances, this can create a new discourse of deaf people as 'poor performers', which undermines the intentions of equal opportunities. The creation of arbitrary divisions between person and Other, personal and political, public and private, in turn creates a division between the concepts of the 'deaf role model' and 'the deaf person' and those of 'the model employee' and 'the professional' who are assumed to be hearing. Thus oppression is created and re-created in relationships based on these divisions.

 **7**

The time has come ...

'The time has come,' the Walrus said, 'To talk of many things'
(Lewis Carroll, *Through the Looking Glass*, 1872)

'That's not a regular rule: you invented it just now.'
'It's the oldest rule in the book,' said the King.
'Then it ought to be Number One,' said Alice.
(Lewis Carroll, *Alice's Adventures in Wonderland*, 1865)

The subtitle of this book is 'towards a human rights perspective' and this is clear in its exposition of human rights as a goal. Along the way, the path has diverged in numerous directions, spanning philosophy, sociology, psychology, history and linguistics; it has taken us through the diverse worlds of people: the communities, movements, societies and cultures they are part of, and the social and political structures and processes which demarcate their relationships. These worlds are in themselves multidimensional; their inherent belief and value systems are often divided by the politics of conflict because each is preoccupied with the essentialist pursuit of its own 'truths'. These multilayered conflicts are complex and contradictory. In their ability to slip into dualisms and rhetoric, they often ignore the middle ground between subject and object, individual and collective, mind and body – and deaf and disabled. Thus essentialism generates exclusion. But it also ignores the postmodern 'realities' of pluralism and individuation along with the political 'realities' of individualist cultures – the struggle between the individual and the group – which are characteristic of contemporary Western society. It could be said that all the recent changes in our thinking about disability (for example the tensions which are now beginning to show themselves between the social model and models of cultural representation), the way disability is researched (for example the move from empirical research to participatory or emancipatory research or the use of biographical narrative), and the way disability is described (for example from the social model to emerging theories of simultaneous oppression) are symptomatic of wider sociocultural change. The changes and challenges seem to be attempts to reunify both personhood or identity and concepts of oppression so that all aspects – both those which are obvious and those which are not so obvious – of the oppressed person and their environment are subject to the same gaze. Much of this book has been concerned with exploring different frameworks which might enable and strengthen a more global and contextualized view of the relationships between deaf and disabled people.

This is not without its dilemmas, however. The 'turn to culture' is already viewed by prominent disability activists with great suspicion, because it is seen to diminish the heterogeneity of power while apparently reducing it to discourses of representation and ignoring its material realities. I have presented a general argument against reification and hegemony, suggesting that few models can claim immunity from these things. People and social structures cannot be reduced to the material level, and so the material alone cannot adequately explain social processes, including social oppression, nor the power structures inherent in different discourses as products of these processes. It is necessary to explore ways in which the material can be contextualized through its relationship to the non-material in the realm of discourse analysis because the term 'discourse' refers to anything which can be 'read'. Individuals and the different characteristics of their social, economic and physical environments all have their associated discourses, all are actors in the networks which construct patterns of inclusion and exclusion. One difficulty with discourse analysis, however, is that in its power to deconstruct, it liberates multiplicity, which brings with it the risk of radical relativism. It seems that acknowledging multiplicity signifies, for the disability movement as disabled people's political wing, a move to a different kind of individualism, which may be perceived as a step backwards. However, *this* individualism, if this is indeed what it might be called, is very different because it is not, I suggest, a product of oppression, but of the collective response to it and the self-worth this has generated. It is as if a compound 'I' consciousness – the individual 'of many masks' (Gergen 1996) – has emerged out of the collective 'we' consciousness – the diverse group. It seems important, then, to hang on to the distinction between *challenges* from within the disability movement – insider perspectives which seek to renew the social model so that it becomes relevant to the diverse challenges, and *denials*, which attempt to deride the social model in order to maintain the primacy which Western society gives to the individual model of disability.

I believe, like Grossberg (1996: 90), that 'politics involves questioning how identities are produced and taken up through practices of representation'. A conceptualization of disability which unifies disabled people under a set of political aims and objectives cannot always be inclusive if it diminishes the relationship between politics, identity production and practices of representation – or the role of culture and language in forging this relationship – because individuation and pluralism tend to be submerged, along with discourse. The context-specific nature of disability, particularly as it relates to different impairments, can be subsumed by discourses which view oppression *only* at the institutional and epochal levels when these discourses are, themselves, presented as metanarratives or dogma. The political struggles of disabled people, and also Deaf people, arose from an awareness of the struggles of other oppressed groups, but we have translated this awareness differently in our actions. As Oliver (1996: 13) emphasizes, disabled people's political task has been to move from this 'general political awareness' of inequality and oppression to the politics emerging from 'the experiences of *disabled people* generally'. But, unlike Deaf people, disabled people are, as a collective, socially and experientially unrelated, even at the levels of impairment and disability. 'General' theories of disability must therefore strike a balance between being representative and acknowledging the threat posed by internal struggles which adversely influence the effectiveness of *collective* empowerment and political action. I feel that in the context of the essentialist way in which relationships between deaf and disabled people are perceived, Deaf people represent such a threat, though the Deaf community may, on another level, teach us something about our unrelatedness. But neither disability theory and practice nor cultural theory which underpins the Deaf world-view have grasped the implications of this for a renewed and more contemporary 'general' understanding of both disability and deafness.

Cultural theorists responsible for developing 'notions of Deaf identity, Deaf community and Deaf culture' might claim that when cultures are viewed in the mutually constitutive terms I am proposing, it diminishes the positivity of a community as the possessor of unique knowledges, language and traditions. However, echoing the comment made earlier about organic and positional critiques in relation to the social model, as long as these notions are conceived, interpreted and developed primarily by hearing academics – which is very much the case in Britain – there is a sense in which it is difficult to own the 'Deaf' origins of the minority group construction. This is the main disadvantage of this construction because supporting fundamental tenets of the minority group construction of deafness (it is distinct and separate from notions of hearingness) is irreconcilable with upholding the positional interpretations of hearing outsiders (at least part of the notions of Deaf identity, Deaf community and Deaf culture are made up of hearingness). Perhaps this criticism has not been addressed beyond alluding to the difference between self-actualization and hedonism. There have been suggestions, too, that perceptions of 'positivity' are relative especially when they become confused with the issue of rights of the few to self-expression and 'pride', both of which are privileged by their legitimation in both the dominant discourses of disability – individual and social. This relates very specifically to the relationship between Deaf and deaf people, particularly aspects of this relationship which are described as 'having' or 'lacking' positivity and pride, which perhaps explains my feelings of inadequacy. The Deaf community is the first 'community of relatedness' to emerge in the disability sphere, though perhaps by a different process. The Deaf community represents a different 'we' consciousness founded on a sociocultural agenda which offers the possibility of affiliation and belonging to those who manifest allegiance to the community without question. I have suggested that the minority group conceptualization of deafness is, in some of its aspects, a consequence of the search for a unifying concept of disability which, in its pursuit of a largely materialist political agenda, has sidelined the social agenda and the need of people to communicate, affiliate and to belong. In Chapter 5, I linked this to Grossberg's (1996) description, in connection with the way in which cultural studies has theorized matters of identity, as 'diaspora'. But because this particular conceptualization of deafness is founded on separatist, essentialist notions, it cannot be politically effective outside of the Deaf community without the use of counter-essentialism.

Historical analysis of minority–majority group relations supports this view. This is in part because a minority group is just that – a minority – and the Deaf community is a very small, oppressed minority which remains under threat from the dominant metanarrative of the individual model of disability, as shown by the community's growing concerns about the re-emergence of sovereign power in the form of cochlear implants and genetic engineering. More importantly, a minority group which is based on cultural and linguistic separatism, particularly a linguistic separatism which rests so much on an experience which is non-translatable without some form of mediation, becomes preoccupied with 'transnationality and movement' and 'with political struggles to define the local as a distinctive community, in historical contexts of displacement' (Clifford 1994: 308). This, in my mind, generates a confusion between the wider political issues of identity and representation which are increasingly evident in disability campaigns and the political struggles which give Deaf people 'the full knowledge, commitment and allegiance *of the partisan*' (Ladd and John 1991: 15, my italics):

> While [diaspora] offers significantly new possibilities for a cultural politics that avoids many of the logics of the modern – by rooting identity in structures of affiliations and ways of belonging, it is, too often, drawn back into the modern. Identity is ultimately returned to history, and the subaltern's place is subsumed within a history of movements and experience of oppression which privileges particular exemplars as the 'proper' figures of identity.
>
> (Grossberg 1996: 92)

Partisanship, it must be remembered, is often unreasoning and biased, and the 'proper' figures of identity (as *exemplars* of how we should be) simply become the metaphorical albatross, an encumbrance when they are weighted down by conditions to our existence and the promise of well-being. Precisely because politics *is* concerned with issues of identity, if we become complacent in our questioning because identity becomes 'fixed' or has reached the status of exemplar, the political process is stunted. 'Figures of diaspora', in these circumstances, can become close to non-translatable, modernist discourses which promote singular concepts of identity and culture in the world of multiple Others where relationships are complex, local, context-bound and time-limited. As such they can embrace oppression:

> As we struggle to agree on appropriate names, we must ever be aware that labels exclude and that rather than defining ourselves we may actually be reducing ourselves only in a different way . . . As a cultural

description, Deaf captures the experience of an identifiable group, but when it is used to question, invalidate, or trivialise the authenticity of someone else's cultural experience it can in itself be an oppressor's term.

(I. King Jordan 1992: 69)

Jenny Morris (1991) rightly implies in the title of her book that *Pride* can be used *Against Prejudice* – we can consciously set out to demonstrate that the images society has of us are narrow in their conception and oppressive by showing who we are and what we are capable of. But I feel uneasy with the word 'pride'. I prefer the terms 'self-acceptance', 'dignity' and 'integrity', because there can be something very supercilious and arrogant about pride if we see it only as *our* right and we exercise prejudice to sustain the privileged position it brings. Jane Austen's analysis of *Pride and Prejudice* carries the message that pride and prejudice are intricately related; we perhaps need to bear in mind that this relationship is not always positive in its outcome. This is difficult to accept when 'pride' is central to our identity and therefore, to our struggles.

I have suggested that non-translatability of discourses, particularly when it appears to be founded on trivializing, invalidating or questioning another group's authenticity – something which, as King Jordan stresses, amounts to prejudice – leads to the politics of compromise. It can be exacerbated when there are aspects of the separatists' existence which mirror something that inclusionists continue to struggle for – to be perceived as having intrinsic value and worth. I will probably be challenged on this point, but Deaf people's unique existence *is* increasingly seen as being of intrinsic value and they *are* getting an increasingly large slice of exposure and resources. Because disabled people do not have human or civil rights, even the most politically active among us still question whether we are perceived to have intrinsic value, irrespective of how we perceive ourselves. This observation is critical because the corollary of it is that, in oppressed communities, the politics of compromise often works against the politics of inclusion and therefore, against collective empowerment. In this context, we might describe our relationships not so much as 'treading the fine line between marginalisation and incorporation' (Oliver 1990: 157) but as existing on the border between fragmentation and inclusion, a position which is maintained by compromise. I use these terms deliberately. What the Deaf élite appear to suggest is that Deaf people do not want incorporation but the right to exist as a minority group. This, for disabled people implies social and, more importantly, political fragmentation because Deaf people conceptualize oppression and their relationship to the oppressor differently. Indeed, this is the crux of my personal struggle in writing this book, because as a disabled, lesbian woman, I am not happy with society as it is and I *do* want society to change so that I am included. As a deaf lesbian woman, I *also* want my linguistic status acknowledged, and the right to social affiliations I feel comfortable with and stimulated by. There is therefore an inner tension which stems from a struggle between the social and the intellectual/political. This influences my personal political struggles because all these elements are necessary for political effectiveness. Much of the analysis which has been presented in this book mirrors my own attempts to make some kind of transition from tension to an alternative and more mutually constitutive relationship. However, as my intellectual and political awareness has grown, I have come to see this personal struggle reflected in the relationship between Deaf and disabled people. I have also come to the recognition that the dynamics of this relationship has caught many deaf people in a subaltern existence, which, at least from the perspective of this relationship, might provide some further thoughts on why 'it is only a minority of disabled people who belong to the BCODP' (Finkelstein 1996: 97) and, for that matter, why a minority of Deaf people belong to the BDA.

I am not disputing the intensity of Deaf people's desire for a separate social existence – to understand this we need only to spend a short time moving between communities. When Deaf and hearing or disabled people come together it can be reminiscent of the old model of locational integration. That is, we exist in the same place but in all other respects we are separate. But this observation only provides a partial understanding of the tension between us, and I have suggested that this is another reason why we need to examine such situations from the point of view of discourse. Discourse and its analysis, we remember, has many levels. It can be used to refer to the language interaction which occurs between people, to how people create and use language to construct knowledge in a particular way and to convey specific and contextualized meanings. Hence discourse analysis can also be employed in dismantling metanarratives and in exposing marginalized discourses within these metanarratives, in addition to focusing on the structural properties of the language that is used (linguistics) and what makes particular languages effective (their rhetorical power) when used in a particular way:

> [Foucault's] point was that if we can understand the origins of our current ways of understanding ourselves, we can begin to question their legitimacy and resist them. In doing this, he also aims to bring to the fore previously marginalised discourses, to give voice to those whose accounts of life cannot be heard within the prevailing knowledges.
>
> (Burr 1995: 69)

That is to say, deconstructing the way in which the separation of Deaf and disabled people is perceived can liberate not only multiplicity but also a deeper understanding of Deaf people's meaning of *incorporation*; they can then place this meaning in the context of their life experiences, both past and present, of either normalization or social withdrawal. This meaning might explain why Deaf people insist that to be part of the disability movement, the movement must accept Deaf people's Deafcentric terms for participation, in the same way that the community says to 'newly arrived' deaf people (Padden and Humphries 1988) that to be part of the Deaf community, one must 'accept that [it has] cultural rules, and that you have to fit in with them'

(Ladd 1996: 121). This is what the disability movement is saying to the dominant culture – inclusion on *our* terms – but both the word and its meaning have changed. What the two groups are asking for is not *exactly* the same, and, on a political level, to accept Deafcentric terms without question means compromising important beliefs about inclusion. That being said, there is absolutely no point in using terms like inclusion if Deaf people remain stuck in images of normalization, withdrawal and threats to Deafcentrism. Similarly, I am aware that how I use the terms 'we' and 'they' – and this is something I have struggled with throughout this book – will be interpreted in terms of an allegiance which signifies the rejection or betrayal of the other. However, such an interpretation is characteristic of thinking in terms of either/or. It does not consider that it is the tension in the relationships between Deaf and disabled people, both overt and covert, that produces difficulties with total allegiance to one or the other – it is not easy to have strong allegiance to both when each denies or compromises important characteristics of the other.

Because of the links between knowledge and power, singular meanings, particularly those which are legitimated within the dominant metanarrative, bring with them the potential for particular social practices, for acting in one way rather than another, and for marginalizing alternative ways of acting. This too takes us into the political realm. By the same token, power is the knowledge that comes from being able to draw upon alternative discourses. When Rachel Hurst (in Campbell and Oliver 1996: 96) notes that 'one of things we have to look at and be confident about is the reality of why most leaders in the disability movement are wheelchair users', and we make a similar observation that Deaf leaders tend to be articulate in *both* sign language *and* English, this point is emphasized. Campbell and Oliver (1996: 96) respond to Rachel Hurst's comment that 'the disabling barriers to political participation are less severe for wheelchair users than for people with other impairments', but they don't take this to the point where they say *why* this is the case. My own answer to this question is predictable but it doesn't relate to disabling barriers: what wheelchair users and bilingual Deaf people *can* do is critical to involvement in political processes. And it is precisely what they can do which indicates to me that there are many others who are excluded because they are not similarly empowered – confined to borderline existences by the politics of identity.

It is this salutary reminder which, again, takes us back to why compromise will not work. But neither will the mutually constitutive both/and perspective of Derrida and other poststructuralists if it is simply conceived as a watered-down version of democracy framed by transparent and ineffectual terms like 'discrimination'. We won't become fully representative unless we recognize *différance* – and for those of materialist disposition, I am reminded of Stiegler's (1994) comment that 'the *what* invents the *who* just as much as it is invented by it'. Indeed, this is why (without getting embroiled in issues of 'us and them') I agree absolutely with disabled activists who suggest that we do need to be extremely careful about how we see our relationships with non-disabled people and what we expect from them. If we ignore the power structures created by these relationships, we ignore our oppression and we run the risk of collusion which, when described in terms of *différance*, contributes to our oppression and the way in which we, at times, oppress each other. It makes sense, then, to be selective in our relationships to our Other in a way which will empower us. To believe in ourselves as a collective, we must see deafness and disability and the individual and society as mutually constitutive, both literally and figuratively, because, in the end, they are all the product of a common history and a common circuit of culture – of people trying to make sense of things in different time-limited and context-related ways – the cycles of which, as a result, have different outcomes. Indeed, this is one of the dilemmas inherent in the framework of simultaneous oppression presented in Chapter 2. It doesn't fully incorporate an understanding of Vernon's (1996a: 51) point that 'until you truly learn to judge yourself, you cannot judge others'. She is inferring, I think, a mutually definitive relationship between the 'person' *and* the 'Other' of racism and disablism which could be usefully extended to incorporate *différance*. In this context, actor-network theory perhaps holds more possibilities, and we could use Figures 1.3 and 3.3 as a starting point in its application.

However, we are still left with the problem of creating new relationships which are based on inclusive meaning. Even here, I think deconstruction can be a useful tool, because power is most effective when we use it in the production of new knowledge. For example, we might consider the term 'Deafcentric', which, as we saw earlier, forms the basis for conditions placed on Deaf people's incorporation in the disability movement. When used by Deaf people, 'Deafcentric' comes quite close to Clifford's meaning of diaspora because it concentrates on linking Deaf identity to 'histories of alternative cosmopolitanisms and diasporic networks' (quoted in Grossberg 1996: 92). What Deaf people are doing in their exposition of Deafcentrism is resisting the dominant discourses of phonocentrism and dactylophobia. But in the context of separatism and withdrawal, this resistance becomes counter-hegemony – the one true way of 'being Deaf' placed in opposition to a narrow conception of being hearing which includes most disabled people – which must be strengthened by the exclusive application of Deaf cultural studies, for example to those 'who are seen to be candidates' of this construction. In the end, this approach to Deafcentrism only has the aim of promoting separation, and therefore self-interest. To begin to move away from self-interest to an outwardly focused interest which uses our positivity, we need to ask if something can be Deafcentric at the same time as optimizing opportunities and equality for deaf people. I think it can if we contextualize *centrism* in a different way which separates it from notions of privilege and pride and joins it with principles of social justice. If, for example, we were to take resistance to oppression as the starting point – in other words, something which deaf and disabled people share – we can then perhaps conceive of an inclusive framework which does not lose the flavour of 'alternative' centrisms, but places them in context and demonstrates how they relate to each other.

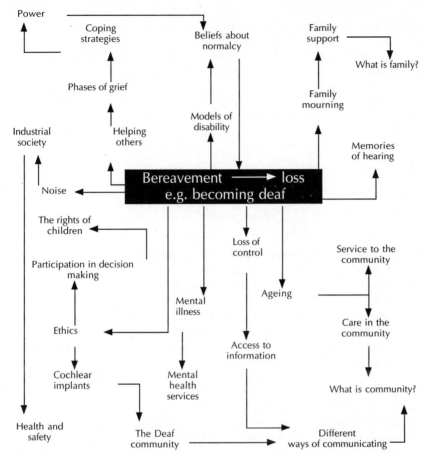

Figure 7.1 Working on bereavement, aged 12–16: a deafcentric supplement

I have started to develop this idea in a practical way with reference to inclusive curriculum development in schools (Corker 1996a), having argued for many years that one of the biggest problems with trying to merge special education with inclusion is that 'special' means separate at all levels of education from policy and planning to teacher training and curriculum delivery. Thus it is not actually compatible with inclusion (see for example Corker 1993a). One example of a more inclusive approach to curriculum is provided in Figure 7.1, which is heavily adapted from a personal-social education framework for looking at bereavement with adolescents aged 12–16 developed by Wagner (1995: 218).

Figure 7.1 is built on a different concept of deafcentrism which removes a bias towards one *or* the other, because it incorporates Williams's (1989) third strategy for liberation from oppression in questioning the primacy given to phonocentric experience at the expense of other attributes and skills. It also accepts that the experiences of deaf, disabled and hearing children and young people are of equal interest and value; *all* can be used to illuminate and explain a wide variety of issues. The framework starts with a general theme of interest to all learners – in this case, bereavement – which then temporarily locates a deaf theme or a particular experience of deafness at the centre of discussion, which are then related to wider issues that affect or are of interest to *all* learners. In this way the experience of deafness and deaf people is:

- set firmly in context;
- treated in an inclusive and equal manner;
- subject to a reduction in stigma;
- used as the basis for shared experiences and cooperative learning;
- used to challenge assumptions and stereotypes of deafness and disability in the context of the dominant culture.

Deconstruction has therefore revealed alternative ways of conceptualizing the deaf–disabled–non-deaf/non-disabled triad. But it is acknowledged that such a strategy, as Williams (1989: 260) suggests, represents 'a Herculean task' because it demands 'a complete reappraisal of the hierarchies of intelligence, competence and skill' based on current essentialist notions. Nevertheless, if such demands are realized, it 'may lead to a better life for everyone', not just deaf and disabled people. This, to my mind, is an important goal – the goal of inclusion – which, in many ways, has triggered this book.

There will be some who have joined me on the journey through the preceding pages who will have found the continued return to the word 'oppression' has evoked a pained and defensive reaction. They will say 'but we put all this time and resources into giving deaf and disabled people a better quality of life, to helping them and to caring for them. Is it not ungenerous of you to throw all that back in our faces?' To this, I want to respond that no one has the right to expect gratitude as long as our oppression continues. Indeed, if this is the only expectation then very serious questions can be asked about the motivation for giving so much. Moreover, I don't think any deaf or disabled person objects to the *principles* of helping and caring – everyone needs them from time to time and very few people need them on a long-term basis. What we object to is when they are forced upon us, or when they are offered to us as a pale substitute for the lives we know we are capable of leading when, and if, the opportunity is there for us to grasp. There is no way that we can see ourselves as separate from this life or outside of it, any more than our Other can see itself as separate from us. We have a relationship, we define each other, though in different ways, and we share a meaning which is open to change.

There are others who have read this book who might ask why has this term 'human rights' been erected as some ideal to which we might aspire? Why human rights and not something else? My answer to this is that I am searching for concepts of rights which bring us together within the same framework, rights which do not discriminate and imply that one right-holder has more right than another right-holder to that right because they are different in some way from an arbitrary 'norm', and rights to which we might all, as human beings, have a claim. I think that statements on human rights come closer than anything else to achieving this at the present time, but that does not mean that they are definitive. *Principles* cannot be definitive, and generally speaking, they are useless without action and without clear legislation to enforce that action. The inability of legislators to be clear, their propensity to mystify us with possibilities, probabilities, maybes and specially designed categories disguises only their inability to commit themselves unquestioningly to objective sets of principles which point the way to social change. The ability of some positional 'experts' to make use of legislative ambiguity so that they are relieved of giving up their power in the interests of our autonomy disguises something equally sinister. When framed in this way, legislation is little better than ideology in its attempts to diminish, to conceal, to ignore paradoxes and contradictions, to invert reality and to produce ideals. Legislation is simply the social production of dominant meta-narratives.

So where do we go from here? Of course much depends on where we want to be, what kind of world we want to live in now and in the future, and on our acceptance of the inevitability of change. I have suggested that this must be a world in which pluralism and individuation are seen as assets; the alternative discourses they create should be regarded as powerful forces of social and cultural resistance and change rather than as threats to the stability of the 'one true voice', because we seem to be approaching the next wave of our struggles where our diversity is uppermost. In developing our analysis on oppression we began by staying within discrete theoretical frameworks which we researched independently and produced descriptions of our experiences in largely discrete ways. We have also searched our different ideologies, stereotypes and discourses – our discourses on feminism, racism, heterosexism, disablism and audism – for differences and similarities in the structure and substantive content of different oppressions. But if we are now to consider a collective pursuit of change which liberates us from these oppressions we cannot simply do this by adding one experience to another or differentiating between them. These experiences are all dimensions of our existence through our person or through our Other, and as long as they remain conceptually separate, there is a risk that we continue to argue that one is more important or more valuable and therefore more powerful than the other. Discourse is something which joins us and separates us, and locates us firmly in the world of social processes. Perhaps this is the unifying concept to take us forward. But in going down this particular road we must be careful that we do not end up in a place – much like the Wonderland and the Looking Glass of riddles – where there are no answers. In the end, perhaps everything does reduce to the language of an inclusive world-view, for language which is removed from 'the stream of life' and from the experience of those who live it, like theory and policy in the same vein, is meaningless, sterile – and exclusive.

Glossary

actor-network theory, a theory which views social processes as consisting of networks of 'actors', both human and non-human, each of whom has a particular role and produces particular discourses which construct the network

ambiguous personhood, a state of personhood where the person's identity is unclear

archæology of knowledge traces the origins of conditions which allowed a specific discourse or knowledge to prevail

archetype, a mental image of, for example, a particular kind of person

attitudinal deafness, a person who thinks, behaves and communicates in a manner which reflects Deaf cultural values is said to be attitudinally deaf

auditory-oral approach, an approach to teaching deaf children which makes maximum use of any residual hearing through the use of appropriate amplification, such as hearing aids, and the provision of spoken language experience

bimodal communication (BC), a combination of two language modes, spoken and signed, in such a way that the benefits of both are optimized

circuit of culture, the circuit formed by the five major cultural processes of representation, identity, production, consumption and regulation

cochlear implants, surgical implants which electrically stimulate the auditory nerve directly to induce a sensation of hearing

collective empowerment, the process by which groups of people who lack power struggle against oppression by those who have power

collectivism, societies in which people are integrated into strong, cohesive in-groups which demand unquestioning loyalty in exchange for the group's protection are called collectivist societies. They emphasize 'we' consciousness and stress collective identity, emotional dependence, group solidarity, sharing, duties and obligations

community has a number of definitions but here it is used in a sociological sense to describe a collective of people – community members – who share and identify with a common experience of deafness and/or disability. The disability movement, as a social movement (q.v.) is part of a disability community but not all members of the community are part of the movement

contingencies, associations or relationships

cued speech, a system of hand signs designed to complement speech

cybernetics, the science of communications and automatic control systems in both machines and people

Deaf/deaf, a convention which was developed to distinguish people who see themselves as part of a linguistic and cultural minority (Deaf people) and people who see deafness as a hearing loss or hearing impairment

deconstruction, the analysis of a piece of text to reveal the discourses and conflicts which operate within it

différance, the meaning of something is always both dependent on its difference from something else and on how it is related to something else. For example, the meaning of strength only emerges from its relationship to weakness but we can still think of strength as being different from weakness

disciplinary power, where people are disciplined or controlled by freely subjecting themselves, often in ignorance, to the scrutiny of others and to their own self-scrutiny

discourse can be used to refer to the language interaction which occurs between people, or to the way in which people create and use language to construct someone or something in a particular way and to convey specific meanings

discourse analysis, the analysis of a piece of text, which can be anything which can be 'read' for meaning such as bodies, facial expressions, emotions, pictures, images, buildings and so on. This is done in order to expose the discourses which are operating within it or the structural properties of the language that is used (linguistics) and to show what makes the language effective (rhetorical power) when used in a particular way

egocentric concept of personhood, the individualist (q.v.) perception of personhood

emancipatory research, research which conceptualizes disability as a political problem and has at its base the principles of reciprocity, gain and empowerment, which are achieved through encouraging self-reflection and a deeper understanding of the research process by those who are being researched

empirical positivism, the belief that we can only know what we can immediately apprehend, so things and people exist only when we perceive them to exist

epistemology, the philosophy of knowledge, what it is and how it is obtained

error analysis, a system of analysis where a set of criteria are set up in advance of analysis to represent some norm against which the characteristics of a person can be compared to see whether and, if so, how they deviate from the norm. For example the spoken language of deaf people might be compared with 'normal' speech and analysed for mistakes

essentialism, the belief that people and things have an essential, inherent nature which can be discovered

false consciousness, a Marxist term which refers to social awareness which is mystified by ideology (q.v.) and ignorant of its own reality

Gemeinschaft, a community tradition where collective trust, cooperation and conservatism were dominant factors in relationships between people and where subsistence economies, largely determined by ecology, were important

genetic engineering, the process of identifying genes which are responsible for serious illnesses, birth defects or impairments and replacing them with 'healthy' genes

Gesellschaft, a community tradition where the relationships were contractual and fuelled by the law of supply and demand and where market economies, created by human intervention, were important

hegemony, the means whereby a politically dominant class maintains its position by force, the threat of force and by consent by creating and recreating particular notions of disability and deafness, for example, through a network of institutions, social relations and ideas

hermeneutics, the philosophy of interpretation of texts

historicity, the belief that the nature of any phenomenon can only be explained and understood by contextualizing it within the process of historical development

identity can be described in two main ways: the personal and the sociocultural. Descriptions of the personal are used mainly by psychologists to describe who someone *is* and what makes them unique or authentic, whereas sociocultural descriptions focus on how identity is socially and culturally constructed or produced in such a way that it cannot be seen as fixed

ideology, a sociological concept which is used to describe the way in which power relations, between oppressor and oppressed, for example, can be obscured by discourses. It is sometimes described in terms of false consciousness (q.v.)

inclusion, the process of social and/or educational integration (q.v.) where everyone, whether disabled or not, deaf or hearing, is able to participate, to engage in self-expression and to determine collectively norms, codes of behaviour and the necessity for change

individualism, societies in which individuals are viewed as separate, discrete units and where autonomy, emotional independence, individual initiative, self-sufficiency are emphasized are said to be individualist. They stress 'I' consciousness

individuation, the social consequence of the multiplication and segregation of roles available to and to some extent forced upon the individual

integration, the process of educating disabled and deaf children alongside non-disabled and non-deaf children in mainstream schools according to hearing and non-disabled norms and codes of behaviour. The emphasis is therefore on deaf and disabled children 'fitting' into a preconceived and often experientially irrelevant framework

internalized oppression, the internalization of oppressive norms, values and practices from the dominant culture by the oppressed and their use in self-discipline, self-abuse and self-oppression

intersubjective theory of meaning, the theory developed by Wittgenstein, which described how meaning is created through relationships between 'subjectivities' or people

intrapreneurialism, the means by which organizations can retain creativity and innovation by creating an infrastructure which rewards entrepreneurial behaviour and protects employees from financial ruin which failure can bring

knowledge worker, a worker who has the ability to apply their knowledge to specific situations, and tailor their skills to the context of the job

legitimation, cultural, the process by which some knowledges or discourses find greater favour than others in a given culture

liberal humanism, serves as a foundation for individualism; it assumes that individuals are rational, able to use reason to make personal choices and that they should be given individual rights to choose freely and define their own goals

liminal, a person who lives between two communities and is a part of neither is said to be living a liminal existence

loop system, an electronic system which when used in combination with a hearing aid can enable the user to focus on and amplify sound within the loop, thus cutting out interference from background noise

materialism, the view that everything can be viewed in terms of physical and/or structural properties; historical materialism proposes that what is fundamental to human history is the productive powers of society and their tendency to grow

metanarrative, all embracing world-view

metaphysics, a branch of philosophy which is concerned with the features of ultimate reality, what really exists and what it is that distinguishes that and makes it possible

mind–body doctrines, different accounts of how mental processes are related to bodily states and processes and what happens when they come together

minicom, a telecommunications device which enables text to be sent down the telephone line in exactly the same way as speech to another minicom user

multiple oppression is sometimes used interchangeably with simultaneous oppression (q.v.). It also refers to the experience of oppression in relation to a number of power differentials based on race, gender, sexuality, disability for example, but generally assumes that the effects of these oppressions are additive and accumulative rather than interactive and complex

nature–nurture, the debate about whether characteristics are inborn or whether they are developed as a result of social processes

neuronal plasticity, the specialization for and localization of specific neurological functions in the central nervous system, and the extent to which these functions can be modified by environmental stimulation

non-manual signs, facial expressions or body postures which convey specific meanings or add meaning to the signed component of sign language

oppression, the process by which power imbalances are created and maintained in society and culture which disadvantage some groups when compared to others

organic is taken from the distinction made by Gramsci between structural or positional (q.v.) intellectuals and organic intellectuals. Organic, here, refers to having subjective, personal 'insider' experience of deafness and/or disability which gives an organic perspective to the development and control of ideas and theories about deafness and disability. It could be said, for example, that the social model (q.v.) of disability is an organic theory because it grew directly from the experiences of disabled people

Other, in anthropology, refers to the West's encounter with non-Western cultures in a way which diminishes the latter and keeps the former intact; can also be used in a broader sense to refer to characteristics or states which are 'other than'; for example, death, madness or the unconscious

Palantype, *see* speech-to-text reporting

paradigm, a pattern of beliefs or ideas

participatory world-view, a world-view which fully acknowledges the interconnectedness between the knower and what is known or the researcher and the researched, for example, and argues that this must be the value base for human inquiry. It therefore seeks to challenge notions of fragmentation and separation such as those which arise from essentialist (q.v.) perspectives and empirical positivism (q.v.)

person-centred counselling, a form of counselling developed by Carl Rogers which has a fundamentally optimistic view of the person, believing that most people have inner resources to deal with life's problems but are not always able to tap these resources. Counsellors place the client centre-stage through the development of empathy, unconditional warmth and genuineness

phenomenology, a theory of knowledge which makes a clear distinction between perceptual and abstract properties, and has strong links to essentialism (q.v.) and idealism – the belief that only minds and their ideas exist

pluralism refers to varieties of humans, individual characteristics, beliefs, ideas, values and so on

positional relates to Gramsci's term 'positional intellectuals'. Positional intellectuals are, for example, non-deaf, non-disabled intellectuals who develop and control ideas and theory about deafness and disability from a positional or outsider perspective

positioning, where we place ourselves in relation to particular ideas, theories or discourses

postmodernism hinges on the celebration of the multiplicity of perspectives, all of which are seen to be equally valid, alongside the rejection of all-embracing theories or truths

poststructuralism, the rejection of structuralism (q.v.) and, in linguistics, the emphasis on the evolving, shifting and contestable nature of meaning

pragmatics, the branch of linguistics dealing with language in use

praxis characterizes the approach of political theorists in studying and influencing the role of free creative activity in changing and shaping ethical, social, political and economic life along humanistic socialist lines

reductionism, in the philosophy of mind is the claim that facts about mentality can be reduced to physical or material facts: for example mental properties can be defined in terms of particular behaviours or behavioural dispositions

reification, the materialization of people or conversion of them into something which can be described in materialist (q.v.) terms

relativism, the view that there can be no ultimate truth and therefore that all perspectives are equally valid

semantics, the branch of linguistics which deals with meaning

simultaneous oppression, oppression on the grounds of more than one power differential, for example, race *and* gender, or disability *and* sexuality

social constructionism takes a critical stance towards taken-for-granted knowledge. It believes that the ways in which we understand the world produce culturally and historically specific knowledges, which are constructed between people in different ways and therefore invite different kinds of social action

Social Darwinism, the practice of interpreting human social phenomena in terms of Darwin's evolutionary theory, of which the most commonly used element was the view of the economy as a competitive arena in which only the 'fittest' would survive

social model of disability separates disability from impairment. It hinges on the belief that disability is a sociocultural creation and that the experience of oppression is a function of disability, not impairment

social movement, new, a social grouping usually formed around marginalized political goals which critically evaluates the dominant society, sets out how society might change and raises issues which transcend national boundaries

sociocentric concept of personhood, the collectivist (q.v.) perception of personhood

sociotechnology, technology which is employed in or is a part of social processes

sovereign power, where people are disciplined and controlled by overt coercion, punishment or death

speech reading (lip reading) attempts to understand the spoken word through reading mouth patterns. A large amount of speech reading is guesswork because only a small proportion of speech sounds can be distinguished by these patterns

speech-to-text reporting, the practice of providing a verbatim text transcript of the spoken word which is projected onto a screen and can then be read by the deaf person. Common types include the use of Palantype and Hi-Linc systems

structuralism, the belief in and search for underlying explanations of, for example, society, human thought or behaviour

subaltern, a marginalized Other

syntactics, the study of syntax or the kinds of expression in a language, and the rules which govern how they combine together

the turn to culture, the upsurge in interest in cultural processes as a result of substantive (matters which have empirical substance) and epistemological (q.v.) factors, which are now viewed as being equally important to economic and political processes

total communication, a philosophy of deaf education which aims to maximize communicative choice by developing skills in as many communication systems as possible

Typetalk, the National Telephone Relay Service based in Liverpool which enables two people with dissimilar telecommunications facilities to contact each other via a third party, the Typetalk operator, who can either voice-over incoming minicom messages or type incoming voice messages on minicom and relay these messages to the receiver

utilitarianism, an approach to morality which sees pleasure or the satisfaction of desire as the only element of human good and regards the morality of actions as entirely dependent on their consequences for human well-being

References

Abberley, P. (1991) The significance of the OPCS disability surveys, in M. Oliver (ed.) *Social Work: Disabled People and Disabling Environments*. London: Jessica Kingsley.

Abel Smith, A., Irving, J. and Brown, P. (1993) Counselling in the medical context, in W. Dryden, D. Charles-Edwards and R. Woolfe (eds) *Handbook of Counselling in Britain*. London: Routledge.

Albrecht, G. L. (1992) *The Disability Business: Rehabilitation in America*. Newbury Park, CA: Sage Publications.

Alderson, P. (1993) *Children's Consent to Surgery*. Buckingham: Open University Press.

Aldrich, H. E. (1992) Incommensurable paradigms? Vital signs from three perspectives, in M. Reed and M. Hughes (eds) *Rethinking Organization*. London: Sage.

Allport, G. (1954) *The Nature of Prejudice*. Reading, MA: Addison-Wesley.

Archard, D. (1993) *Children; Rights and Childhood*. London: Routledge.

Atterhed, S. G. (1985) Intrapreneurship: the way forward? in D. Clutterbuck (ed.) *New Patterns of Work*. Aldershot: Gower.

Barnes, C. (1992) *Disabling Imagery and the Media: An Exploration of Media Representations of Disabled People*. Belper: The British Council of Organizations of Disabled People.

Barnes. C. (1996a) Disability and the myth of the independent researcher, *Disability and Society*, 11(1): 107–10.

Barnes, C. (1996b) Theories of disability and the origins of the oppression of disabled people in western society, in L. Barton (ed.) *Disability and Society: Emerging Issues and Insights*. Harlow: Longman.

Barton, L. (ed.) (1996) *Disability and Society: Emerging Issues and Insights*. Harlow: Longman.

Bateson, G. (1972) *Steps to an Ecology of Mind*. NewYork: Chandler.

Bauman, Z. (1992) *Mortality, Immortality and Other Life Strategies*. Cambridge: Polity Press.

Bayliss, P. and Thacker, J. (1995) Personal-social education for children with special educational needs, in R. Best, P. Lang, C. Lodge and C. Watkins (eds) *Pastoral Care and Personal-Social Education*. London: Cassell.

Begum. N. (1992) Disabled women and the feminist agenda, *Feminist Review*, 40: 70–84.

Bhaskar, R. (1979) *The Possibility of Naturalism: A Critique of the Contemporary Human Sciences*. Brighton: Harvester Press.

Bochner, J. H. and Albertini, J. A. (1988) Language varieties in the deaf population and their acquisition by deaf children and adults, in M. Strong (ed.) *Language Learning and Deafness*. Cambridge: Cambridge University Press.

Bones, C. (1994) *The Self-Reliant Manager*. London: Routledge.

Braden, J. (1994) *Deafness Deprivation and IQ*. NewYork: Plenum.

Brah, A. (1992) Difference, diversity and differentiation, in A. Rattansi and J. Donald (eds) *Race, Culture and Difference*. London: Sage Publications and The Open University.

Brechin, A. and Walmsley, J. (1989) *Making Connections: Reflecting on the Lives and Experiences of People with Learning Difficulties*. London: Hodder and Stoughton.

British Deaf Association (1996) *Education Policy*. Carlisle: British Deaf Association.

Brown, R. (1986) *Social Psychology*, 2nd edn. NewYork: Free Press.

Brown, R. H. (1994) Reconstructing social theory after the postmodern critique, in H. W. Simons and M. Billig (eds) *After Postmodernism*. London: Sage Publications.

Bumiller, E. (1991) *May You Be the Mother of a Hundred Sons: A Journey among the Women of India*. Calcutta: Penguin Books India.

Burr, V. (1995) *An Introduction to Social Constructionism*. London: Routledge.

Butler, J. (1993) *Bodies that Matter*. London: Routledge.

Campbell, J. and Oliver, M. (eds) (1996) *Disability Politics: Understanding Our Past, Changing Our Future*. London: Routledge.

Carroll, L. (1865) *Alice's Adventures in Wonderland*. London: Macmillan.

Carroll, L. (1872) *Through the Looking-Glass*. London: Macmillan.

Chadwick, A. (1996) Knowledge, power and the Disability Discrimination Bill, *Disability and Society*, 11(1): 25–40.

Chang, J. (1991) *Wild Swans: Three Daughters of China*. London: HarperCollins.

Cheney, G. (1987) On communicative praxis and the realisation of our discipline's potential. Paper presented to the Central States Speech Communication Association, Columbus, OH.

Christiansen, J. B. and Barnarrt, S. N. (1995) *Deaf President Now! The 1988 Revolution at Gallaudet University*. Washington, DC: Gallaudet University Press.

Clegg, S. R. (1989) *Frameworks of Power*. London: Sage.

Clifford, J. (1994) Diasporas, *Cultural Anthropology*, 9: 302–38.

Coleman, L. M. and DePaulo, B. M. (1991) Uncovering the human spirit: moving beyond disability and 'missed' communications, in N. Coupland, H. Giles and J. M. Wiemann (eds) *'Miscommunication' and Problematic Talk*. Newbury Park, CA: Sage Publications.

Connors, J. L. and Donnellan, A. M. (1993) Citizenship and culture: the role of disabled people in Navajo society, *Disability, Handicap and Society*, 8(3): 265–80.

Corbett, J. (1989) The quality of life in the 'independence' curriculum, *Disability Handicap and Society*, 4(2): 145–63.

Corbett, J. (1994) A proud label: exploring the relationship between disability politics and gay pride, *Disability and Society*, 9(3): 343–57.

Corbett, J. (1996) *Bad Mouthing: The Language of Special Education*. London: The Falmer Press.

Corker, M. (1982) 'The relationship between auditory perception and ascriptive language use in hearing and hearing impaired individuals', unpublished MPhil thesis, University of East Anglia, Norwich.

Corker, M. (1989a) *A Mockery of Needs? Parents' Experiences of Assessment, Statementing/recording and Appeals under the Education Act 1981 and the Education (Scotland) Act 1981*. London: National Deaf Children's Society.

Corker, M. (1989b) *What about Me? A Guide for Mainstream Teachers with Deaf Children in their Classes*. London: National Deaf Children's Society.

Corker, M. (1989c) Deaf–hearing integration: bridging the gap within, *Deafness*, 3(5): 4–5.

Corker, M. (1990) *Deaf Perspectives on Psychology, Language and Communication*. Coventry: NATED/Skill.

Corker, M. (1993a) Integration and deaf people: the policy and power of enabling environments, in J. Swain, V. Finkelstein, S. French and M. Oliver (eds) *Disabling Barriers – Enabling Environments*. London: Sage Publications in association with The Open University.

Corker, M. (1993b) An open letter to the powers that be, *Disability, Handicap and Society*, 8(3): 317–28.

Corker, M. (1994a) *Counselling – The Deaf Challenge*. London: Jessica Kingsley.

Corker, M. (1994b) The cloak of denial, *Deafness*, 10(2): 4–11.

Corker, M. (1994c) *A Consultative Policy Document for a Unified Service to Deaf Children and their Families in Lincolnshire*. Lincolnshire: Lincolnshire Deaf Services.

Corker, M. (1995a) 'Bimodal communication and interpreting – oral anarchy or linguistic oppression', unpublished paper given at Issues in Interpreting 2 Conference, University of Durham.

Corker, M. (1995b) Mental health services and counselling – are they the same? *Deafness*, 11(3): 9–15.

Corker, M. (1996a) Personal-social education for deaf children and young people: changing concepts of need and creating caring communities, *Journal of The British Association of Teachers of the Deaf*, January: 9–21.

Corker, M. (1996b) *Deaf Transitions*. London: Jessica Kingsley.

Corker, M. (1996c) Inside out or outside in? Language, culture and inclusion. Paper presented to ESRC-funded seminars *Disability Dialogues and Theory*, London, October 1996.

Coupland, N. and Nussbaum, J. F. (1993) *Discourse and Lifespan Identity*. London: Sage Publications.

Crow, L. (1996) Including all of our lives: renewing the social model of disability, in J. Morris (ed.) *Encounters with Strangers*. London: Women's Press.

Crystal, D. (1987) *The Cambridge Encyclopaedia of Language*. Cambridge: Cambridge University Press.

Dallos, R. (1991) *Family Belief Systems: Therapy and Change*. Buckingham: Open University Press.

Dalrymple, J. and Burke, B. (1995) *Anti-Oppressive Practice: Social Care and the Law*. Buckingham: Open University Press.

Davis, K. (1990) The crafting of good clients, *Coalition*, September: 5–9.

Davis, L. (1995) *Enforcing Normalcy: Disability, Deafness and the Body*. London: Verso.

Denmark, J. C. (1994) *Deafness and Mental Health*. London: Jessica Kingsley.

Derrida, J. (1974) *Of Grammatology*. Baltimore, MD: Johns Hopkins University Press.

Derrida, J. (1978) *Writing and Difference*. Chicago: University of Chicago Press.

Derrida, J. (1981) *Dissemination*. Chicago: University of Chicago Press.

Dimmock, A. (1980) Chairman's report to the Second Convention of the National Union of the Deaf, *Report of the Second Convention*. Guildford: NUD.

Dimmock, A. (1986) Chairman's report to the Fifth Convention of the National Union of the Deaf, *Report of the Fifth Convention*. Guildford: NUD.

Doyal, L. and Gough, I. (1991) *A Theory of Human Need*. Basingstoke: Macmillan.

Doyle, B. J. (1996) *Disability Discrimination: The New Law*. Bristol: Jordans.

Drucker, P. F. (1977) *People and Performance: The Best of Peter Drucker on Management*. New York: Harper and Row.

du Gay, P., Hall, S., Janes, L., Mackay, H. and Negus, K. (1997) *Doing Cultural Studies: The Story of the Sony Walkman*. London: Sage Publications in association with The Open University.

Dworkin, R. (1977) *Taking Rights Seriously*. Cambridge, MA: Harvard University Press.

East, P. (1995) *Counselling in Medical Settings*. Buckingham: Open University Press.

Elton, F. A. (1996) Cross cultural communication between Deaf and hearing people. Paper presented at the conference *Deaf and Disabled People: Towards a New Understanding*, organized by the Policy Studies Institute and the Alliance of Deaf Service Users and Providers. London, December.

Emanuel, J. and Ackroyd, D. (1996) Breaking down barriers, in C. Barnes and G. Mercer (eds) *Exploring the Divide*. Leeds: The Disability Press.

Erikson, E. H. (1959) Identity and the life cycle, *Psychological Monographs* (Monograph 1). New York: International Universities Press.

Fairclough, N. (1992) *Discourse and Social Change*. Cambridge: Polity Press.

Fairclough, N. (1993) Discourse and social change in the enterprise culture, in B. Graddol, L. Thompson and M. Byram (eds) *Language and Culture*. Clevedon: British Association for Applied Linguistics in association with Multilingual Matters, 44–54.

Fancher, R. T. (1995) *Cultures of Healing: Correcting the Image of American Mental Health Care*. New York: W. H. Freeman.

Featherstone, M. (1990) Global culture: an introduction, *Theory, Culture and Society*, 7(2/3): 1–14.

Feinberg, J. (1973) *Social Philosophy*. New York: Prentice-Hall.

Fenton, D. (1989) *Passivity to Empowerment*. London: RADAR.

Fineman, S. (ed.) (1993) *Emotion in Organizations*. London: Sage.

Finkelstein, V. (1996) From an interview in J. Campbell and M. Oliver (eds) *Disability Politics: Understanding Our Past, Changing Our Future*. London: Routledge.

Finkelstein, V. and Stuart, O. (1996) Developing new services, in G. Hales (ed.) *Beyond Disability*. London: Sage Publications, in association with The Open University.

Firestein, D. (1996) *Bisexuality*. London: Sage Publications.

Fishman, J. (1982) A critique of six papers on the socialisation of the deaf child, in J. B. Christiansen (ed.) *Conference Highlights: National Research Conference on the Social Aspects of Deafness*. Washington, DC: Gallaudet College, 6–20.

Fishman, J. (1989) *Language and Ethnicity in Minority Sociolinguistic Perspective*. Clevedon: Multilingual Matters.

Fitouri, A. (1983) Working with young bilingual children, *Early Child Development and Care*, 10: 283–92.

Foucault, M. (1972) *The Archæology of Knowledge*. London: Tavistock.

Foucault, M. (1978) On power (interview with Pierre Boncenne), ed. L. D. Kritzman (1988) *Michel Foucault, Politics Philosophy and Culture: Interviews and Other Writings 1977–1984*. London: Routledge.

Foucault, M. (1976) *The History of Sexuality: An Introduction*. Harmondsworth: Penguin.

Foucault, M. (1979) *Discipline and Punish*. Harmondsworth: Penguin.

Franklin, B. (1995) *The Handbook of Children's Rights: Comparative Policy and Practice*. London: Routledge.

French, S. (1992) Equal opportunities? The problem of time, *New Beacon*, 76(1) March: 97–8.

French, S. (1993) Disability, impairment or something in between? in J. Swain,

V. Finkelstein, S. French and M. Oliver (eds) *Disabling Barriers – Enabling Environments*. London: Sage Publications in association with The Open University.

French, S. (ed.) (1994) *On Equal Terms: Working with Disabled People*. Oxford: Butterworth-Heinemann.

Frost, P. J., Moore, L. F., Louis, M. R., Lundberg, C. C. and Martin, J. (1985) *Organizational Culture*. Beverly Hills, CA: Sage.

Further Education Funding Council (1996) *Inclusive Learning: Report of the Learning Difficulties and/or Disabilities Committee* [The Tomlinson Report]. London: HMSO.

Fuss, D. (1989) *Essentially Speaking*. London: Routledge.

Geertz, C. (1973) *The Interpretation of Cultures*. New York: Basic Books.

Gergen, K. J. (1989) Warranting voice and the elaboration of the self, in J. Shotter and K. J. Gergen (eds) *Texts of Identity*. London: Sage.

Gergen, K. J. (1992) Organization theory in the postmodern era, in M. Reed and M. Hughes (eds) *Rethinking Organization*. London: Sage.

Gergen, K. J. (1996) The healthy, happy human being wears many masks, in W. Truett Anderson (ed.) *The Fontana Post-Modernism Reader*. London: Fontana.

Gergen, K. J. and Kaye, J. (1992) Beyond narrative in the negotiation of a therapeutic meaning, in S. McNamee and K. J. Gergen (eds) *Therapy as Social Construction*. London: Sage Publications.

Gill, D., Mayor, B. and Blair, M. (eds) (1992) *Racism and Education: Structures and Strategies*. London: Sage Publications in association with The Open University.

Gillespie-Sells, K. (1994) Getting things right, *Community Care Inside*, 31 March.

Gilligan, C. (1984) *In a Difference Voice: Psychological Theory and Women's Development*. Cambridge, MA: Harvard University Press.

Goffman, E. (1968) *Stigma: Notes on the Management of Spoiled Identity*. London: Penguin.

Golan, L. (1995) *Reading Between the Lips*. Chicago: Bonus Books.

Gooding, C. (1996) *Blackstone's Guide to the Disability Discrimination Act, 1995*. London: Blackstone Press.

Gramsci, A. (1971) *Selections from the Prison Notebooks*, ed. and trans. Q. Hoare and G. Nowell Smith. London: Lawrence and Wishart.

Gregory, S. (1995) *Deaf Futures Revisited*, Block 3, Unit 10, Course D251, Issues in Deafness. Milton Keynes: The Open University.

Gregory, S, and Bishop, J. (1989) The integration of deaf children into mainstream schools: a research report, *Journal of the British Association of Teachers of the Deaf*, 13(1): 1–6.

Griffin, S. (1984) Split culture, in S. Kumar (ed.) *The Schumacher Lectures Volume II*. London: Abacus.

Groce, N. E. (1985) *Everyone Here Spoke Sign Language: Hereditary Deafness on Martha's Vineyard*. London: Harvard University Press.

Grossberg, L. (1996) Identity and cultural studies, in S. Hall and P. du Gay (eds) *Questions of Cultural Identity*. London: Sage Publications, 87–107.

Habermas, J. (1977) Hannah Arendt's communications concept of power, *Social Research*, 44(1): 3–24.

Hall, E. T. (1994) Deaf culture, tacit culture and ethnic relations, in C. J. Erting, R. C. Johnson, D. L. Smith and B. D. Snider (eds) *The Deaf Way: Perspectives from the International Conference on Deaf Culture*. Washington, DC: Gallaudet University Press.

Hall, S. (1991) The local and the global: globalisation and ethnicity, in A. King (ed.) *Culture, Globalisation and the World-System*. London: Macmillan, 19–39.

Hall, S. (1996) Introduction: who needs identity? in S. Hall and P. du Gay (eds) *Questions of Cultural Identity*. London: Sage Publications.

Hall, S. (ed.) (1997) *Representation, Cultural Representations and Signifying Practices.* London: Sage Publications in association with The Open University.

Harré, R. (1981) The positivist-empiricist approach and its alternative, in P. Reason and J. Rowan (eds) *Human Enquiry: A Sourcebook of New Paradigm Research.* Chichester: John Wiley.

Harré, R. and Gillett, G. (1994) *The Discursive Mind.* London: Sage Publications.

Harris, J. (1995) *The Cultural Meaning of Deafness.* Aldershot: Avebury.

Harris, P. L. (1994) *Children and Emotion.* Oxford: Blackwell.

Harvey, D. (1989) *The Condition of Post-Modernity.* Oxford: Basil Blackwell.

Hearn, J. (1987) *The Gender of Oppression: Men, Masculinity and the Critique of Marxism.* Brighton: Wheatsheaf.

Hearn, J. and Parkin, W. (1993) Organizations, multiple oppressions and postmodernism, in J. Hassard and M. Parker (eds) *Postmodernism and Organizations.* London: Sage.

Hearne, K. (1991) Disabled lesbians and gays are here to stay, in T. Kaufman and P. Lincoln (eds) *High Risk Lives: Lesbian and Gay Politics after the Clause.* Bridport: Prism Press.

Heartfield, J. (1993) Why children's rights are wrong, *Living Marxism*, October: 13–15.

Herdt, G. (1993) *Third Sex, Third Gender: Beyond Sexual Dimorphism in Culture and History.* NewYork: Zone Books.

Hevey, D. (1992) *The Creatures that Time Forgot.* London: Routledge.

Hill, M. (1992) Conference address, in *Race and Disability: A Dialogue for Action.* London: Greater London Association of Disabled People.

Hoffman, E. (1989) *Lost in Translation.* NewYork: Minerva.

Honey, S., Meager, N. and Williams, M. (1993) *Employers' Attitudes towards People with Disabilities.* Brighton: Institute of Manpower Studies, Report 245.

Hugman, R. (1991) *Power in Caring Professions.* Basingstoke: Macmillan.

Ingstad, B. and Reynolds-Whyte, S. (1995) *Disability and Culture.* Berkeley, CA: University of California Press.

Kagitçibasi, Ç. (1995) A critical appraisal of individualism and collectivism: Towards a new formulation, in U. Kim, H. C. Triandis, Ç. Kagitçibasi, S-C. Choi and G.Yoon (eds) *Individualism and Collectivism.* Thousand Oaks, CA: Sage Publications.

Katz, I. (1996) *The Construction of Racial Identity in Children of Mixed Parentage.* London: Jessica Kingsley.

Kaufman, W. (1950) *Nietzsche: Philosopher, Psychologist, Anti-Christ.* Princeton, NJ: Princeton University Press.

Kenyon, D. (1994) Reaction–interaction, in L. Keith (ed.) *Mustn't Grumble.* London: Women's Press.

Kim, U. (1995) Individualism and collectivism: conceptual clarification and collaboration, in U. Kim, H. C. Triandis, Ç. Kagitçibasi, S.-C. Choi and G.Yoon (eds) *Individualism and Collectivism.* Thousand Oaks, CA: Sage Publications.

King Jordan, I. (1992) Language and change, in M. D. Garretson (ed.) *Viewpoints on Deafness: A Deaf American Monograph,* Vol. 42. Silver Spring, MD: National Association of the Deaf.

Kleinman, A. (1980) *Patients and Healers in the Context of Culture.* Berkeley, CA: University of California Press.

Kritzman, L. G. (ed.) (1988) *Michel Foucault, Politics, Philosophy and Culture: Interviews and Other Writings 1977–1984.* London: Routledge.

Kyle, J. G. (1991) *The Deaf Community,* Block 1, Unit 2, Course D251, Issues in Deafness. Milton Keynes: The Open University.

Kyle, J. G. (1996) Issues of deaf–hearing professional relationships, in C. Laurenzi and S. Ridgeway (eds) *Progress through Equality: New Perspectives in the Field of Mental Health and Deafness*. London: British Society of Mental Health and Deafness.

Laclau, E. (1983) The impossibility of society, *Canadian Journal of Political and Social Theory*, 7: 21–4.

Laclau, E. (1990) *New Reflections of the Revolution of Our Time*. London: Verso.

Ladd, P. (1992) Deaf cultural studies – towards an end to internal strife, in M. D. Garretson (ed.) *Viewpoints on Deafness: A Deaf American Monograph*, Vol. 42. Silver Spring, MD: National Association of the Deaf.

Ladd, P. (1994) Deaf culture: finding it and nurturing it, in C. Erting, R. C. Johnson, D. L. Smith and B. D. Snider (eds) *The Deaf Way: Perspectives from the International Conference on Deaf Culture*. Washington, DC : Gallaudet University Press.

Ladd, P. (1996) from an interview, in M. Oliver and J. Campbell (eds) *Disability Politics: Understanding Our Past, Changing Our Future*. London: Routledge.

Ladd, P. and John, M. (1991) *Deaf People as a Minority Group: The Political Process*, Block 3, Unit 9, Course D251, Issues in Deafness. Milton Keynes: The Open University.

Lane, H. (1992) *The Mask of Benevolence: Disabling the Deaf Community*. New York: Alfred Knopf.

Lane, H. (1995) Constructions of deafness, *Disability and Society*, 10(2): 171–90.

Lane, H., Hoffmeister, R. and Bahan, B. (1996) *A Journey into the DEAF-WORLD*. San Diego, CA: DawnSign Press.

Lang, P. (1995) International perspectives on pastoral care (affective education), in R. Best, P. Lang, C. Lodge and C. Watkins (eds) *Pastoral Care and Personal-Social Education: Entitlement and Provision*. London: Cassell.

Latour, B. (1991) Technology is society made durable, in J. Law (ed.) *A Sociology of Monsters*. London: Routledge.

Lee, R. A. (1990) There is nothing so useful as an 'appropriate theory', in D. C. Wilson and R. H. Rosenfeld (eds) *Managing Organizations: Texts, Readings and Cases*. London: McGraw-Hill.

Levine, E. S. (1981) *The Ecology of Early Deafness*. Columbia, NY: Columbia University Press.

Liggett, H. (1988) Stars are not born: an interpretative approach to the politics of disability, *Disability, Handicap and Society*, 3(3): 263–76.

Llwellyn-Jones, M. (1991) Bilingualism and the education of deaf children, in S. Gregory and G. M. Hartley (eds) *Constructing Deafness*. London: Pinter Publishers in association with The Open University.

Lukes, S. (1974) *Power: A Radical View*. London: Macmillan.

Lynas, W. (1994) *Communication Options in the Education of Deaf Children*. London: Whurr.

Magee, B. and Milligan, M. (1995) *On Blindness*. Oxford: Oxford University Press.

Marcia, J. E. (1994) The empirical study of ego identity, in H. A. Bosma, T. L. G. Graafsma, H. D. Grotevant and D. J. de Levita (eds) *Identity and Development: An Interdisciplinary Approach*. London: Sage Publications.

Maryanski, A. and Turner, J. H. (1992) *The Social Cage: Human Nature and the Evolution of Society*. Stanford, CA: Stanford University Press.

Maxwell, M., Bernstein, M. E. and Mear, K. M. (1991) Bimodal language production, in P. Siple and S. D. Fischer (eds) *Theoretical Issues in Sign Language Research, Vol. 2, Psychology*. Chicago: University of Chicago Press.

McLeod, J. (1993) *An Introduction to Counselling*. Buckingham: Open University Press.

McNay, L. (1992) *Foucault and Feminism*. Cambridge: Polity Press.

Mearns, D. and Thorne, B. (1988) *Person-Centred Counselling in Action*. London: Sage Publications.

Michael, M. (1996) *Constructing Identities*. London: Sage Publications.

Mill, J. S. (1969) *Utilitarianism*, in M. Warnock (ed.) *Utilitarianism*. London: Fontana

Miller, G. A. (1964) *The Psychology of Communication*. Baltimore, MD: Penguin Books.

Miller, J. G. (1984) Culture and the development of everyday social explanation, *Journal of Personality and Social Psychology*, 46: 961–78.

Mithaug, D. E. (1996) *Equal Opportunity Theory*. London: Sage Publications.

Montgomery, G. (1996) *Oceans Divide Us: The Experience of Deaf and Hearing Minorities at Work in America and Britain*. Edinburgh: Scottish Workshop Publications.

Montgomery, G. (1997) Review of 'Progress through Equality', *Deaf Worlds*, 13(1): 30–1.

Montgomery, G. and Laidlaw, K. (1993) *Occupational Dissonance and Discrimination in the Employment of Deaf People*. Edinburgh: Scottish Workshop Publications.

Moorhead, D. (1995) Knowing who I am, in S. Gregory (ed.) *Deaf Futures Revisited*, Block 3, Unit 10, Course D251, Issues in Deafness. Milton Keynes: The Open University.

Morris, J. (1991) *Pride Against Prejudice*. London: Women's Press.

Morris, J. (1992a) Personal and political: a feminist perspective on researching physical disability, *Disability, Handicap and Society*, 7(2): 157–66.

Morris, J. (1992b) *Disabled Lives*. London: BBC Educational Publications.

Morris, J. (ed.) (1996) *Encounters with Strangers: Feminism and Disability*. London: Women's Press.

Murphy, R. F. (1987) *The Body Silent*. New York: Henry Holt.

Murphy, R. F., Scheer, J., Murphy, Y. and Mack, R. (1988) Physical disability and social liminality: a study of the rituals of adversity, *Social Science and Medicine*, 26(2): 235–42.

Oliver, M. (1990) *The Politics of Disablement*. Basingstoke: Macmillan and St Martin's Press.

Oliver, M. (1996) *Understanding Disability: From Theory to Practice*. Basingstoke: Macmillan.

Padden, C. (1989) The Deaf community and the culture of Deaf people (1980), in S. Wilcox (ed.) *American Deaf Culture: An Anthology*. Silver Spring, MD: Linstok Press.

Padden, C. and Humphries, T. (1988) *Deaf in America: Voices from a Culture*. Cambridge, MA: Harvard University Press.

Parkinson, R. (1995) *Ideas and Realities of Emotion*. London: Routledge.

Peters, S. (1996) The politics of disability identity, in L. Barton (ed) *Disability and Society: Emerging Issues and Insights*. London: Longman.

Preston, P. (1994) *Mother Father Deaf: Living between Sound and Silence*. Cambridge, MA: Harvard University Press.

Putnam, L. L. and Mumby, D. K. (1993) Organizations, emotion and the myth of rationality, in S. Fineman (ed.) *Emotion in Organizations*. London: Sage.

Rawls, J. (1971) *A Theory of Justice*. Cambridge, MA: Belknap.

Reason, P. (1994) *Participation in Human Enquiry*. London: Sage Publications.

Reid, C. (1994) Voice-over training needed, *British Deaf News*, February: 19.

Ricœur, P. (1986) *Lectures on Ideology and Utopia*, ed. G. H. Taylor. New York: Columbia University Press.

Ricœur, P. (1992) *Oneself as Another*. Chicago: University of Chicago Press.

Riddell, S. (1996) Theorising special educational needs in a changing climate, in L. Barton (ed.) *Disability and Society: Emerging Issues and Insights*. Harlow: Longman.

Rieser, R. and Mason, M. (1991) *Disability Equality in Education: A Human Rights Issue.* London: Disability Equality in Education.

Rogers, C. M. and Wrightsman, L. S. (1978) Attitudes towards children's rights: nurturance or self-determination, *Journal of Social Issues*, 34(2): 41–57.

Rojek, C., Peacock, G. and Collins, S. (1988) *Social Work and Received Ideas.* London: Routledge.

Roscoe, W. (1995) *Queer Spirits: A Gay Man's Myth-Book.* Boston, MA: Beacon.

Rotter, J. B. (1966) Generalised expectancies for internal versus external control of reinforcement, *Psychological Monographs*, 80(1): 609.

Rowe, D. (1995) *Dorothy Rowe's Guide to Life.* London: HarperCollins.

Ruebain, D. (1996) *Notes on the Disability Discrimination Act as at October 1996.* London: David Levene and Co. Solicitors.

Ruesh, J. (1964) Clinical science and communication theory, in D. McK. Rioch and E. A. Winstein (eds) *Disorders of Communication.* Association for Research in Nervous and Mental Disease, Research Publications, Vol. 42. Baltimore, MD: Williams and Wilkins.

Sampson, E. E. (1989) The deconstruction of the self, in J. Shotter and K. J. Gergen (eds) *Texts of Identity.* London: Sage.

Sampson, E. E. (1990) Social psychology and social control, in I. Parker and J. Shotter (eds) *Deconstructing Social Psychology.* London: Routledge.

Saussure, F. de (1974) *Course in General Linguistics.* London: Fontana.

Scanlon, T. (1978) Rights, goals and fairness, in S. Hampshire (ed.) *Public and Private Morality.* Cambridge: Cambridge University Press.

Senge, P. M. (1990) *The Fifth Discipline: The Art and Practice of the Learning Organization.* London: Century Business.

Shakespeare, T. (1992) A response to Liz Crow, *Coalition*, September: 3–4.

Shakespeare, T. (1993) Disabled people's self-organisation: a new social movement? *Disability, Handicap and Society*, 8(3): 249–64.

Shakespeare, T. (1994) Cultural representation of disabled people, *Disability and Society*, 9(3): 283–300.

Shakespeare, T. (1996) Disability, identity, difference, in C. Barnes and G. Mercer (eds) *Exploring the Divide: Illness and Disability.* Leeds: The Disability Press.

Shakespeare, T., Gillespie-Sells, K. and Davies, D. (1996) *The Sexual Politics of Disability.* London: Cassell.

Shweder, R. A. and Bourne, E. J. (1982) Does the concept of the person vary cross-culturally? in A. J. Marsella and G. M. White (eds) *Cultural Conceptions of Mental Health and Therapy.* Dordrecht: Kluwer.

Simon, W. (1996) *Postmodern Sexualities.* London: Routledge.

Simons, H. W. and Billig, M. (1994) *After Postmodernism: Reconstructing Ideology Critique.* London: Sage Publications.

Sinha, D. and Tripathi, R. C. (1995) Individualism in a collectivist culture: a case of coexistence of opposities, in U. Kim, H. C. Triandis, Ç. Kagitçibasi, S.-C. Choi and G.Yoon (eds) *Individualism and Collectivism.* Thousand Oaks, CA: Sage Publications.

Sisson, K. (ed.) (1989) *Personnel Management in Britain.* Oxford: Blackwell.

Smither, R. D. (1988) *The Psychology of Work and Human Performance.* NewYork: Harper-Collins.

Stiegler, B. (1994) *La technique et le temps, 1: La faute d'Epiméthée.* Paris: Galilée. Eng. trans. Richard Beardsworth and George Collins as *Technics and Time, 1: The Fault of Epimetheus.* Stanford, CA: Stanford University Press (forthcoming).

Stohl, C. (1995) *Organizational Communication: Connectedness in Action.* London: Sage.

Strauss, A. (1978) *Negotiations*. San Francisco, CA: Jossey-Bass.

Stuart, O. (1992) Race and disability: just a double oppression? *Disability, Handicap and Society*, 7(2): 177–88.

Taylor, C. (1985) *Philosophy and the Human Sciences: Philosophical Papers* (Vol. 2). Cambridge: Cambridge University Press.

Taylor, G. and Bishop, J. (1991) *Being Deaf: The Experience of Deafness*. London: Pinter Publishers in association with The Open University.

Thompson, M. (1987) *Gay Spirit: Myth and Meaning*. Boston, MA: Alyson.

Thompson, M. (1994) *Gay Soul: Finding the Heart of Gay Spirit and Nature*. Boston, MA: Alyson.

Thoutenhoofd, E. (1997) Vision/deaf: vision as a constitutive element of Deaf communities, *Deaf Worlds*, 13(1): 19–29.

Tizard, B. and Phoenix, A. (1993) *Black, White or Mixed Race*. London: Routledge.

Tönnies, F. (1957) *Community and Society*, ed. and trans. C. P. Loomis. New York: Harper and Row (original work published in 1887).

Turner, B. (ed.) (1990) *Organizational Symbolism*. Berlin: De Gruyter.

Turner, G. H. (1994) How is deaf culture? *Sign Language Studies*, 83(Summer): 103–25.

Turner, V. (1967) *The Forest of Symbols*. Ithaca, NY: Morrow.

Van Deurzen Smith, E. (1988) *Existential Counselling in Action*. London: Sage.

Vasey, S. (1992) A response to Liz Crow, *Coalition*, September: 5–6.

Vernon, A. (1996a) A stranger in many camps: the experience of disabled black and ethnic minority women, in J. Morris (ed.) *Encounters with Strangers*. London: Women's Press.

Vernon, A. (1996b) Fighting two different battles: unity is preferable to enmity, *Disability and Society*, 11(2): 285–90.

Wagner, P. (1995) Schools and pupils: developing their responses to bereavement, in R. Best, P. Lang, C. Lodge and C. Watkins (eds) *Pastoral Care and Personal-Social Education*. London: Cassell.

Walkerdine, V. (1981) Sex, power and pedagogy, *Screen Education*, 38: 14–23.

Walzer, M. (1983) *Spheres of Justice*. New York: Basic Books.

Watzlawick, P., Beavin, J. H. and Jackson, D. D. (1967) *The Pragmatics of Human Communication*. New York: Norton.

Williams, F. (1989) Mental handicap and oppression, in A. Brechin and J. Walmsley (eds) *Making Connections*. London: Hodder and Stoughton, in association with The Open University.

Wilson, D. C. and Rosenfeld, R. H. (1990) *Managing Organizations: Text, Reading and Cases*. Maidenhead: McGraw-Hill.

Woodford, D. (1993) Towards a perception of a 'hearing culture' and its relationships with a 'deaf culture', *Deafness*, 9(3): 13–15.

Woolfe, R., Dryden, W. and Charles-Edwards, D. (1993) The nature and range of counselling practice, in W. Dryden, D. Charles-Edwards and R. Woolfe (eds) *Handbook of Counselling in Britain*. London: Routledge.

Zarb, G. (1995) Modelling the social model of disability, *Critical Public Health*, Winter: 2–11.

Zola, E. (1983) *Socio-medical Inquiries*. Philadelphia, PA: Temple University Press.

Index

compared to Sex Discrimination Act,
117–21
definition of disability and, 116, 117
Genuine Occupational Qualification
and, 118–21
reasonable adjustment and, 116,
119–20
sensory disability and, 55–6
disability movement
Deaf community and, 31, 37
divisions in, 16, 21, 37
political action and, 26–7
disabled people
communication and, 48
social identification and, 23
discourse, 7, 51–4, 56–8, 71–3, 145
of access and support, 114
cultural, 38
dominant, 64, 73
knowledge and, 51
legitimation of, 73
material contributors to, 52, 71
as meaning and representation, 52, 71
social power of, 52
translatability of, 68, 136
discourse analysis, 52–3, 71, 134, 138,
145
du Gay, P., 34, 38, 40, 46
Dworkin, R., 11, 80

Education Act, 1981, 76–9
embedded individuality, 45
empirical positivism, 14, 145
employment organizations, 121–32
communication in, 120–5
cultures of, 114
deaf people as Other in, 123
emotional labour in, 123
grapevines in, 124–5
'learning disabled', 121
negotiated order in, 122–3
postmodernist view of, 122
recruitment practice in, 121
reproduction of power in, 114
scapegoating in, 124
work environments, 114
work patterns, 114
epistemology, 34, 145
equal opportunity theory, 12, 25, 76, 90
optimum conditions for, 91

optimum prospects and, 91
error analysis, 52, 145
essentialism, 13–21, 133–4, 145
dilemma of, 17

Fairclough, N., 53, 57, 70, 97, 106
family
of choice, 23–4
of origin, 23–4
at risk, 88
Fancher, R., 12, 100
Fineman, S., 122, 123, 124
Finkelstein, V., 37
Fishman, J., 13, 20
Foucault, M., 9, 19, 34, 38, 40, 46, 62, 138
French, S., 14, 19, 21, 70, 119

GCSE League Tables, 90
Gemeinschaft, 20, 145
genetic engineering, 61, 136, 145
Gergen, K., 34, 73, 98, 106, 134
Gesellschaft, 20, 145
Goffman, E., 21, 46
Gregory, S., 21, 67, 86
Grossberg, L., 57, 98, 134, 136, 140

Hall, S., 44, 53, 56
Harré, R., 58, 64, 105
hearing impairment, 60
disability and, 37
as distinct from Deaf, 10, 21
marginalization of, 63
hegemony, meaning of, 8, 145
hermeneutics, 36, 38, 145
historicity, 13, 145
Hugman, R., 106, 110
human rights, 84, 133, 142
entitlement and, 92
objective human needs and, 83, 91
utilitarianism and, 82

identity
border-crossing and, 57, 98–9, 139
complex, 22, 98–9
construction of, 56–8
cultural, 13, 21
Deaf, 21, 56
definitions of, 146
diaspora, 99, 136
discourse and, 56–8